The Book of
MINIATURES
❁ Furniture & Accessories ❁

The Book of
MINIATURES
✤ Furniture & Accessories ✤

Helen Ruthberg

With Foreword by Sybil Harp, Editor
Creative Crafts Magazine

CHILTON BOOK COMPANY
Radnor, Pennsylvania

Library of Congress Cataloging in Publication Data
Ruthberg, Helen.
   The book of miniatures.
   (Chilton's creative crafts series)
   Bibliography: p. 232
   Includes index.
   1. Miniature furniture.   2. Miniature rooms.
I. Title.
TT175.5.R87   1977   749   76-451
ISBN 0-8019-6365-6
ISBN 0-8019-6366-4 pbk.

7 8 9 0   5 4 3 2 1

In memory of my great-nephew,

Gregg Bennett Stein

Foreword

To explore the world of miniatures is to discover a source of fascination and enjoyment that is seemingly inexhaustible. More and more people are beginning to find their way into the Land of Lilliput, where all the problems are little ones, but where the imagination has no bounds, and craftsmanship and creativity find continual challenge.

The wonders of miniaturia reveal themselves to different people in different ways. One of my own first inklings of them came when I saw some miniature shell arrangements created by Helen Ruthberg. Shells have long been a popular medium for craft hobbyists, but Helen's work in them was, to my mind, unique. Instead of using large, spectacular looking shells as most craftsmen do, she sifted out the tiny ones that washed up in the sand on the edge of the waves. From these ordinary appearing little bits and pieces she created exquisite miniature pictures, meticulously displayed in tiny frames. To me they illustrated the singular beauty of art on a small scale, the insignificant given importance and, above all, the fascination (there seems to be no better word for it) of things that are tiny and lovely and perfectly done.

I was soon to discover that I was far from alone in my appreciation of miniature crafts. Readers of *Creative Crafts* began to request more articles on "minis." A special issue devoted to the subject brought such an enthusiastic response that, two years after the issue was published and long after it was sold out, we received frequent orders for it. I also learned of the formation of organizations for miniature enthusiasts, of museums of miniature art, of special publications devoted to the subject and of the many collectors and craftsmen who apparently are everywhere.

While there are many ways to enjoy miniature crafting, the roads of Lilliput all seem eventually to lead to the dollhouse, that ultimate vehicle for miniature craftsmanship. It is in a dollhouse that ingenuity and craftsmanship can be given full scope, and it is here that one can fully enjoy the indulgence of his own taste and fancy. And happily a dollhouse, like its full-scale counterpart, is almost never really finished, but seems to offer continual opportunity to implement new ideas and to perfect one's skills.

The secret of successful miniature craftsmanship lies in the ability to "think small." Since the most popular scale in dollhouses is one-twelfth (one inch equals one foot), the eye and mind must learn to perceive the possibilities that exist in a multitude of small and ordinary items. The truth is that materials for miniature crafting are everywhere at hand; it is simply a matter of seeing them. One must begin to notice the shape and texture of hundreds of tiny objects that we use and discard every day. The fun of it all comes when our perspective alters to the point where we see things, not as they are, but as they can be in one-twelfth scale. Suddenly the world becomes full of discovery.

Helen Ruthberg brings to this book not only the ability to think small, but also artistic talent and high standards of craftsmanship. Most importantly, she possesses an enthusiasm for miniature crafts that she is eager to share with others. She will tell you how to furnish your own dollhouse on (or with) a shoestring . . . or a bottlecap, bits of fabric or lace, and many other odds and ends that will cost you next to nothing. But in spite of the extensive use of "found" materials, there will be nothing "junky" about your creations, for she will also teach you the techniques and give you the helpful hints you need to turn out finely crafted, perfectly scaled miniatures.

Sybil C. Harp
Editor, *Creative Crafts* Magazine

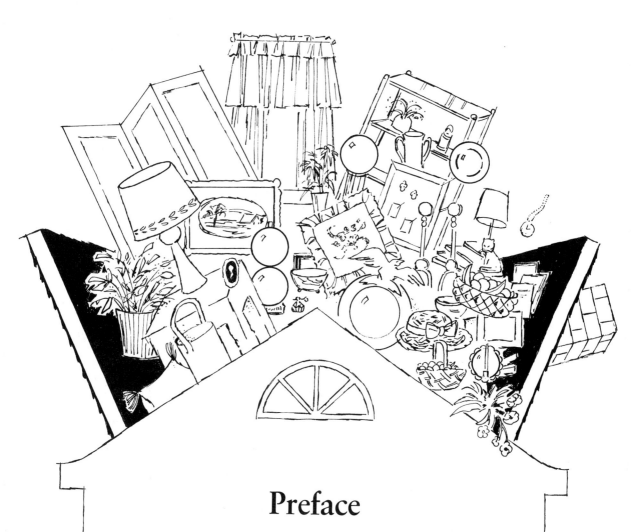

Preface

Did you ever see a little girl who wasn't enchanted by a miniature dollhouse? As a matter of fact, did you ever see a *big* girl who wasn't enchanted by a miniature dollhouse? Young or old, the intrigue is the same; even little boys and big boys have been captivated by its charm.

Plaything or hobby, miniature dollhouse furniture and accessories have become a part of the business world. There are countless sources of stores, dealers, artisans and mail-order catalogues that allow the miniature fancier to satisfy every whim.

Creating your own furniture is time consuming and requires great patience, but accessories are easier and even more fun to indulge in. This book is devoted to the creation of the miniature, consisting of all the odds and ends that help make a wee room livable and lovable.

Acknowledgments

Although my hand may be limp from writing, drawing and crafting, my heart is nevertheless full, and my sincere thanks are extended

. . . to Sybil Harp, Editor of *Creative Crafts*, whose faith and intuition reactivated a long-desired dream to produce a book on miniatures

. . . to Elyse Sommer, my agent, whose expertise and guidance helped set a positive course

. . . to Ed Erdman, formerly of Dremel Manufacturing Company, and Jim Doyle of Northeastern Scale Models, Inc., for their extreme generosity and willingness to help

. . . to Rhoda and Norman Pollock of Fotomart, who developed my photos and offered mountains of advice

. . . to Donna Murray of Fabric Outlet, who graciously allowed me to raid her fantastic shop

. . . to Stephen Markovits, Crafts Manufacturing Company, Thrall Library and Lyons' Millwork for their respective aid

. . . to Ilse Goldsmith, who heard me out scriptwise and otherwise when I needed it most

. . . to Marge Purdy, typist, who conquered the task of deciphering my handwriting

. . . to Elaine Brandon, Ceil Millman and Roberta Moore for their undimmed faith in my ability

. . . to all those who permitted me to use their work and who will be properly credited where their work is shown

. . . to Brad, my wonderful son, who was conveniently away at college, thus abdicating his room for a Lilliputian takeover

. . . and, above all, to my understanding husband, Jack, who always has and always will continue to awe me with the wealth, breadth and scope of his knowledge, which he placed unceasingly at my disposal.

Contents

Contents

List of Illustrations

List of Color Illustrations

Part I Getting Started

1

Introduction to Miniaturing

Miniature is my love.

For many years it seemed that no matter what I did, any creativity ultimately dwindled down to the size of the miniature. When seashell plaques were created, I soon found myself involved with petite designs. As a professional artist, it was impossible to resist the lure of the miniature painting and the thrill of exhibiting in national miniature shows. It was inevitable that I should be smitten with dollhouse fever and succumb to all the itty-bitty goodies that go into making up the wonderful world of dollhouse miniaturia.

Miniaturing is like a brilliant gem: multifaceted, admired and capable of producing awesome reaction. The producer of this "gem" can achieve a glow by developing talent in many directions. Creativity takes shape in different ways: design, cut, glue, paint, carve, mold, decorate, build, stitch, embroider—these are the facets of the miniature world, and you can be a part of it (Fig. 1-1).

The miniature dollhouse is not a new hobby. In fact, it goes back for centuries, having once been the hobby of royalty. In this respect it is an important craft, be-

cause the dollhouse, more than being just a plaything, has contributed much of historical significance by showing the way of life that existed at the time it was conceived.

This book does not pretend to be an exclusive accounting of the history of miniature dollhousing. There is excellent literature already available on the subject. My primary purpose is to try to lay as much groundwork as possible, to acquaint interested miniaturists with most aspects of *creating* and encourage them to indulge in the very gratifying task of crafting their own accessories and furnishings.

Since most miniature households present living at its best and truest, there are snatches of relevant history throughout the book to help the reader relate to various phases of household planning. Miniatures are authentic copies of their real-life counterparts, so I went directly to the sources and relate throughout the book pertinent facts designed to help you see the trend of development in the world of furnishings and accessories. Limitation of space prevents thorough involvement but, hopefully, this small taste of history will encourage you

Fig. 1-1 Creating miniatures can develop talents in several directions; involvement is self-determined.

Fig. 1-2 A Victorian farmhouse is the result of team effort by Carolyn and Robert Conley of DORMOUSE DOLLHOUSES. The main section features board and batten siding and has a wraparound front porch with gingerbread; the roof section of the main house also has gingerbread. The front door on the main section features two "edged glass" panels and a paneled door. All windows have paneled shutters. (*Robert Conley, photograph*)

Fig. 1-3 Shaker home. Bedroom: notice the Shaker dress on wall at left. In front of dress is a bonnet on a bonnet stand, used to shape the bonnets as they were made. Shakers were famous for their oval boxes, seen on top of bureau. Shaker rooms contained a row of pegs around the walls. These were used to hang items such as candleholders, towel racks, mirrors and chairs (when not in use or when cleaning floors). Chair hanging on pegs is similar to those used around the dining room table when benches were not used, with low backs so they could be pushed under the table and out of the way. The bed has rope springs and all drawers open. Living Room: man's hat above desk on left, pin cushion and spool holder on desk. Picture above woodbox is of famous Shaker Tree of Life. Made by Sally and Wayne Lasch of SHAKER MINIATURES. Hats, chairs, boxes made by the Schwerdtfegers of Maine. (*Wayne Lasch, photograph*)

to investigate, thus helping you to mold your thoughts and ideas regarding the direction you wish to take.

Getting started with a dollhouse involves many decisions but perhaps the most raking is choosing the style of house and furnishings.

Although this book is not devoted to the structure of the dollhouse itself, there are numerous sources for acquiring houses of various architectural styles (see Sources of Supply). Some houses are already assembled; others are available in kits. Some are mass produced by the manufacturer and others are hand-crafted by individuals (Fig. 1-2). The individual artisan will restore and custom design, and your decision of involvement may be honestly decided by costs—for dollhouses and miniaturing can range from reasonable to preposterous—depending upon your needs, goals, desires and limited only by your imagination and financial resources.

Selecting a Theme

Breaking furnishings down into three parts, there is a choice of period, traditional or contemporary.

Period involves all aspects that are true and believable of that period in time which you are trying to portray, whether it's French Louis, English or Italian Renaissance, American Puritan, Revolutionary or any era in history that appeals to you.

Traditional involves the use of some period pieces with an updated handling of lighting, window treatment, kitchens and other areas of home decor that make both past and present time what they are.

Contemporary goes a step further than traditional and includes the use of fine examples of modern styling, including that of Swedish and Danish. Designs become functional, the mod look is used and plastic—which is often abhorred by the purists—is acceptable. Let's face it! Plastic has been introduced to the modern scene and it's here to stay.

The best factual impression is, of course, achieved if one remains within the era of that which is being portrayed; this is the decision that you alone will have to make. If you are intrigued by the simplicity and charm of the past, then you may wish to recreate a room reminiscent of the Shaker period (Fig. 1-3). If you desire to show a home that exemplifies our present way of life, and there are variations on this, then you will be contributing something for the future—a blueprint of this particular era that will become an heirloom to be cherished by someone else.

Fig. 1-4   A narrow shadowbox, 2″ deep, allows room for a wall arrangement. A plastic plant in wicker basket, a Gone-with-the-Wind lamp on a small skirted table, a print from Williamsburg notepaper and an umbrella-hat stand complete the arrangement.

Displaying Miniatures

Once in awhile I hear people comment that they've been interested in starting a dollhouse but have delayed because they haven't found their desired house. They believe that before collecting any furnishings they *must* start with a house. What a pity! There is really no necessity to have a house for a beginning. There are so many different, attractive or suitable ways for showing off a miniature room, and if you start off with one room, it may not seem so overwhelming. Little by little you ease into a more complicated unit.

There are advantages to a single room. If you desire to exhibit your miniature achievement in a show or if you are asked to talk about miniature furnishings to a group, there is less hassle involved in packing and transporting an individual unit. Shadowboxes are sold for single room units or, if you are handy, you can construct your own (Fig. 1-4).

There are other modes of display, too. A cabinet with closing doors to conceal the rooms is a charming and unexpected way to show off your hobby. The bookcase style dictates a frank, bold display and Faith Bradford's house at the Smithsonian is a perfect example of this (Fig. 1-5). Two or three rooms placed atop each other in a townhouse arrangement are popular and take up little space; don't overlook the possibility of the inside of the case of an unused clock. Some units can be made to fit a lazy susan and there are self-made shelf wall units, both

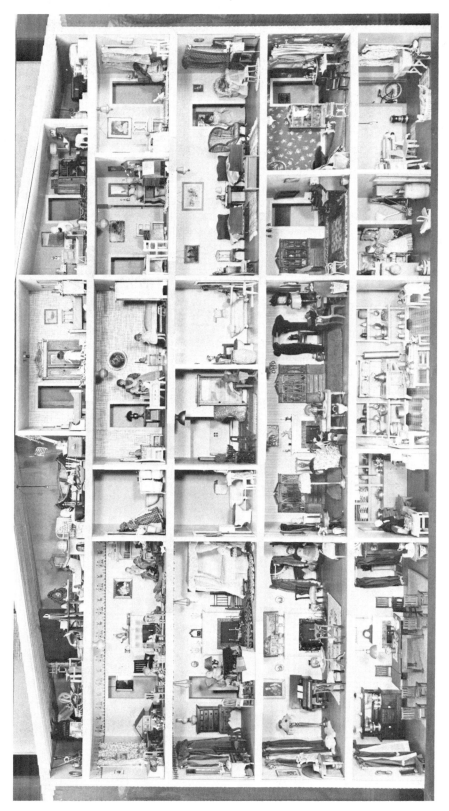

Fig. 1-5 Typically displayed in bookcase fashion, the miniature house by Faith Bradford shows the way of life of an American family during the period 1910–1914. It's a big house and, judging from the occupants in it, it's a big family, too. (*The Smithsonian Institution, photograph*)

Fig. 1-6　Although scaled a little tall, the extra height of this shop dramatizes the vast amount of goods available. In addition to fabric, there are beads, buttons, ribbons, trims, boutique items and all the desirable decorative necessities for the creative individual. Donna Murray enjoyed re-creating her own shop in miniature.

straight and corner. A china cabinet makes an unusual display area and remains conveniently visible through glass front doors. The simple primitive shoebox and corrugated box can be elevated to new heights by dollhouse additions. And the smallest of miniatures can even be housed in an eggshell (see color section, Figure 5).

Sources of Inspiration

A popular fad is recreating one's very own home, or at least a room or two, in miniature. This is a delightful idea and certainly the very personal nature of the whole scheme should reward and gratify anyone who's conscientious and determined enough to see this through to completion.

When you began to put your own real home in order, did you accomplish it within a week, a month or even a year? Of course not! So don't expect to complete a miniature house in a short time just because it's small. Much thought and consideration should go into the makeup of your tiny abode and the more forethought you use, the better will be your result.

Use books and magazines for sources of inspiration and information. Visit your local library and mull over the many books that explicitly detail eras of years gone by. Exact antique reproductions of furnishings and accessories will make you knowledgeable and confident. Home and decorating magazines suggest room arrangements, color schemes and styles of furnishings. Even the advertisements in your daily newspaper and direct-mail department store advertising can provide suggestions. And, of course, observe your own home and the homes of others and visualize all possibilities. Many of your contemporaries' homes have either authentic antique furnishings or excellent reproductions, and a closeup viewing is a

8

real blessing. If you live near historical sites that feature period rooms, this is another bonus. The important thing is to "become involved" and then you will enjoy, enjoy, enjoy putting your room or house together.

When we think of miniature furnishings we automatically turn to the home and its contents. But let us remind ourselves that there are many other fascinating and interesting sources of ideas to duplicate. Surely, the shops of the past played dominant roles in everyone's life. Consider bakery, ice cream parlor, grocery, hardware, fabric, apothecary, silversmith, blacksmith, variety, printers, toy, dry goods, millinery, dressmaker and pet shops, the schoolroom, studios of photography and art and others that contribute to our heritage (Figs. 1-6, 1-7, 1-8). Once you begin to look into these you may become quite smitten with their charm and succumb forevermore to just doing shops of vocational nature.

Another attraction is the possibility of duplicating the office of the old-time professional doctor, lawyer or dentist; consider the great possibilities of the antique railroad waiting room. Unless our citizens save them, our stations are doomed to become a memory, but your miniature rendition can live on and on.

Do you have a hobby? If not, then cultivate one especially for your own little house. Do you enjoy the sea, plants, boating, fishing, gardening, hunting, golf, tennis, traveling—or is your love horses or another animal? Whatever you like, make it the dominant theme in one of your rooms. A theme room turns out with more charm than you can ever imagine and as you unexpectedly find little expressive things for this special room you will experience incomparable happiness.

Don't leave nature outside. Invite it into your home for a natural, comfortable warm feeling. Use it in and among your furnishings. Bring in lots of natural resources, using dried flowers, plants, wood, twigs, rocks, water, seashells and even earth dirt. Help your house come alive with the use of animals, a bird, fish and, of course, little dollhouse figures. If you don't have a figure available, then do

Fig. 1-7 Trims and more trims are all wound up, ready and waiting for the customer to unwind. Shop by Donna Murray.

have some clothing and food here and there to let your viewer know that the house is inhabited.

As I have already stated, miniaturing is not something that you turn on and off in a year. The true enthusiast often goes on and on for several years. As you continue to collect through purchases and your own making, you will find that you may have more than you can accommodate in a house. You have a choice of either hiding these mini items away in boxes until needed or you can display them as extra added attractions with wall groupings, on shelves or in cabinets. A neat little compartmental idea is the use of the old printer's type drawer which has become very popular—so popular in fact that it is even being duplicated. When upended these small cubbyholes become

Fig. 1-8 As the happy day approaches, the bride-to-be makes her decision in this rendition of a bridal salon created by Donna Murray. The cases are complete with tiny headpieces and other items that a bride might need. (This is scaled larger than $1/12$.)

Fig. 1-9   Once you begin collecting, you're going to find yourself with an excess of little things. Rather than hide them away in a closet, proudly display them as collectors' items. An old printer's type drawer makes an excellent background piece. Secure them with a tiny dab of Stickum or they'll be falling down off their perches more times than you care to pick them up.

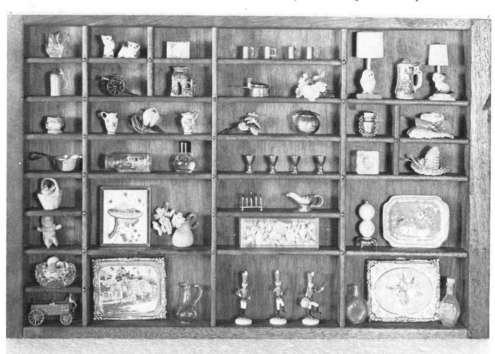

nice little niches for your minis, as shown in the example in Figure 1-9. Obsolete drawers from broken desks and bureaus can be salvaged and refinished. You can also use the inside of cigar boxes, set in a few shelves using wood strips, and these are delightful when stained, painted and decorated. Several can be attached together with strong ribbons. But you're clever and you'll think of your own way to display and dismay your family and friends.

We grow with learning and crafting for a miniature house will surprisingly turn you into a miniature architect, carpenter, decorator, artist and more. Significantly, each learning experience will benefit not only your hobby but you as well.

There will be times when making projects in this book that you may say, "But I don't have that, so how can I duplicate it?" True, you won't be able to exactly duplicate everything, but the contents of this book are primarily to help you get your thought vibrations activated and, through your own ingenuity, use substitutions that you may have and I don't have.

Some of you may have been avid miniaturists for quite awhile now and others may only recently have embarked on a new adventure into this little world. Taking into consideration that different abilities do exist, I have tried to introduce different projects for variable skills. Some furnishings are simple with unworkable parts, designed to help the beginner in getting started; the chest-on-chest in Chapter 20 is an example of an easier pattern. On the other hand, the more accomplished craftsman may welcome trying the painted settee or bookcase console. Each is a challenging and interesting piece of furniture.

If you make a mistake, don't be discouraged . . . begin again. I've made more than my share of errors and I must admit that I learned something from each correction.

To do total justice to the whole world of miniaturing would require volumes. What I am trying to do is acquaint you with a bit of this and that from as many aspects of dollhouse furnishing and accessories as this book will allow me to cover. Hopefully, it will entice you to try, experiment, get involved and pursue a most gratifying hobby.

Unlock your imagination and make miniature *your* love, too.

Collecting and Getting Organized

Where do you begin? What will you need and where will you find what you want? Let me begin by saying that almost anything small can become a treasure (Fig. 2-1). Just start collecting.

Although many suggestions in this book are the happy result of discards—and it has often been said, "One man's trash is another man's treasure"—some items are also devised or started from an initial purchase. A tiny ceramic animal can start you on the road to creating the most darling lamp that you have ever seen; once you start, your imagination begins to take off like a soaring kite. Soon you will find yourself absorbed in one of the most fascinating hobbies of miniaturia.

Any store can produce an unexpected find, whether it's variety, department, drug, supermarket, interior decorator, hardware, antique, craft, boutique, flower, fabric, hobby or import. And don't overlook the marvelous possibilities of auctions, antique sales, garage and rummage sales, flea markets, bazaars, forgotten drawers and attic trunks, where you may find discarded pieces of jewelry, chains, fabrics, buttons, trims and other small ornamental objects. These sometimes become just the items that you've needed to complete a clever little idea that's been rattling around in your brain since the day you conceived it while washing the dishes.

Collectibles

Before we get carried away by unexpected finds, it must be clarified that the bulk of your collectibles will include basic items that provide the backbone for miniature creations. These essentials include paper, fabric, plastic, metal, wood, glass, jewelry and odds and ends.

To give you a more extensive idea of what to acquire, and to further help you, the following descriptive listing will keep you alert for these necessary ingredients. Many of these items are already in your possession; with the cooperation of relatives and friends you can acquire several more. Other items will necessarily have to be purchased, but your own ingenuity will best prevail. As you gather them, keep them together for your own convenience.

PAPER

Illustration board and two-ply bristol board from art store

12

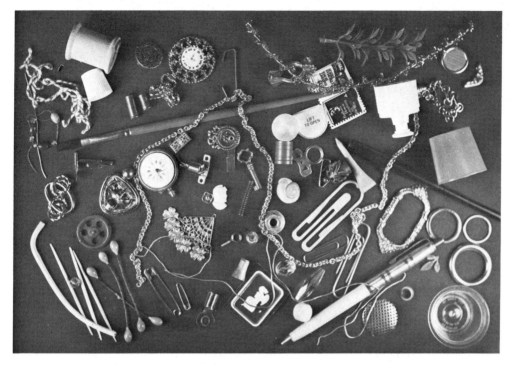

Fig. 2-1 Ordinarily, these might be discarded as a lot of junk . . . but the miniaturist will oftentimes find these items both useful and necessary to complete a small project.

Cardboard from dress boxes, shirts

Index cards (file cards) henceforth referred to as "card"

Cigar boxes

Strong gift boxes, especially with surface designs, cut into flat pieces

Tiny gift boxes—leave intact

Unusual cosmetic boxes and packaging

Cardboard tube from waxed paper, plastic wrap or paper toweling—each has different thickness and strength

Contact paper—wood grain, marble pattern, solids and other small patterns

Gift wrapping paper designs that appeal to you for wallpaper or murals—colored foil, petite patterns, flock designs

Colored and gold paper and borders saved from greeting cards

Greeting cards showing landscapes and other small designs

Notepaper with designs of animals, children, flowers, scenes, etc.

Paper drinking cups—small juice and jigger size, jelly cups, cream containers from restaurants

Direct mail advertising, booklets, brochures, catalogues from department stores, specialty shops and publishers

Usable pictures from advertisements in magazines

Doilies, white or gold

Gold filigree embossed borders and designs from crafts shop

FABRIC

Handkerchiefs—white and pastel with hemstitched or lace edges, designs, embroidered (Fig. 2-2)

Upholstery fabric—samples or on bolt, sold in department stores, decorator shops and fabric departments

Lightweight materials—solid colors and very small patterns, remnants from fabric shop, discarded clothing, such as lingerie, night clothes, ties

Linens—old doilies, lace and embroidery

Leather—soft, pliable and thin; old handbags, shoes, gloves, belts, etc.

Fig. 2-2   A pinwheel of handkerchiefs indicates the assortment of designs and edgings that are available as fabrics. There's a choice of many—modern or traditional, bold or conservative, colorful or quiet.

Vinyls and leatherette
Acrylic pile and imitation fur
Foam rubber—block and shredded; art foam
Cotton balls, cotton batting
Felt
Tiny ribbons—velvet-covered ribbon
Embroidered ribbon trim (Fig. 2-3)
Laces of all varieties and widths—delicate in design
Feathers of small size, for example, molted from parakeet
Yarns—embroidery floss, crewel, acrylic
Tassels, white string, brown cord, crochet thread, etc.
Assorted place mats
Hem bindings and bias tape—assorted colors
Elastic cording

PLASTIC

Curtain rings—all varieties, sizes and colors
Pill containers—assorted sizes
Acrylic—available from glass dealers
Acetate—firm and flexible; available in art stores

Deodorant roll-on balls
Used ball-point pens—both transparent and click-top cartridge styles; save the *whole* thing
Place mats
Scraps of Formica and Marlite
Clear, curved domes from vending machines and spray bottles
Ping-Pong balls
Clear plastic straws, other assorted straws, clear tubing, clear capsules from pills
Containers from photography film; other doodads from photographic equipment
Bag ties from plastic bags, unused
Old shower cap with small pattern

METAL

Wire dress hangers
Paper clips—all sizes
Staples—all kinds, all sizes, large ones from corrugated packaging
Caps from soft drink bottles and similar containers
Wire—gold and silver beading wire; picture wire, copper wire (18 gauge); electrical wire and scraps of radio wire in assorted colors; florist's wire
Aluminum—frozen dinner plates, baking containers; sand smooth any cut edges of pieces when using
Pouring spouts from food boxes
Square support framework around frozen food packaging
Cocoa can covers, small bouillon package bottoms
Safety pins—all sizes
Straight pins—flat heads and round heads
Screen scraps, tea strainer
Hairpins—black and silver
Eyelets of all sizes
Grommets; washers; hooks and eyes; snappers
Discarded watch and clock parts
Used bullet shells; used primers (*dented*) from cartridges and bullet shells
Sliding-door finger pulls

WOOD

Miniature wooden items, specially made for dollhouses (see Sources of Supply)

14

Quality wood—cherry, pine, birch, walnut, mahogany, oak, etc.; available from dealers or your local cabinetmaker

Veneers—obtained from dealer

Balsa wood—flat broad pieces of various widths; strips of different thicknesses

Dowel sticks—especially widths of $1/8''$, $3/16''$, $1/4''$, $5/16''$; other sizes available if needed

Box of round toothpicks; flat too, if needed

Wooden spools—all sizes (Fig. 2-4)

Flexible wood trim, flexible gold trim

Sticks—cotton-tipped swab applicators, Popsicle sticks, tongue depressors

Used artists' or children's paintbrush handles

Cedar from cigar boxes

Old shoebrush handle

GLASS

Sample perfume bottles

Mirrors—decorative and plain; purse and compact size; round, oval, etc. from crafts store

Used ampules

Test tubes

Microscope slides

Stained glass—smooth surfaces, marble pattern

JEWELRY

Beads—assortment of all kinds and sizes; glass, ceramic, lucite, opaque, pearl, wooden, painted, mottled, round, square, oval, faceted, gold; visit your bead shop

Bracelets with links and decorative styles; odd children's bracelets; oval and round

Pendants, brooches and pins

Earrings—especially those with clusters of beads, dangle styles, both screw-on and clip-on styles

Cuff links

Chains—jeweler's chain; other various assortments from fine to heavy; assorted costume chains (Fig. 2-5)

Filigree fastenings, choker clasps, necklace hooks and clasps, bead caps, bell caps

Jewelry accessories—jump rings (jump

Fig. 2-3 Embroidery trims, edgings, braids, ribbons, from wide to narrow, are supplemental and useful to have available. Even a 2″ piece of trim can become a pillow or an applique, so collect all scraps.

links), head pins, eye pins (fastening pins), bails; acquire these in various sizes from craft or bead dealer

Bolo tie ends and string fasteners

Sequins—assortment of sizes and colors

ODDS AND ENDS

Tops from perfume bottles, shaving lotions, nail polish, toothpaste tubes, liquid dishwashing caps, cleaning containers, cocoa boxes, plastic bottles

Fig. 2-4 Pillars of empty spools support shelves for collectible bottle tops, restaurant containers and other odd items all destined to be glamorized for dollhouse miniatures.

Spools—all sizes from thread; both wooden and plastic

Buttons—decorative, flat, painted, heraldic

Buckles from shoes and belts

Toys—broken pieces from larger toys; fastenings, etc.

Miniature seashells

Tiny polished semiprecious stones

Bristles from old brushes—all kinds and textures

HIDDEN TREASURE

Dig in and look around. Visit your familiar shops and inquire about small discards. Perhaps there will be woodsy scraps that you can garner from your local cabinetmaker. They probably won't appreciate you for coming in to bother them, but smile bravely and pay for the wood and their time. Cabinetmakers are better equipped to cut fine slices. Those long splintery slivers of wood on the floor come in handy. They won't mind if you take those and help clean up their floor.

Visit your local glass and mirror distributors, too. Many of their small broken pieces end up in the scrap pile. The interior decorator may be willing to oblige you with an obsolete sample book. Don't overlook the trash cans of a man's workshop; I snooped and found a beautiful fine-haired brush and wonderful radio wire being discarded by my husband. When my son went off to college, either because of laziness or sentiment, I delayed cleaning out his closet which had become laden with boyhood toys. Eventually I got to the job, and that's where the gold mine was! Among the goodies was a new Sculpi-Clay set, begging to be used. This clay can be easily molded or sculptured and can be hard baked in the oven. So don't discard those broken toys before you've examined them for possibilities. An old wooden wheel can become the beginning for a wheel-topped table or a wheel chandelier. Small metal pieces that fit together for a combined piece make excellent little fittings for many miniature projects. So be wary about throwing out "the junk."

FILIGREE

Collect filigree ornaments! They are in a beautiful world all of their own and should be treated as individual entities (Fig 2-6).

Filigree is so versatile that it's used for projects in many different chapters of this book and will turn up unexpectedly at any turn of the page.

It can become an elegant compote dish, a teeny delicate napkin ring or a bracelet . . . or it's suddenly transformed into a letter holder or decorates a frame Victorian in motif . . . and for sheer, beautiful light fixtures, there's little that competes with this ornament.

There's a wide variety of miniature goodies that will result from experimentation. Filigree can be glued, bent, cut apart, twisted and the most unexpected results attained. Because filigree provides so many different designs, shapes and sizes, it's just something that you alone will have to work with—but I really shouldn't say work, because once you start to manipulate your filigree, you'll soon admit it's "play" and pleasurable.

Recall the old adage, "Waste not, want not!" If you have been a steadfast, avid collector of "anything" you will be rewarded for your diligence. If you find that the purchase of extras for finishing off projects can become a mite weighty on the budget, consider sharing materials and such with two or three other dollhouse enthusiasts. Sharing supplies will go a long way in miniature and will help stretch your dollar, too.

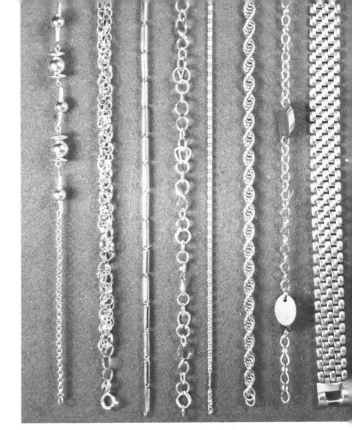

Fig. 2-5 Infinite variety, beautiful design, useful to the miniaturist: when broken apart and cut, long jewelry chains offer vast possibilities and help complete many a project. Purchase a few or you might even snitch an inch from one of your own lengths of chain—it will never be missed.

Tools and Supplies

TOOLS

Good basic tools are a necessity of the craftsman's trade and quality of work often suffers or flourishes depending upon selection and use. A selection of many important items discussed below is shown in Figure 2-7. Three essential items, small in size, are a set of chain-nose, serrated-jaw pliers, also called needle-nose; a diagonal semiflush wire cutter, also called parrot-nose and dike; and gripping pliers. Fortunately, I have a very good set, gifted from my husband, Jack, and I value it more than a luxury item. When one is involved in miniatures, gift giving and receiving is indeed simplified.

Purchase an X-acto carving set (#77 is adequate) which includes the knife and

Fig. 2-6 A small variety of metal filigree pieces can help your crafting of miniatures. Collect a few bell caps, bead caps, flat rounds and other ornaments and also acquire eye pins, head pins and jump links.

teeny-tiny saw. All the extra pieces will prove indispensable for your quick carving needs. X-acto also manufactures other inexpensive, simple tools including a cordless battery-run power drill, most essential for making those clean tiny holes which are endlessly necessary in miniature work. A small miter box, saw, suction base, vise, steel files and a pair of electrician's pliers with a side cutter are also recommended. Include a pair of pointed tweezers, which will become your best friend, and lots of round toothpicks for applying glue, cleaning up glue and even in helping to structure many of your handmades.

Like the whipped cream on the top, the Dremel Moto-Shop is something very special for miniaturists. This wonderful, complete multipurpose power workshop makes minicrafting a delight, eliminating the drudgery and time-consuming lot of handcutting every piece. For the harder and thicker pieces of wood I consider this tool an absolute necessity. Small in size, lightweight and adaptable in any area, the Moto-Shop is one item that should be high in priority on your list of gift suggestions—a gift to you, of course.

Following in its wake is Dremel's other fascinating tool, the Variable Speed Moto-Tool kit. A hand-held instrument, it proves itself very worthy in miniature work as it performs many functions for the crafter. Equipped for various size drills, routers, sanders and more, this tool, with a bit of practice, produces easier performance and better crafting.

For the real diehard miniaturist, a mechanical bonus is the miniature lathe, equipped to make all those intricate turnings for posts and legs.

WORKING MATERIALS

Additional working tools in the following list will prove convenient and make for better working conditions.

8″ × 10″ sketch pad
8″ × 10″ tracing pad
Graph paper
Cutting board—wood or plastic
Large sharp scissors
Small sharp scissors
Cuticle scissors
X-acto knife and blades; if you purchase a carving set, knife handle is included
Single-edge razor blades
12″ metal-edge ruler
6″ ruler
Masking tape
Cellulose tape
Ice pick, awl, or large drapery hook, for piercing holes in plastic
Cardboard juice cans for paint
Sandpaper—fine, 200–220; medium, 400—emery boards
Waxed paper or waxed freezer-wrap paper
Drawing compass
Rubber bands, hair clips, clip clothespins to hold flat, glued pieces together
Pencils—HB, 2H
Kneaded eraser
Small paintbrushes—rounds #000, #0, #3; others if preferred
Small paintbrushes—brights #00, #2
Felt-tipped permanent coloring pens (Sharpie)

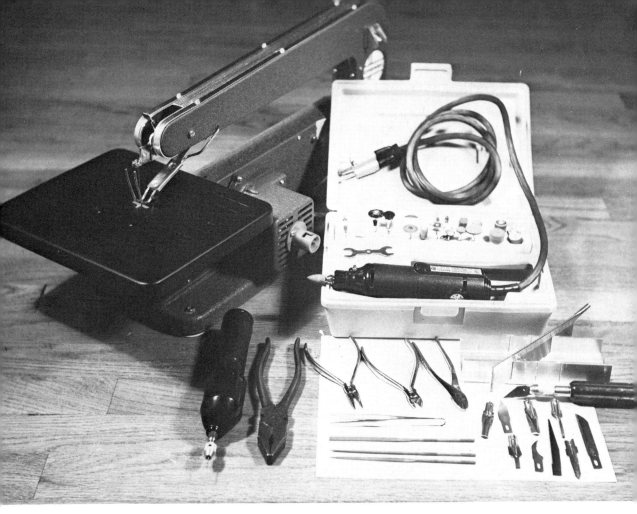

Fig. 2-7 Power tools and hand tools help the craftsman achieve his goal. Dremel's Moto-Shop and Variable Speed Moto-Tool are shown at the top of photo. At the bottom are X-acto battery-run drill, an electrician's side cutter pliers, Snap-on set of serrated pliers, diagonal cutter, gripping pliers, a miter box, sculpture set, tweezers and needle files.

Wood stains—dark mahogany, walnut, others
Shellac, satin varnish, or polyurethane satin finish and glossy finish
Crystal clear acrylic spray
X-acto soldering iron/hot knife

PAINTS

Although I have every classification of painting equipment available for my use, I prefer and use acrylic for miniaturing. It's versatile and serves many needs. It can be applied thickly for an *impasto* (raised) effect or, since it is water soluble, it can be used to create a watercolor "masterpiece." It's useful for decorating furniture and walls, too. Advantageously, the paint dries quickly. It also adheres to a variety of surfaces and, when thoroughly dry, it is smearproof. A small-size set of tubes with a wide range of colors will answer your needs, but remember that a brush used in acrylic *must* be cleaned with soap and water immediately after use. Craft manufacturers have come out with mouth-watering colors of acrylics in jars, and whether these tempt you for special projects is another consideration.

Gesso, a white compound used by artists as a primer and filler, is useful to cover over areas that have been glued together. It's supportive and prepares the surface for further painting, which is often required.

Gold and silver are essential in miniature finishes. Testor's PLA Enamel is favorable for plastic surfaces and is obtained in model hobby sections. Other colors may be required as you produce more minis. Quick-drying spray enamels for certain projects are often feasible, providing a smooth finish in hard-to-reach areas with a brush, but this is optional.

The product Floquil-Polly S has produced a stain and finish which are used on plastic surfaces and attain the appearance and color of wood (available at craft and hobby stores).

GLUES

Glue plays a prominent role in crafting miniatures and there's such a variety on the market, with differing methods of application, that it almost boggles the mind. As you do more work you will discover by yourself which glues best suit *your* needs. In my own experience, the following have been successful:

Elmer's Glue, Sobo and Duco Cement are good for porous surfaces, and dry clear. The white glues can be diluted with water (3:1) and used for such diverse needs as providing a gloss or protective coating over paper accessories. Duco can advantageously be combined with different surfaces, for example, bonding metal to wood

Orinico cement, usually sold for seashell work, is quick setting and has been very useful for nonporous surfaces

Velverette, a craft glue, is ideal for fabric and trimmings and for quick set-up

Plastics require a special glue and Testor's polystyrene plastic is favorable

Epoxy glues are strongest and are especially good for metals. They now come conveniently premixed

Instant bonding glues (Pliobond) are quick and fast adhering, also good for metals, but be careful you don't glue your fingers together

Most permanent tried-and-true glue (not clear) is the animal hide glue used for wood; this is slow setting and may require a press until set

Since there are so many new glues on the market, it might be best to consult your local hobby, craft or hardware store and also be advised that some of these glues may be toxic and should not be used by children.

WOODS

Creating with wood may be a completely new experience for many readers. There are the softwoods, such as balsa and basswood, or the harder, more durable varieties, such as pine, walnut, mahogany and cherry. Cedar and soft pine might be in the middle, but no matter which, miniatures can really be made from any selection (Fig. 2-8). Although balsa and basswood are soft enough to require only an X-acto knife for cutting, they can be a little tricky because of their tendency to split. Basswood is the better of the two, a bit more durable without the tendency to pit. With care they can produce a satisfactory piece of work and, for the beginner, this might even be the logical selection. Spruce is sometimes available at model shops and is cut to various widths. This is medium hard and well worth trying for some of the small projects.

Softwoods take paint nicely but remember that glue will resist staining, so always apply your color before gluing pieces together. Sand softwoods carefully and slowly, especially balsa. They corrode quickly under a fast, hard rub—and suddenly there you are, with a skimpy surface and a warped-looking edge. So use the gentle touch.

Hardwoods are something else: special in color, tone, texture, grain and versatility. They are class! They respond to a subtle application of wax, or glow through the right amount of shellac, varnish or lacquer. You will become fascinated by the beautiful difference and respect each wood for its own merit. Cherry is fine grained and oak is coarse; technically, if the grain of oak were enlarged to life size, it would be ridiculous, but we tend to overlook this and appreciate it, as is, in miniature. Of course, hardwoods are tougher to slice so you may look around for a mechanical assist from someone else or, even better, invest in

Fig. 2-8 The different color tone is evident in this small variety of wood. Balsa, cherry, pine, oak, mahogany and walnut offer a choice. Dowels and strips are often useful and should be readily available.

your own little tool. You may be reluctant to try mechanical devices, but in order to swim you have to get your feet wet, so take the plunge and at least investigate. Today there are wonderful power tools available in small, manageable sizes; as already mentioned, the Dremel Moto-Shop is a real blessing.

As I proceed to craft both furnishings and accessories, I will be using a variety of woods, both soft and hard. Each effort will be specifically mentioned so that you may see the result. This does not mean that each piece must be made of that particular wood. I am offering this variety for the benefit of the reader, but feel free to make your own selections. However, try to remain within the realm of authenticity, for different periods did favor certain woods.

Storage

Storing all your collectibles so that they are conveniently accessible is a "must." Miniatures have a sneaky way of hiding and if you have to go looking high and low for some little item that you "know" you have but can't remember "where," you will waste precious time and wear your patience thin. A regular, orderly

place to work is something to strive for. My husband says, "miniatures don't take up space . . . it's only the boxes." Acknowledged—but still, boxes help set your miniature world in order.

You probably won't use all of these, but the list gives you a choice.

> Clear plastic sweater boxes or several shallow, well-constructed store boxes about 10″ × 14″; section off the inside of each box with smaller boxes (milk cartons are good)
>
> Shoeboxes—regular or clear plastic; if you use the regular cardboard box, label contents on outside
>
> Fisherman's clear plastic tackle boxes (Fig. 2-9)
>
> Mini organizer boxes and trays
>
> Silverware utility trays
>
> Partitioned candy boxes
>
> A large-size jewelry box with lift-up top, complete with small sections and a bottom pull-out drawer, is great for traveling with your minis (Fig. 2-10)
>
> Sectional jewelry boxes used in drawers
>
> Bottom halves of 1-quart and 2-quart milk containers

STORING YOUR THOUGHTS

Our kitchen has a second counter—not for food preparation, but for "me." That

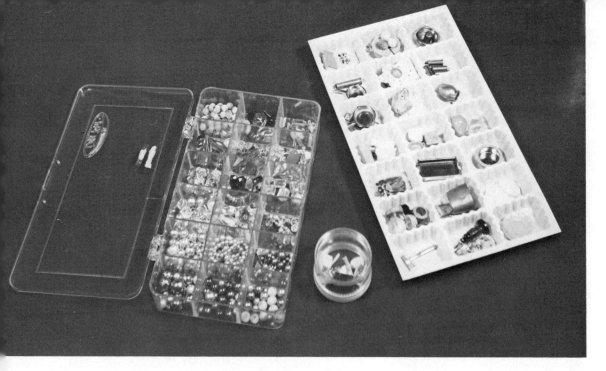

Fig. 2-9   A tackle box, candy box and small plastic container help keep miniatures, beads and other trivia orderly and organized.

Fig. 2-10   A jewelry box can help keep small items neatly accessible and becomes a satisfactory traveling case for your littlest possessions.

counter takes a lot of abuse. It's never really all cleaned off at any one time and I've long ago ceased to apologize for it. The kitchen is where I get most of my ideas. Something suddenly hits me and if I don't jot it down, or make a sketch or start to cut, clip, snip, twist, turn or glue, then my fantasies begin to fade. So whether you do or don't have an extra counter, do at least have a looseleaf notebook handy—I suggest a normal $8'' \times 10''$ size—so you can quickly record your brainy new thoughts as they expound and expand. Also treat yourself to pocket-envelope folders that are sold in office-stationery departments (Fig. 2-11). These are looseleaf and they help to organize your ideas and compartmentalize all the good things that you will be clipping for source material. Also I recommend that you carry a small notebook in your purse at all times to be able to record any ideas, measurements or quickie sketches of something that you wish to duplicate.

Sizing Your Miniatures

There are different scales in size on the miniature scene; but the most popular

22

one, probably because manufacturers and artisans had to arrive at a common denominator, is $1'' = 1'$ (one inch equals one foot). When the metric system takes over this will change, but until then we'll stay conventional. Since I'm not a mathematical genius at quick calculations, it can be a nuisance to rapidly decipher sizes when needed. Hence, the following breakdown of sizes scaled $1/12$ is convenient to use and if you want to scale this down even more, the pleasure is yours. Copy this on a stiff white cardboard and on one side of the board also include the specifications of a ruler up to $5''$ or $6''$. It's surprisingly useful at the most unexpected times and you'll be glad to have both available when needed.

Dollhouse Measurement	Real Measurement
(1 inch) 1″	12″ (12 inches or 1 foot)
$15/16''$	$11 1/4''$
$7/8''$	$10 1/2''$
$13/16''$	$9 3/4''$
$3/4''$	$9''$
$11/16''$	$8 1/4''$
$5/8''$	$7 1/2''$
$9/16''$	$6 3/4''$
$1/2''$	$6''$
$7/16''$	$5 1/4''$
$3/8''$	$4 1/2''$
$5/16''$	$3 3/4''$
$1/4''$	$3''$
$3/16''$	$2 1/4''$
$1/8''$	$1 1/2''$
$1/16''$	$3/4''$

Sharing

Since miniaturing has blossomed into an all-out hobby, there have been several good miniature newsletters and magazines appearing on the scene. These are wonderfully informative, graciously inspiring and generously complete with notable suggestions and comments from miniaturists all over the globe. These periodicals are available at a cost and are well worth acquiring. They are listed in the Sources of Supply at the back of this book.

There are also a goodly number of clubs and associations that are being formed. If

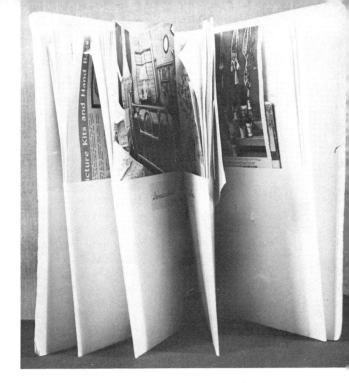

Fig. 2-11 Keep your overflowing ideas neatly stashed away in a handy envelope folder. When it begins to bulge, you may end up acquiring a folder for each room in your house.

this is your fare, there may be one already organized in or near your area.

Workshops are making their presence known in a few localities and hopefully more will be made available. The newsletters are the best source for information concerning locations of organizations, workshops, miniature shows and conventions.

Before you start, read everything carefully and reflect for awhile. Observe everything in your home, in your drawers and in the stores. Soon the pieces will begin to fit together and you will be on your way to creating many tiny miniatures. Before you know it you'll be stumbling all over yourself with new ideas. Unlock your imagination and have fun.

Helpful Hints

✔All patterns for tracing are laid out to exact size for finishing except in cases where grid marking is used. Grid marks are a grouping of squares and the drawing over the grid is smaller, but kept in scale. Therefore, enlarge grid marks to 1″. Complete new drawing, copying the placement of the artwork in the book into new 1″ squares. The new enlarged drawing can be transferred to your working surface.

✔ When looking at fabric, laces, embroidery, decorative lace, embossed gold paper, wallpapers or anything, don't just look at the whole pattern and stop—look at the individual small parts that make up the whole pattern. There's a wonderful miniature world hiding in the overall design, waiting to be discovered.

✔ Cotton, plain fluffy cotton, becomes the indispensable filler, useful in gluing one thing to something else. Use it sparingly, as needed, or in larger amounts, soaked in glue. Whichever way you use it, though, don't let it show.

✔ To bend thin pieces of balsa wood or pine, submerge wood in a container of very *hot* water and allow to soak thoroughly. When wood is ready, carefully bend around a curved surface. A small cardboard salt shaker or small juice glass is a good starter. When you have desired curvature, hold wood in place with masking tape. When dry, glue thoroughly to desired surface with Elmer's glue. Use tape again for holding in position.

✔ Leather can sometimes prove to be too thick for a project. Some leather can be thinned out by carefully pulling away excess back surface. Apply a warm iron to leather to smooth out frayed areas, also to secure folds when necessary.

✔ Waxed paper resists glue. If you need to glue something on a flat surface, leaving it there to dry, place waxed paper underneath. I prefer the stronger freezer waxed wrap, especially when using contact glues or instant bonds. For gluing two thin areas together (paper on acetate), place between two sheets of waxed paper and set under heavy object to flatten while drying.

✔ Waxed paper is also useful if you are machine sewing a very sheer fabric, which may tend to catch. Place waxed paper under fabric before you sew. After stitching, paper can be pulled away.

✔ To pick up a very tiny piece of "anything," moisten tip of toothpick with tongue and toothpick will stick to small item—paper, bead, seashell, pearl or anything small that needs to be picked up. Place small item in position.

✔ Sanding in small curved areas of wood can be troublesome. If you don't have needle files, cut a piece of sandpaper 1″ × 3″. Fold sandpaper over round toothpick and proceed to sand.

✔ To pierce a hole through plastic, heat an ice pick or pointed end of drapery hook over flame and quickly push point through plastic (great for deodorant balls).

✔ Save all the little scraps of wood that accumulate from cuttings. Many times those seemingly insignificant pieces are just what you need for something else that's very tiny and they're already conveniently cut.

✔ Use a hole puncher for making perfect little round pieces when needed.

✔ When working with fabric, you will sometimes finish off edges with hemming or a trim. However, if material is too thick for hemming or undesirable for finishing off in another way, smear a very thin application of white glue along edges on reverse side of material. When dry, cut away edge and material will not ravel. Of course, allow an extra measure of ⅛″ of fabric when planning to do this and always test material first.

✔ To obtain smooth folds, lay paper or cardboard on sharp edge of counter and press two sides around counter edge. Another method to fold cardboard is with a steel edge ruler and razor blade; *gently* run a very delicate indentation along all fold edges.

✔ Sewing will become an impossible task at times. Thanks to the wonderful craft glues that are available, glue your tiniest projects together. After material has dried, add a few stitches with needle and thread for extra security.

✔ Wax Stickum is the best adherent for affixing things to walls, tables and floors.

Fig. 2-12 Some recommended beads, bits and things that are used or can be used in the creation of miniatures; most are available through shops or mail-order dealers.

There is also clay Stickum. However, be advised that these will stain.

✔An emery board makes a fine sander for small pieces of wood.

✔For adhering wallpaper to a wall, use a regular wallpaper paste or thin application of white glue. Do not use rubber cement—this dries out and turns brown.

✔When working with miniatures, there can sometimes be a frustratingly long period of waiting for glue to become firm. To eliminate impatience, work on several items at one time and shift from piece to piece, allowing proper time for glue to take hold.

✔Two small flat pieces glued together can be held in place until glue sets by clipping on a two-pronged hair-setting clip.

Larger pieces can be held by clip clothespins.

✔If you have wood cut $1/16''$ thick and a project also needs $1/8''$ thick, glue two pieces of $1/16''$ wood together, weight under heavy books overnight. Proceed to cut pattern.

✔Add papier mâché to plaster and the mixture will not crack.

✔Spraying a tiny object or flat piece of wood will cause it to "fly away" from you. Secure tiny piece in place by holding pointed end of toothpick on it, then spray.

✔Felt material can be molded into curved shapes: wet material, squeeze out excess fluid, wrap around curved object, secure firmly, and allow to dry.

✔Cafe curtain rings may sometimes be too

large for your needs. To make perfect smaller circles ½" and less is easy. Cut 2" of 18-gauge copper wire, depending upon size you want, wrap tightly around stem of marking pen, pen holder, paintbrush holder; with diagonal cutter, snip through the two wires; excess wire will fall away, leaving round circle. Separation point can be covered with tiny jump link or piece of cut filigree or just left as is.

✔Observe the chains at the jewelry counter. They are beautiful in design and many, when disconnected, become useful for handles, legs, decorations, links, fasteners and other projects.

✔Lengths of beads also come in multiple designs. You can often acquire several different styles of beads and chains, all in one long strand.

✔Lastly, if you make a mistake, repeat the project. You'll do better the second time around. I always do!

Part II Accessories

3

Frames, Artwork and Sculpture

A room looks undistinguished and bare until there is something on the walls; framed art, reproductions, photographs and other artistic endeavors magically contribute to the finished effect.

Fashion influences many things, including frame design and styles of painting. Heavy gold-leaf ornamentation was popular in the seventeenth and eighteenth centuries. Elaborate frames are still available and used today in period style homes as long as the painting and furnishings are compatible—but perhaps the best rule of thumb for a contemporary house is to individually judge each piece of work and appropriately blend your art and frame. (See color Fig. 11.)

The one regrettable aspect about the advent of photography is the lost art of family portraiture as an esteemed wall decoration. Portraits in oil, pastel or watercolor were the only way of personifying and permanently identifying important members of family and society. In addition to distinguished portraiture of the late 1700s and 1800s, landscape paintings depicted areas of historical interest and regional scenes.

Reverse glass paintings enjoyed popularity during the nineteenth century and these even found their way into the decoration of mirrors and clocks. Profile and silhouette portraits were an expedient method for attaining likenesses of individuals. Portraiture or full-figure cutouts were mounted on contrasting white or black paper or material. Whether it's folk art or fine art, paintings add much to the home.

Prints are another artistic contribution to wall decoration. These, too, represented personal likenesses, landscapes, still life and other genre. Most notable are Currier and Ives, Godey's ladies and Audubon's famous birds.

Photography became the answered prayer for the quick and accurate recording of pictorial subjects. Although commercial sources benefit the most, walls can still be beautified by some very artistic renderings of landscape and still life. Family portraiture, most popular during the late nineteenth and early twentieth centuries, added a very personal touch. But if you were to ask the young teens in the family of today, they'd probably vote for the popular wall posters that decorate their rooms.

It's the unexpected that makes miniaturing a beautiful world. Our local arts

Fig. 3-1 *Across top and down:* A photograph of a great aunt looks regal in a daguerreotype frame; Chinese paper cutout horses on red velour paper in a white and gold plastic frame; a bauble of a gold plastic soldier in profile rests in a handmade lace-decorated, gold-painted frame; snapshots are in gold rings with filigree top, on ribbon caught with a choker clasp; greeting card portion of deer sets in a pearl buckle; catalogue picture of a ship is mounted on a handmade frame; the hand-painted duck on ceramic dome (Oriental) is on blue velour paper set in a handmade frame. On the background screen (originally a cologne box) are a pair of hand-painted silhouette profiles in a pair of bracelet links; a watercolor of roses is set off by a gold-embossed paper mat in a handmade frame. Victorian tic-tac-toe holds a cut print from a catalogue; a three-dimensional plastic profile sits on red velour, surrounded by a pearl finding, a cafe curtain ring and topped with cut filigree. Handmade frame matted in red check contains a cute little original drawing. Top right presents a picture hook (with bottom hook removed)—the little round center is perfect for paper cutout. The lady, hand painted by yours truly, is just right in a metal pin with clasp removed. Tinsel paper art is in a handmade frame; a tiny cherished locket from a long-ago dance frames my two favorite people. The gentleman, who was painted by your author, is matched to a beautiful stained basswood frame complete with gold liner. All handmade frames are described with directions accompanying Figure 3-4.

council presented a very talented artistic paper cutter, Cheng Hou-Tien, in an exhibition and demonstration. His large cuttings were outstanding but when I saw his miniatures, which were less than ½″, I melted. Did I get one? You better believe it! Two tiny horses (Fig. 3-1)!

Sculpture, although not confined to a frame, makes its appearance in many forms. Primitive art has its appeal in the wooden weather vane, figureheads, shop signs, eagles, ducks, the cigar store Indian and so on. Carved work in stone and scrimshaw (carvings on whale's tooth or

Fig. 3-2 Two "dog whistle" posts mounted on wooden buttons rope off a collection of sculpture. Man's head was molded from Sculpey; rolled piece of copper glued to marble and twisted paper clip constitute modern offerings; bas relief plaster head and ceramic fish were both purchased. Handsome clay sculptured Oriental figure is from China; hand-carved, painted duck, a "modern" hand-carved owl from marble and a purchased plastic bird complete the collection.

tusk) offer the diminutive in this craft. Notable Grecian sculpture is copied from museum pieces and graces many a tabletop. Parian statuary is a form of sculpture, conceived from pottery, which reached great heights of popularity during the nineteenth century. Prominent people have been immortalized in busts and figures of frosted glass, wood, marble and bronze. Modern sculpture is in a world of its own and can range from stylized renditions of figures to lumps of gracefully carved, polished marble or twisted, agonized pieces of metal (Fig. 3-2).

A few generalized suggestions for framing can help. *Oil paintings* ordinarily use a wide frame, sometimes a liner, no mat and no glass. Frames may be stained, painted, gilded or finished off in some other manner. *Watercolors* and pastels are used in shallow, narrow frames with white or colored mat, and covered by glass or acrylic. *Theorem* (*painting on velvet*) and *reverse glass painting* look best in simple, medium-size frames. *Black*

and white graphics are used in very narrow frames, white or black mat, glass or plastic covered. *Photography* requires a narrow frame or no frame for contemporary look, white mat, glass or acrylic covered. *Three dimensional* work is best displayed in a glass-fronted shadowbox frame.

While these suggestions are more or less designed to set you on the proper track, I must confess that in dollhouse frames, I have sometimes departed from the rules and in a weak moment succumbed to using other available materials.

Of course, you will want to make an elegant wooden frame and you can (Fig. 3-3). Real honest-to-goodness frame moldings are available from the model shops or dealers (see Sources of Supply), which offer a varied basswood assortment from narrow to wide in authentic scale.

Being able to make your own frame has an advantage. You can ascertain the size you need from small to extra large and that means you're in control of the situa-

only the use of a sharp blade. With a little effort and practice, you too can become a qualified framer. You may construct a single frame or extend your talent by adding a liner—second frame within the first frame. These are quite professional in appearance and upon completion of one of these, your ego will surely escalate.

Helpful Hints

Finished frames are available to the miniaturist through dealers and mail-order accommodations, but for more resourceful individuals who derive satisfaction from hunting for their own unique frames, here are some suggestions.

✔A beautiful frame, ready to be used, is the famous daguerreotype case, found in antique shops and shows, flea markets or great grandma's dresser drawer. It comes in assorted styles and sizes. Prices do vary, but inquiries will soon make you knowledgeable about the best value for your purpose. Let me digress for a moment as I launch into other attributes of the daguerreotype. The outer case of this frame can also be valuable since it resembles a recessed frame when disjointed from the metal insert. Cut tiny shelves of balsa wood for a catchall display of little things. If you wish to strip off this covering you will have a wooden base which can be painted or stained. This outer case could also become the top for a trunk, and the inside velvet padding can be used as a background for memorabilia or the lush material can also become an upholstery covering for a stool or chair. Ornamental buttons, painted ceramics or discarded pieces of jewelry would also look handsome mounted on the velvet. The embossed outer cover, soaked off, dried and cut to shape, becomes a beautiful fireback. If you're not using the glass to cover a print or water-color painting, save the glass for a tabletop, window or framed cabinet door. This glass is desirably thin. The little latch can be transferred to a cupboard door. You can probably think of ideas, too.

Fig. 3-3 A mahogany-stained basswood frame with an added gold liner will do wonders for your artwork. In this case it's a portrait of a gentleman from a past generation.

tion. You can finish off the moldings to your discretion, but if you wish to stain the wood, then do it first before gluing the corners together. Stain doesn't take too well if glue is stuck to wood. However, if you plan to paint or gild the frame, then joints can be completed first.

There are tiny miter boxes available at hobby shops but if you don't have one, you can try cutting a frame by using a 45°-angle triangle as a guide. Since basswood is soft, it responds to cutting with

✔ Buckles from shoes and belts may become frames, too. And they come in a variety of materials and styles from the simple to the ornate.

✔ Craft stores and mineral and gem shops have jewelry findings in stock.

✔ Brooches, bracelets, lockets and rings come in different sizes and designs and make perfect frames.

✔ Small box covers can often be utilized for a box frame.

✔ If you need a truly small and simple frame, try using a button. Insert a picture cut to the size of the inside area of the button, leaving the rim to serve as the frame.

✔ The white plastic and gold rings used for cafe curtains are also useful and inexpensive. Add a small jump link to the top of the circle to resemble a small holder.

✔ Keep alert for obsolete links from bracelets and other pieces of jewelry.

✔ If you have a dollhouse in the dollhouse, use a jump link for a frame.

✔ Small matchboxes (especially decorative ones from weddings) can be the start for a three-dimensional picture or shadowbox frame.

✔ Balsa wood (in flat pieces and strips) is usually sold in art departments or model hobby and craft shops. The strips can easily make a frame; just cut the strips to a size that is best suited for your need. Glue the four corners together as indicated. When thoroughly dry, paint the frame the color of your choice. Decorate, if desired.

✔ What you intend to put into a frame is unlimited. Save all assortment of small, small reproductions, photographs that feature water colors, oils, portrait and graphic material. When it comes time to select for your walls, you'll be glad to have a variety from which to choose.

✔ Notepapers are versatile today, featuring a marvelous selection of flowers, animals, birds, children, scenes and many other subjects.

✔ Designs on stationery are also eye-catching and provide an additional source of framable artwork.

✔ Magazines, direct-mail advertising and gift catalogues provide some good material, too.

✔ Try to avoid surfaces with a shiny finish. A soft matte effect produces a more elegant result.

✔ Tallys for card games are petite and their designs offer an additional choice. Tally cords can be used for hanging up a picture.

✔ Match covers come in an assortment of designs—minus advertising, of course.

✔ Tear open restaurant sugar packets carefully . . . the design may be just what you're looking for.

✔ Many U.S. commemorative stamps are beautifully designed, engraved and color printed. Matted and framed, they are eye-catching.

✔ Create the personal touch . . . use small snapshots of you and your family. Include a photo of your household pet, too.

✔ Dig out those old, old family albums and either photograph some pictures yourself or have them reduced in size. This will really be a meaningful wall accessory.

✔ If you admire a prominent historical figure, allow his or her photo or painting to become part of the miniature scene.

✔ Hang two or three pictures of a related subject, for instance, floral prints or birds, together as a grouping.

✔ Create a grouping of three or more pieces of art which can be similar in concept or contrasting in size and technique.

✔ Group several pictures in one big frame on one mat, cutting appropriate size openings to fit around each picture.

✔ Create a tinsel painting.

✔ Try a reverse painting on glass.

✔ Do a simple folk painting on a wooden panel.

✔ Suspend some work from the ceiling with tasseled cord or chain.

✔ Save the acetate covering that is used in packaging stationery box tops and cosmetics. This duplicates a glass covering over your prints.

✔ Notice that the glass in small, old-fashioned frames is often very thin—good for miniature use.

✔ Whatever pleases you will look beautiful

either inserted into a frame; simply matted on a piece of decorated cardboard; glued onto a thin piece of wood; or bordered with some braid, cord, string, ribbon or metallic trim.

How to Make Formal and Casual Frames

The following instructions for frame styles shown in Figure 3-4 may be altered to accommodate the size of the artwork you have in mind. The moldings, although specified in the text, may also be changed for the effect you want.

FORMAL FRAME WITH LINER

Moldings are Northeastern PFC-8 and PFD-6 for the frame in Fig. 3-4A.

If you don't have a small miter box, it can be a mite tricky cutting your corners, but let's try it the second best way with a 45°-angle triangle and lots of luck. Lay the 45° angle on your molding for a corner and cut straight through the wood with a very sharp knife blade or razor blade. Reverse triangle and cut molding from other side, determining the length that you want. Measure cut molding for a second similar piece and repeat the process. Cut two more pieces for third and fourth sides, determining their length. Try for fit. If they need a bit of trimming for a good right angle fit, trim *very* little. Stain. Glue two corners together. Allow to dry thoroughly. Try for fit, then glue other two corners together.

Liner is made the same way, but it must fit snugly within the rabbet area of outer frame. The enlarged cross section of two moldings shows the larger molding as the outer frame and the inset as a separate smaller frame which fits within the rabbet of the larger frame. Paint inset gold and stain outer molding walnut (or color of your choice). When thoroughly dry, glue two frames together.

This frame also becomes the basic structure for a tray with an inset, which can be finished off in various ways (see

Ch. 6). It can also be used to construct some lovely mirrors (see Ch. 4) and it proves itself useful in the construction of furniture doors (Ch. 19). When all is said and done, it just might be wise to invest in a mini miter box. The saw is also very useful for sawing other small pieces of wood.

FRAME WITH ROPE

For the frame in Figure 3-4B, first cut large back rectangle of 1/16″ wood or cardboard and cover with material. Cut smaller rectangle of 1/16″ cardboard and glue an appropriate picture onto it. Trim. Center and glue onto background. Using a heavy string, start with a knot at one corner, proceed to glue a stretch of string, knot, string, knot, etc., until the border is complete.

FILIGREE CORNER

No molding for this frame (Fig. 3-4C). Just use four simple strips of balsa or another wood 1/16″ thick and glue together. Cut a small circle of flat filigree into quarters and glue ornaments in corners. Spray gold.

LARGE CARVE

Selecting a thin molding, such as Northeastern PFB-4, make outer frame. Cut a bristol board mat to fit within frame. Glue a heavy lace trim to mat (Fig. 3-4D). Glue into frame and spray everything white.

DELICATE CARVE

Make outer frame from a molding, such as Northeastern PFB-4. Fit a mat for the frame. Glue delicate lace onto the mat, taking care to miter the corners (Fig. 3-4E). Spray everything gold.

TIC-TAC-TOE

Cut the pieces as indicated in Figure 3-4F out of 1/32″ balsa. Stain dark walnut. Glue together. Cut six-prong bead cap in half. Flatten and glue in corners. Repeat. Stain four corners brown to match walnut stain.

Fig. 3-4 Formal and casual frames.

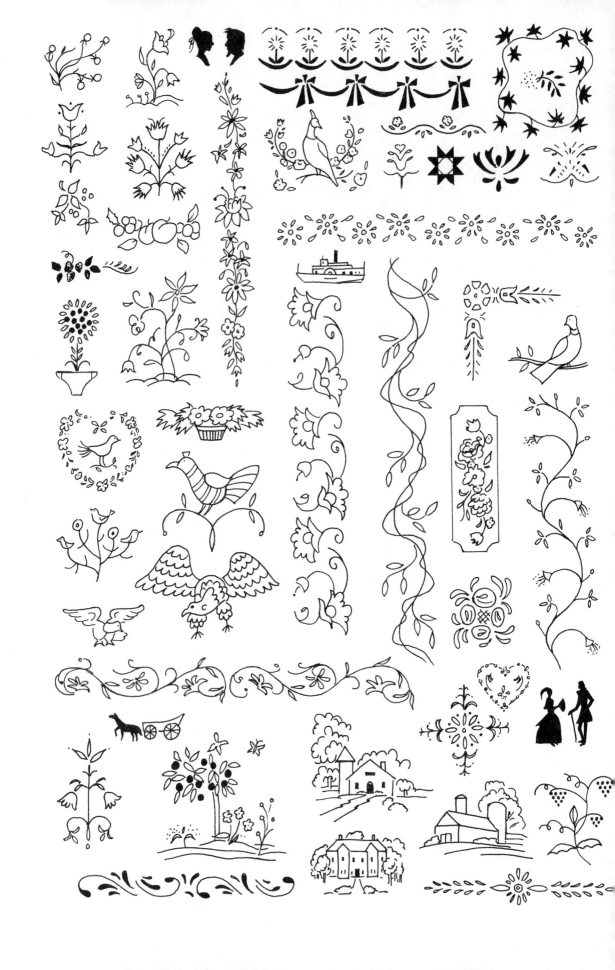

BAMBOO

Cut antiseptic stick into needed lengths. With diagonal cutter, gently twist into the wood to create bamboo look (Fig. 3-4G). Miter corners and glue together. Paint black or red. Add a teensy gold stripe at each cut if you want.

SHADOWBOX

Use balsa wood $1/32''$ thick, cut to strips $1/4''$ wide. Decide length and width and glue together. Cut a back piece to fit over the edges and glue. Select a molding and make one to fit around front of box for an attractive frame, as shown in Figure 3-4H.

COVERED MAT

Cut shape of mat out of index card to fit your frame. Apply glue to surface and place on back of material or gold or colored paper. Cut material in opening as indicated by dotted lines in Figure 3-4I. Apply glue to material on sides and pull back over edges of the mat.

How to Make Framable Miniature Designs

I'd be remiss if I didn't provide my readers with some petite designs to use for their convenience (Fig. 3-5). Knowing how advantageous it can be to have some line drawings readily available, I've compiled an assorted group of multipurpose designs. These can be incorporated into a variety of accessories, depending upon your purpose and ingenuity.

Some of these drawings can be used as source material for paintings and then framed. Other drawings will prove themselves useful for some other media, as mentioned further along in the book or as outlined below.

✔ Transfer a design to bristol board; outline design in black and fill in rest of areas with transparent colors, using ink, felt-tipped pens or watercolor.

✔ Fill in areas of design with an opaque paint, blending areas as they meet.

✔ Create a stark black and white design on a colored background.

✔ Create a tinsel painting. Trace off black lines on glass with fine-lined marking pen and fill in areas with felt-tipped colored inks. Lay wrinkled aluminum foil directly on the painted surface. Turn over and frame.

✔ Do a theorem painting on velvet with acrylic paint; fruit and/or flowers are the designs most often used.

✔ Make a reverse glass painting. Start with dark accent areas first, applying opaque paint in order of objects that project to forefront of picture first; then work to background.

✔ Adapt a design for a folk art painting on wood.

✔ Designs can be applied for stencil art on walls and floors.

✔ Designs can be used for furniture: paint trim on chests of drawers, dowry chests, chairs, etc.

✔ Adapt a portion of a larger design for use in decorating toleware and woodenware.

✔ Several designs can become patterns for embroidery work (crewel) for pillows, bedspreads, bed hangings, linens, clothing, cornices, etc.

✔ Continue some of the long panel designs to create your own wallpaper.

There, that's a dozen assorted suggestions for you to think about. Refer to other chapters, too—there may be something along the way that inspires other usage.

Fig. 3-5   Miniature artwork designs for framing and other decorative uses.

Mirrors, Clocks and
Other Wall Accessories

Walls can sometimes tell little secrets. The sentimentalist will hang photos of family, the achiever will display hobbies, the investor will show off collections and, of course, the patron of the arts will share her walls with renditions of fine art. Walls can be fun to decorate and they can be anything you choose to make them (Fig. 4-1).

MIRRORS

Venice, Italy, long known as the glass center of the world, was the first locale to create the looking glass in the sixteenth century. About 1670, England began to make mirrors and American produced mirrors in limited amount in the late 1700s.

In the beginning, mirrors were a luxury and they became cherished possessions. Even small broken pieces were prized. Mass production changed the status of mirrors from elegant to commonplace.

Like furniture, styles in mirrors change, too. Chippendale, Queen Anne, Hepplewhite, Sheraton and others all leave their mark of distinction; with a little resourcefulness, a pinch of ingenuity and a bit of modification, some of these beauties can be reproduced in miniature (Figs. 4-2 and 4-3).

Because of reflective value, mirrors were used to good advantage with lighting appliances. Placed appropriately in sconces, they increased light value twofold.

Mirrors today are not just used for reflection. They have gained a place for themselves as a means of decoration, too, and many a home has been enhanced by a mirrored fireplace and a mirrored wall.

CLOCKS

Useful, wonderful clocks! Our days and nights are ruled by time, whether it's spent in work, leisure, daydreams or sleep. The clock is not only a functional item, but is indeed a work of art. Artisans and craftsmen over the past few hundred years have created masterpieces of design which today command great respect as both *art d'objets* and financial investments. Whether a clock is for wall, mantel, shelf or floor, variety is infinite.

Reaching back into time, a sundial may rest comfortably in a garden; let's not forget the sand glass which gained prominence in the 1300s. In spite of the advance

Fig. 4-1 Embroidery can be fun, beautiful and *easy!* Find a piece of cotton fabric that has a tiny printed pattern and embroider right over the design. The bouquet pattern (upper left corner) shows before and after. The profile of the little girl also starts with a print and portions of outline and the hair are completed with embroidery chain stitch. The bird on the mailbox was cut from embroidered Swiss notepaper. The two oval frames were children's bracelets. The big bird tapestry was taken from purchased ribbon trim. The shadowbox has a miniature arrangement. The small collection box has spices and the larger box holds nature's wonders—polished stones, seashells, driftwood and a rosebud. The lion is a separated cuff link, the roses are three tiny gift cards transposed into three-dimensional papier tole, the upper round decoration is a pendant, the lower round decoration is a plastic bauble. The bulletin board of cork rests in outer case of daguerreotype. The heraldic bauble was a pin. The calendar is a calendar. The cherubs resemble Wedgwood and are framed in a pin finding. A decoupaged art print and an enameled round of copper complete this photo of wall suggestions. The handmade wall accessories in this photo are described with instructions in this chapter.

in timepieces, these two are still popular in limited usage or as decorative accents.

Mechanical clocks were only conceived 700 years ago, but there are too many clocks to individually identify by name. Suffice it to say that early domestic clocks

from Europe, starting in 1500, were beautifully and ornately constructed: modeled in bronze or brass, they were a foretaste of finer and more accurately run mechanisms.

French and English clocks were elabo-

Fig. 4-4 The bracket clock, so named because it was originally intended to sit upon a wall bracket, has often been placed on other satisfactory surfaces, including mantels, shelves and tables. (*Jack Ruthberg, photograph*)

Fig. 4-2 Framed mirrors can be created from scratch or devised from what's available. The mirror at top left is set within a pearl buckle. Below is a handmade frame with lace inset, all painted gold. The Colonial mirror is mahogany and uses miniature frame molding. My favorite, the Sheraton country style, is handmade with reverse glass painting. The three round styles show twine encircled, a doodad back and pink pearl lights added for a cosmetic mirror.

Fig. 4-3 Tiny white baby cups and the smallest of univalve seashells combine to become a beautiful border for a circular mirror. This can also be done with a rectangular shape.

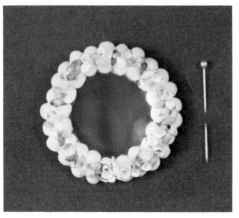

rate with decorations of brass, tortoise shell and ormalu. American clockmakers rejected ornateness and concentrated on simplicity in design, augmented by beautiful wooden cabinets. The most heralded clock for graceful design is the banjo, which is a wall clock. A mantel clock, the Terry is also a popular model, but for clean simple lines the schoolhouse clock is most precious and popular. Grandfather clocks, tall, stately and dignified, earn a respectable place in any home.

For the updated household, clock cases can test the ingenuity of everyone. A modern stylized design can be copied from any number of sources or you can be inventive and design your own creation.

Has anyone made a cuckoo clock in miniature?

NEEDLEWORK

Samplers set the pattern for a young lady's introduction to needlework, for there was nary a lass who didn't learn this art a few centuries ago. The sampler was an "exemplar" of embroidery stitches, which formed the basis for future work on household linens and such. There were many stitches involved but the fundamental ones were cross stitch, tent stitch (needlepoint), satin stitch and outline stitch. Early samplers were comprised of

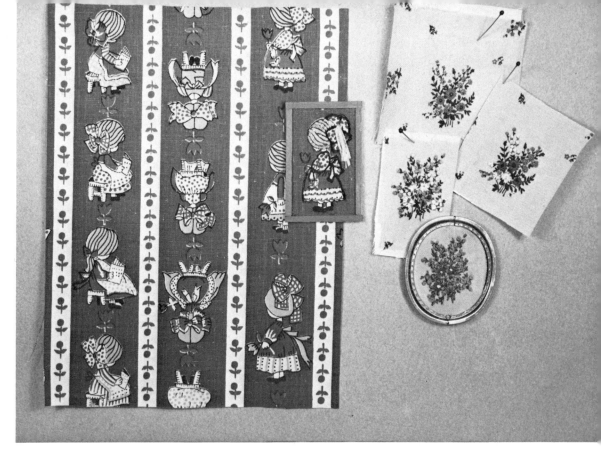

Fig. 4-5 Small prints in fabrics can range from beautiful florals to whimsical figures. Designs are cut out and glued onto another, sturdier piece of fabric. Using one or two strands of embroidery floss, embroider right *over* the design, copying the colors already imprinted, or change to your own choice. The little girl pattern was placed in a balsa wood frame. The floral on the right is finished off in different color schemes and the one on the bottom is framed in a child's bracelet.

fruit and flowers, birds and animals, borders, alphabets and, oftentimes, a verse. The "house" made its appearance around the middle of the eighteenth century and remained popular all through the nineteenth century as did other designs.

The embroidered picture became another type of needlework, sometimes complex and elaborate. They were worked on linen in the petit-point stitch and also on silk in a variety of stitches. Romantic, religious and pastoral scenes were composed.

Needlework has always enjoyed a place on the wall and once upon a time crewel embroidery was synonymous with Jacobean design. In this great revival of needlework, crewel and needlepoint are enjoying great popularity. Anything seems to be acceptable in today's feast of designs: petite or huge, formal or casual, sty-lized or modern, sedate or bizarre. Take your pick.

HOBBIES

Hobbies can take in a lot of territory, but in this case we're interested in the ones that can benefit a wall. Collectibles are one answer and these will have to identify with the century for which you're planning. There are some items that can be fastened to a wall, others will sit on shelves and still others are best confined in a cabinet. I dare say, in many instances your own preference and even your own personal hobby will take form and shape in miniature.

Since seashells are my second love, that brings me to shelling (Figs. 4-6 and 4-7). If you reside near or visit a good shelling beach, your miniature wall arrangements will flourish. The smallest of the small

41

Fig. 4-6 A seashell arrangement is displayed in a daguerreotype frame. A sample pill container is painted red and lodges a different miniature in each section, and one specimen shell is proudly displayed on a bracket. The small dried fish, mounted on wood, was purchased years ago, but that's the reward for "fishing for collectibles"—you've got it when you need it.

ways throughout this book. I love them and any secrets I have about them, I like to share with you.

POTPOURRI

Decoupage and *papier tole* are two old-time crafts that have been resurrected, updated and popularized again. Treat them as an antique craft or modernize them for an up-to-date look. *Quilling* is another beautiful decoration that deserves consideration.

Dry pressing flowers and arranging them under glass is another old-fashioned art cultivated by devotees (Fig. 4-8). Colonial Williamsburg still has remnants of this craft on some of its walls.

Memorabilia boxes bring us right on up to the present time. It's a little bit of old, a little bit of new, but whichever, it's pure nostalgia. You really have to scrounge for the smallest of the small and be very inventive to find your miniature memorabilia—but where there's a will, there's a way and, somehow, I think you'll conquer this one, too.

Although the essentials in wall decoration seem to be covered, let's not forget some of the functional items. Humbly speaking, where would we be without the *calendar* and *bulletin board* to remind us of our daily commitments? With that statement I now stand committed to show you how to make some of the aforesaid items.

shells are usually found in the mounds of seemingly crushed shell that wends its way along the shoreline. Scoop up a few good handfuls and place in a plastic bag, box or milk container. At home leisurely sift through small amounts at a time and with a tweezer, extract your tiny finds. The best locations for miniatures on the East coast are Sanibel Island and in the Florida Keys, Lower Matacumbe. Shell supply sources may also sell miniatures, but not always the variety in petite sizes that the beaches can yield. Small shells can also be shown as a hobby collection on a shelf or in a cabinet. In fact, don't be surprised to see shells popping up in various

Helpful Hints

✔Make an accent mirror. Paint wooden framework around a mirror a bright color and add some tiny painted flowers for decoration.

✔Early modern style featured large plate-glass mirrors over mantels, behind sofas, buffets, dressing tables and in front foyers.

✔Add a long mirror to a closet door.

✔Make a mirror to hang above a console table.

✔Make a long mirror to hang above a pier table.

✔A small Oriental rug can be hung as a tapestry.

- For fine embroidery work use one or two strands of embroidery floss. For very fine work use regular sewing thread.
- Take advantage of printed cotton fabric with petite designs. Leave some of the printed pattern showing and edge the design with embroidery work.
- Miniature needlepoint kits and cross-stitch kits are available (see Sources of Supply).
- Sometimes a greeting card features embroidery as a design. These are often available at Christmas time. Once framed, this makes an elegant wall-piece.
- How about that handkerchief with the small embroidery in the corner? It resembles crewel and when framed it's lovely.
- Even an embroidered initial, simply mounted, can say so much.
- Embroider a miniature map. These were popular in the nineteenth century.
- For clock faces, cut out illustrations from advertisements and catalogues.
- Look for very small pocket watches. If you find one that works, incorporate this into a clock for a real working clock. If not working, the face still provides a very authentic look, complete with hands. A wristwatch may also be serviceable.
- When a clock requires weights (Grandfather's clock) use cylindrical beads, or cut dowel sticks and paint bright gold or cover with gold foil paper.
- A pendulum can be made from one cut round piece from a metal pouring spout. Glue the round to a fastening pin. Paint gold.
- Metal filigree pieces and gold embossed paper help decorate the baroque or ornate style of clock.
- Glue seashells, each a different variety, onto a background. Make a frame from driftwood. Glue shells onto a thin piece of bark as another method.
- Make a tiny seashell "sailor's valentine." This is a symmetrical, closely set grouping of many shells with borders, flowers and designs, set within a box—originally made for sweethearts, wives and mothers.
- Collect a coarse hairnet. Using a small

Fig. 4-7 A miniature seashell grouping set within a daguerreotype frame will enhance any wall. Other accessories are dried alyssum in glass bead vase on glass button base; a pair of lamps—beads on baubles; a buddah—earring—on wooden base; and purchased ceramic fish, all resting on a console table and small wall bracket. (*Jack Ruthberg, photograph*)

portion of net, catch small seashells up in an arrangement with glue. Spray well with clear acrylic or hairspray. When dry, transfer to a background or directly onto wall. Glue into place.
- For the contemporary youngsters' room decoupage their favorite cartoon character. Snoopy and Mickey Mouse are both destined to become collectors' items.
- Combine pressed flowers with tiny lace

43

for the daintiest dry flower arrangements.

✔ For the all-girl bulletin board, use green felt for a background and place within a very pretty oval frame. Tack up miniature greeting cards, a flower or corsage, a dance program, a piece of jewelry or anything else that's sweet and sentimental.

✔ An entire yearly calendar, on a single card and usually dispensed by banks or businesses, can be dressed up and used in an office or store.

✔ Small metal spread eagles turn up unexpectedly. Paint gold or black and mount on the wall.

✔ Make a collage out of your favorite materials or use the inside parts of an unworkable watch.

✔ Create a weather vane. Cut out "two" of a rooster, whale, or whatever, from card. Glue back to back with an upright rod of wire between the two pieces. Extend another rod across the bottom, right angled to the upright. Add the letter N to front of wire. Paint black. Mount on wall.

✔ Acquire a collection of one of the following: plates, mugs, steins, glass birds or other birds, animals, candlesticks, etc. Show them off on wall shelves.

✔ Do memorabilia boxes "grab" you? Select a member of the family—baby, boy, girl, teenager, adult—then proceed to plan box fillers related to the person's interests. Or fill a box with kitchen items, needlework, school subjects or flowers.

Fig. 4-8 Nature's wonders are the most gratifying to work with: a dried pressed flower arrangement of alyssum and bramble bush flower buds sparkles on a dark blue velour background. The lower dried arrangement is typical of nature's phenomena. The tiny "floral" birds flying and sitting on a silver bead wire are really wildflower Vetches (blue and purple)—individually plucked off and pressed. And if they're dried in silica gel they retain a lovely three-dimensional quality. Don't look at the whole item and stop! Look at all the individual parts, too. The birds were placed on a light blue chintz for sky background and a few sprigs of tiny dyed dried grass were added. The effect is awesome, so look for *Vetches* in the summer-fall season. They grow throughout the United States.

How to Make Bracket Clocks, Memorabilia Boxes and Extra Wall Accessories

The step-by-step instructions in this section supply the details for making the assortment of wall accessories shown in Figure 4-9.

BRACKET CLOCK

Materials: Walnut wood, $^1/8''$, $^1/16''$ and $^1/32''$; balsa wood, $^1/4''$; gold cardboard;

Fig. 4-9   Bracket clock, memorabilia boxes, framed shadowbox, other ideas for attractive wall hangings.

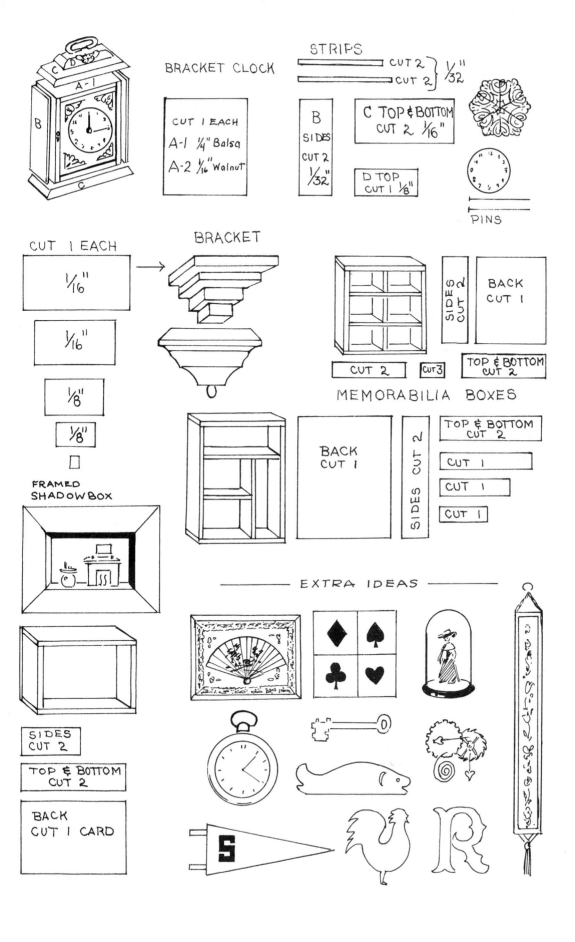

BRACKET CLOCK

STRIPS

CUT 2 } 1/32"
CUT 2 } 1/32"

CUT 1 EACH
A-1 1/4" Balsa
A-2 1/16" Walnut

B
SIDES
CUT 2
1/32"

C TOP & BOTTOM
CUT 2 1/16"

D TOP
CUT 1 1/8"

PINS

CUT 1 EACH

BRACKET

1/16"

1/16"

1/8"

1/8"

SIDES
CUT 2

BACK
CUT 1

CUT 2   CUT 3

TOP & BOTTOM
CUT 2

FRAMED
SHADOWBOX

MEMORABILIA BOXES

BACK
CUT 1

SIDES CUT 2

TOP & BOTTOM
CUT 2

CUT 1

CUT 1

CUT 1

SIDES
CUT 2

TOP & BOTTOM
CUT 2

BACK
CUT 1 CARD

EXTRA IDEAS

S

clock face, which can be cut from a catalogue, no larger than $9/16''$ in diameter; filigree for corner trim; gold pins for hands; link for handle.

Directions:

1. Glue gold cardboard to front of balsa wood (A-1) and glue walnut back (A-2) to back of balsa wood (A-1).

2. Glue sides (B) into position.

3. Sand and bevel three sides of top and bottom pieces (C). Glue into place.

4. Sand and round four top sides of top piece (D) and glue on the top.

5. Glue face of clock in center of gold cardboard. Add four cut pieces of filigree to corner (or lace can be used and painted gold).

6. Drill hole in center of face; glue two hands made from cut pins into position and glue top portion of pin into hole covering over ends of pins.

7. Glue strips of wood along front sides and top and bottom. Add filigree lock on left, trim on top and, lastly, glue a flattened link onto top for handle.

BRACKET SHELF

1. Cut the four patterns out of $1/8''$ and $1/16''$ walnut.

2. Glue four pieces together, lining up all backs flush. The front will "step in." Dry overnight.

3. Using steel files, shape and curve under areas. Except for top shelf, eliminate squared look. Just have fun and file away. Add small ball-shaped piece to bottom.

MEMORABILIA BOXES

Materials: Balsa wood, $1/16''$ thick; clear acetate.

Directions:

1. Cut out balsa wood pieces in sizes that are indicated (these are shown same size).

2. Glue together as shown in Figure 4-9.

3. Paint box the color of your choice with acrylic.

4. Fill cubbyholes with your own choice of items; glue them into position.

5. Hold acetate in place with glue or four corner pieces (cut filigree, pin heads).

FRAMED SHADOWBOX

1. Cut out pattern of $1/16''$ thick balsa or pine.

2. Glue together as shown in Figure 4-9.

3. Fit and make a frame for front using frame molding. Stain or paint.

4. Decorate inside of box anyway you want.

EXTRA IDEAS

✔Some pieces of jewelry feature a fan, or you can make an accordion-pleated one. Glue down on satin or velvet. Trim with lace and border with a very delicate gold frame.

✔Glue cut corners of playing cards together for a different, modern look. Trim as you like.

✔Place an HO gauge little figurine under dome and adhere button base. (HO gauge is used in model railroad sizing; figurines and other miniatures are available in model railroad supply stores.)

✔Make a wall "watch" clock. Add a curtain ring to face of a clock cutout, mounted on card. Add top pieces with real expendable watch parts, if possible.

✔Add a small metal key or carve a key out of wood.

✔Cut a fish out of wood. Sand front edges round and polish well.

✔Make a collage out of watch parts or from other interesting small articles.

✔Cut a banner out of felt, saluting your alma mater or some other school.

✔Make a rooster out of thin wood or aluminum. Hang on the wall or make into a weather vane decoration.

✔Carve an initial out of wood. Sand front areas round and smooth. Polish or lacquer.

✔Make a bell pull using very narrow embroidery trim, or do your own crewel embroidery needlework.

BULLETIN BOARD

Thin sheets of cork are available in crafts stores. Cork can be inserted within a frame and adorned with notes, push pins (ball-head pins) and whatever else you choose to tack up (see Figure 4-1).

CALENDAR

Sometimes a tiny calendar finds its way into your home via direct-mail advertising. If not, variety stores or stationery stores may be able to oblige. Mount this in an attractive way and, depending upon the room it's used in, dress it up or dress it down. It does become an excellent way of forevermore dating your little house—if it's contemporary.

How to Make Mirrors, Tapestry, Flower and Seashell Arrangements

Instructions are supplied in this section for making several mirror styles and other elegant and casual wall accessories shown in Figure 4-10.

COLONIAL MIRROR

1. Cut $1/32''$ thick back (A) from mahogany or pine (can be stained mahogany).
2. Make a frame (B) using Northeastern PFA-6 molding.
3. Cut a thin mirror to fit within frame molding; glue everything together and securely down onto (A).

SEASHELL MIRROR

Materials: 1″ round mirror (craft shop) —if unavailable, a square shape can also be used; miniature seashells—assorted and white baby cups; bristol board.

Directions:
1. Cut a round of bristol board, $1^{5}/_{16}''$ in diameter.
2. Glue mirror to board.
3. Wind strip of cotton into a length and glue around mirror; keep moist.
4. Glue white baby cupshells all around mirror, extending beyond the edge of board.
5. Creating a pattern, glue variety of mini univalves and bivalves on top of cup shells.

COUNTRY-STYLE SHERATON MIRROR

Construct a frame, using Northeastern molding PFA-8. Stain all parts mahogany before gluing. Fit and glue crossbar into place. Cut one glass to fit into top area and one mirror to fit into lower area. Using acrylic, carefully paint in the house and background on glass in the following manner. Place drawing under glass and fill in colors in this order: black windows and door; white house; gray or red roof; red chimneys; dark green bushes in front, dark green trees; light green grass—extend a little up in back and sides of house, mixing with darker green; beige walk; blue sky.

Turn the painting over and you will have a reverse painting on glass. Glue painted glass and mirror into frame.

ROPE MIRROR

A piece of good quality twine is glued to the edge of round mirror. This can be done with a square-shaped mirror, also.

SEASHELL ARRANGEMENT

Seashells in miniature are an awakening experience, perhaps because these tiny miracles of beauty are lost in vast stretches of beach. Reach out and find them and possess a miniature seashell arrangement of your very own.

Materials: Natural miniature seashells; frame with covered background of material or elegant paper.

Directions:
1. Start out by selecting a "base" shell (scallop) to represent a vase.
2. Create a stem effect by shaping an arrangement that resembles a spray or glue down fine green florist's wire.
3. Create little flowers with tiny cup shells, buds with univalves, etc.
4. Leaves are not necessary in seashell work but if you prefer some, cut tiny ones out of flower pictures in catalogues, shape some out of Velverette ribbon, or use tiny plastic leaves.

HANGING TAPESTRY

Search through embroidered ribbon trims and look for those that pertain to animals, birds, flowers, etc. These can be turned into delightful wall hangings in the following way.

Prepare tapestry: When cutting, allow extra design on each side for fold back

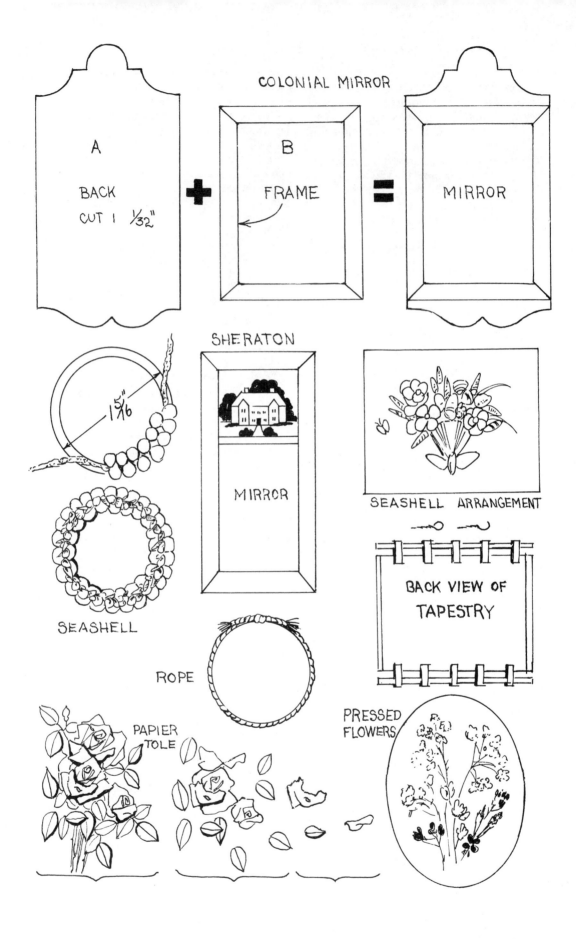

COLONIAL MIRROR

A
BACK
CUT 1 1/32"

+

B
FRAME

=

MIRROR

SHERATON

MIRROR

SEASHELL ARRANGEMENT

1 5/16"

SEASHELL

ROPE

BACK VIEW OF
TAPESTRY

PAPIER
TOLE

PRESSED
FLOWERS

and gluing, for neat finished appearance. If threads from embroidery push over onto your main design, pull out threads carefully, first.

1. Cut two pieces of dress hanger wire as wide as your tapestry will be.

2. Cut several strips of Velverette ribbon, $1/8'' \times 3/4''$ long.

3. Fold each strip over the bars and glue tips together (see Fig. 4-10).

4. Glue strips to back of tapestry on top and bottom.

DRY PRESSED FLOWERS

The subject of flowers is discussed in detail in Chapter 10 and will be helpful for this project.

Materials: The tiniest picked flowers; frame; glass or acetate; material or colored paper for background, mounted on bristol board or card.

Directions:

1. Place your fresh picked flowers between pages of a telephone book and leave until dry.

2. Cover cardboard with background material to fit within frame.

3. Make an arrangement of flowers, tacking flowers with a dab of glue. Use ribbon, too, if you like. Cover over with glass or acetate and secure firmly within frame. Glue heavy brown paper on back to keep in place.

PAPIER TOLE

To achieve dimensional depth, portions of a second and third print are pasted down with a silicone sealer, directly over a matching area.

Materials: Two or three tally cards (same picture) or any paper subject that is small; clear silicone rubber sealer; bristol board.

Directions:

1. Paste complete first picture down on bristol board or another background.

2. With a second matching picture, cut out all areas that appear *closer* to view (set aside); on third picture, cut out all areas that are *closest* to view (set aside).

3. Gently curve each cutout piece backward. Start with first group of cutouts. Using a dab of clear silicone sealer, glue each piece directly over matching area. Repeat with second group of cutouts. This will produce a raised effect.

4. Place in a frame. This may or may not be covered with acetate.

DECOUPAGE

Materials: Small pictures from catalogues; small thin pieces of wood, $1/16''$ (walnut, birch, pine); sandpaper; stain or paint; white glue.

Directions:

1. Sand wood smooth, rounding edges.

2. Stain or paint wood.

3. Dilute glue to solution: two parts glue, one part water.

4. Apply solution to wood and place picture where desired; press out extra bubbles so picture is smooth; allow to dry.

5. Continue to brush on solution several times until glossy sheen is acquired. Dry thoroughly between each brushing.

Fig. 4-10 Mirrors, seashell and pressed flower arrangements and tapestry.

Lighting Fixtures and Appliances

Today we bask in light and it's awesome to realize that for centuries our ancestors had to combat darkness. Although we may look upon candles as meager illumination, they were nevertheless considered a luxury during the eighteenth century. A grease-soaked rag or a burning rush provided the only light for many a home.

Eventually candlesticks became a very important household item. They were needed to hold candles for light and every home or shop contained several. They were made of iron, tin, carved stone, wood, pottery, brass, glass, silver and pewter. Holders varied according to their placement and use (Fig. 5-1). There were different varieties for tabletop, ranging from one candle to multiple candleholders. The sconce was attached to the wall, and the candlestand was floor based, conveniently shifted from place to place as needed. When candles were replaced by whale-oil-burning lamps, candlesticks still remained as beautiful, if not useful, decorative household articles. The advancement of fuel-burning appliances made life more endurable.

Chandeliers also ranged from the simple to the ornate and were constructed of materials from plain tin to glittering crystal. Wrought iron, brass and pewter were also used as multiple lighting fixtures, popular in the latter part of the eighteenth century.

Later, when electricity became a reality, chandeliers and lamps of bygone days were duplicated and, augmented by light bulbs, enhanced many beautiful homes (Figs. 5-2 and 5-3).

Yes, indeed, electricity wrought many changes. Lamp styles took assorted directions and the different lamps and chandeliers that resulted over the years up to the present time were either unbelievably beautiful or invariably atrocious.

Table lamps of hand-decorated glass urns and graceful porcelain figurines vie for attention with modern marble bases and globes. Contemporary pole lamps leap from floor to ceiling and hanging contraptions suspend precariously from chains attached to ceilings. Lamps are small and demure or big, bold and brassy.

Miniature lighting fixtures can provide a great choice in variety. You may be strictly attracted to contemporary or a devotee of period, but whichever you choose to do, the best results depend upon your selection of materials and much imagination. Many lamps can be minia-

Fig. 5-1 Antique illumination consists of candleholders, oil lamps and wall sconces. Several are described with directions for Figures 5-7 and 5-8, but the general materials used are a motley collection of assorted beads, earring findings, cuff links, choker clasps, necklace clasps, ampules, curtain rings, mirrors, used bullet shells, fancy bracelet links, inner pen tube, bolo tie clasp, jump links, paper clips and bits of copper.

ture replicas of varied electrical appliances (Fig. 5-4), while gas and candle-lit varieties will add nostalgic charm from the past.

For the miniaturist whose house is destined to be electrified, there are workable fixtures available through dealers. For those who are more resourceful or fortunate enough to have a helpmate who's an amateur electrician, there are other materials available on the market. With the use of transformers, bulbs, solder, wire and other essential tools, your little domain can brightly glow with the flip of a switch. Whether you proceed to have an electrified home or not will depend upon your time, available talent, finances and, of course, the time "period" of your structure. But most important is to know your home will still be most charming even if not electrified.

Helpful Hints

CANDLES

- The easiest candle is a shortened round toothpick, painted white; add a thread wick at the top.
- Roll a thin piece of white paper to the size that you want, then glue together.
- Modern candles are large. Cut a birthday candle down in length and set in anything small and attractive.

Fig. 5-2 The modern ceiling fixture is the silver top off of a deodorant can plus a big clear bead from a pendant. The next three fixtures are described with directions for Figure 5-8. The last two small ones are a bauble and an earring. The floor lamps, described with directions for Figure 5-7, are a spotlight, a torchere, a pull-chain, a candlestand and a modern globe creation.

🖝Try carving a design out of a large birthday candle—square it, too.

🖝Fill a miniature ½" to 1" univalve seashell with melted wax. Quick!—add the wick before it hardens.

🖝Holders for candles can be beads, buttons, eyelets, bead caps, jewelry findings, metal findings or anything handmade.

SCONCES AND WALL FIXTURES

🖝Large earrings (bead ornaments removed) become sconces.

Fig. 5-3 Revival means popularity and the Tiffany lampshade is back in style. Our miniature table lamp, made by gluing colored tissue paper to a plastic dome, looks quite at home on a dark green velvet skirted table topped with an old-fashioned lace doily.

☑ Flat cufflinks and buttons can also be used.

☑ Small round mirrors set within a scoop metal button or trimmed about the edge are adaptable.

☑ Belt tips become spotlight lamps.

☑ Necklace hooks or lanyard hooks help to complete a sconce (see directions).

☑ Use a sequin for a drip catcher under a candle.

☑ Check the hardware department for night lights. Some are very small and mighty clever.

CEILING FIXTURES

☑ If a glass blower is in your area, prevail upon one to "blow a fixture."

☑ Jeweler's chain is the best for use in chandelier work. It's most flexible and fits nicely through the smallest beads.

☑ Purchase an additional assortment of chains at jewelry counters and keep a watchful eye out for sale days.

☑ Use clear glass faceted teardrop beads for drop crystals.

☑ Use other clear beads that resemble bulbs . . . pearls are good.

☑ Filigree circles and other pieces are decorative and easy to tie onto with jump links and chains.

☑ Pierce holes along edge of bottle cap, suspend beads from wires and hang entire piece from a chain.

☑ Buttons that resemble light fixtures are inverted and glued to ceiling.

☑ Dangle earrings very often resemble a hanging fixture and a pair doubles the interest.

☑ Roll-on deodorant balls are marvelous for large impressive lights. Glue one into a gold bottle cap and hang upside down.

LAMP BASES

☑ Good sources for bases are lipstick containers, small glass perfume bottles, cologne bottle tops, small salt shakers, marbles, small spools, golf tees and flat buttons for under the bases.

☑ Beads, beads, beads are the answer to everyone's need for an assortment of decorative lamp bases from the tiniest to the largest. Visit your bead store.

☑ Petite ceramic or wooden animals, mounted on wood, are most attractive and eye-catching.

☑ Tiny blown glass objects make very pretty bases, too.

☑ Small figurines are appealing (especially him and her).

☑ For a unique lamp, use a colorful seashell mounted on a small driftwood base.

☑ A small, clear plastic pill container can be filled with ornamental items, such as rice, assorted colored beads, or small seashells.

☑ Lamp finials come in a wide assortment of designs and they are beautiful. Watch it!—you may be tempted to become a finial snatcher.

☑ Decoupage small designs onto a painted wooden spool; or paint some wild design on it.

☑ Bases for standing floor lamps are attractive buttons, dapped filigree findings, upside-down lids.

☑ The stand can be ⅛" dowel, paintbrush-handle, metal insert from within ballpoint pen, dress wire hanger, chopstick.

LAMPSHADES

☑ Lampshades can be made from small paper drinking cups, cut down to size; paper roll tubes, cut down; plastic res-

Fig. 5-4   All manner of table lamps, ranging from small to large, are concocted from many collectibles. Bases are combinations of beads and buttons, animals, nature's products, bottles, replicas and more. Shades are caps, cups, covers, containers, lace, trim, filigree and more. Whimsical, tiny animals become an adorable base for lamps in a suitable setting. Animals and birds are available in ceramic, wood, plastic, metal and glass.

taurant cream containers or plastic ice cube containers; bottlecaps and tube tops from toothpaste, glues, or paint. The smallest tube tops from artists' small paint tubes are especially good for night table lamps.

✓Bottlecap tops which come in assorted sizes and colors make good modern shades. Toothpaste tops are also good for pole lamps. Small tops can be used for wall lights.

✓Within table lampshade, glue a pearl which will resemble a light bulb.

✓A paper cup shade can be left white or colored with acrylic paint. Draw a tiny design on shade, using a fine felt-tipped pen. Create flowers, leaves, dots or modern designs.

✓Trim top and bottom with tiny rickrack or other narrow trim.

✓Decoupage some cutout designs onto colored paper shade.

✓Carefully glue tiny dried flowers (alyssum, spirea, baby's breath, or others) to paper shade, then spray with lacquer.

✓Paint a shade silver or gold; better, gold leaf a shade. Instructions for application accompany the gold leaf.

✓Using a sharp needle, pinprick a pattern into the shade from a preplanned design.

✓Match shade to wall fabric, covering with same material used on wall, and trim.

✓Ruffled lace topped with a velvet ribbon offers the delicate touch.

✓With needle and thread, gather soft sheer material and wrap around shade; secure it with tiny ribbon and a bow.

54

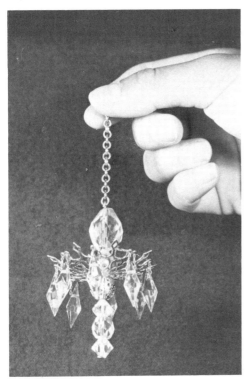

Fig. 5-5   Faceted crystal beads will glitter and seem to glow even without benefit of electricity.

✔Filigree bell caps, silver, gold or painted white, are very delicate.
✔Using the cap from a pill container, glue embroidered ribbon trim around the edge—or glue plain ribbon, velvet, grograin or satin trim.
✔Accordion pleat a length of thin paper and glue to paper shade.
✔Make tiny finials out of bead caps and other cut bits of filigree, or use a small bead.
✔Circular dome tops from spray cans look big, beautiful and modern.
✔And don't forget the roll-on deodorant balls. They're the greatest globes for table, floor, wall or hanging.

How to Make Floor Lamps, Tiffany Lamps and Sconces

Instructions are given in this section for making all the lighting fixtures shown in Figure 5-7.

PULL-CHAIN LAMP

The stand is the metal insert from a ball-point pen glued to an earring finding. The shade is a deodorant roll-on top cover; fine chain, glued to inside top, has bugle bead pulls. Pearls are inserted for light bulbs.

CANDLESTAND

This lamp is made from dowel stick and a large wooden oval bead. Crossbar and three feet are shaped. Stain all wood dark color and glue together. Add two small rolled aluminum pieces for candleholders. Add white toothpick candles.

SPOTLIGHT LAMP

The stand is a child's paintbrush handle, painted gold and mounted on an open metal piece over a wooden button. The shades are metal belt tips, glued into place with twisted copper wire, then glued *into* brush handle (drill for holes).

MODERN GLOBE LAMP

The stand is an artist's brush handle, painted gold and mounted in a decorative gold bead. The top is two filigree pieces glued together and topped with an extra large roll-on ball (the only one I have and I can't remember where I ever got it).

Fig. 5-6   Three perky uniformed soldiers were purchased and one was glorified by being turned into a lamp base. Note the lampshade, made from matching embroidery trimming.

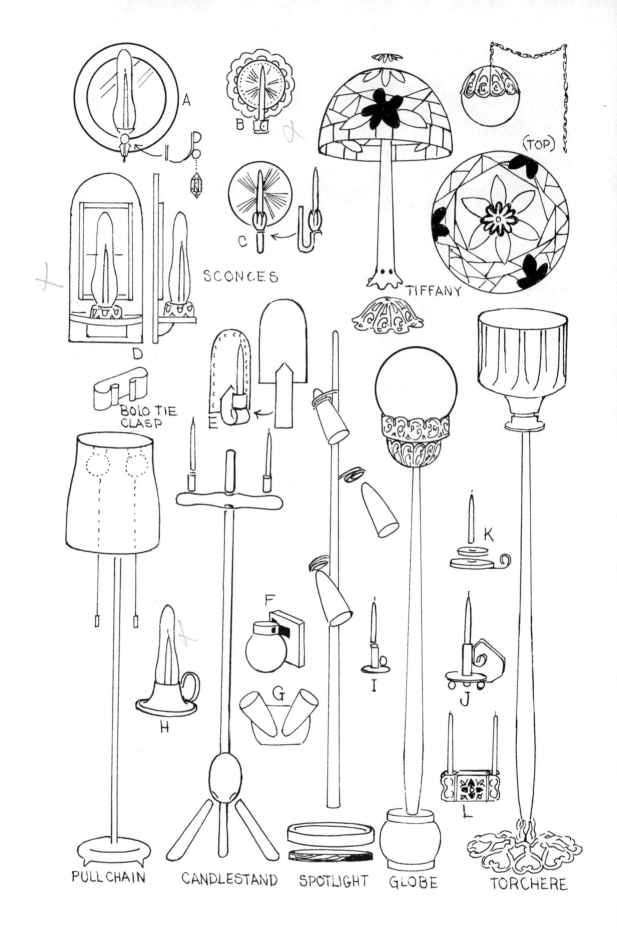

A

B

C

SCONCES

D

BOLO TIE
CLASP

E

TIFFANY

(TOP)

F

G

H

I

J

K

L

PULL CHAIN   CANDLESTAND   SPOTLIGHT   GLOBE   TORCHERE

TORCHERE LAMP

Again the stand is a paintbrush handle, but this one is ivory plastic. It's mounted on a bead cap and dapped filigree base. The top is an inverted detergent bottle top with a little gold brushed over it to eliminate the stark white appearance.

TIFFANY LAMP

Although the shade of this lamp can be colored with stained glass paints or permanent color pens, I'm presenting a different way to do this with colored tissue paper—an extra learning experience. *All tissue cutouts are glued inside the shade* and the glue is applied little by little to the area of shade that will "receive" the tissue piece. Apply glue sparingly and use your tweezers for positioning pieces.

Materials: Clear plastic dome (Love bottle top); 1¾″ bolo tie tip; ⅝″ filigree bell cap; ⅜″ filigree circle; colored tissue paper; Elmer's or Sobo glue.

Directions:

1. Cut three flowers out of red tissue and glue at equidistant intervals around inside of shade.

2. Cut out dark green tissue leaves for sides of flowers and for top of shade and glue into position.

3. Cut out alternating rectangles of yellow and light green tissue for border design along bottom of shade. Glue into position.

4. Cut out an odd assortment of triangular pieces of colors pink, fuchsia and orange tissue. These are carefully pasted down next to each other in all different ways. There is no set design for this. Try not to have colors overlap too much.

5. With the design glued into place, brush a thinned coating of glue over everything. Allow to dry.

6. On *outside* of shade, thinly outline the design with permanent black felt-tipped pen.

7. Bend out the prongs at wide bases of both bell cap and bolo tie tip. Glue bolo tip onto top of bell cap and glue top into center of shade. Use a "smidgen" of

cotton, if necessary, to help hold in place. Glue small circle (black or painted black) on top of shade.

Note: If you are unable to obtain the proper length of bolo tie tip, substitute a post. Cut a length of tapered brush handle and paint it gold.

SCONCES

Sconces can be made from scratch using copper, aluminum or whatever; others are contrived using what's available with a bit of ingenuity.

A round mirror (purchased from craft store) is glued under a metal curtain ring to make the sconce in Figure 5-7A. A portion of earring finding is glued to front and a faceted bead is added to bottom, if desired. A discarded ampule rests on top of a sequin and the toothpick candle is within. (Confession: I don't have any luck cutting the tops off my ampules so I leave them as is. Better luck to you.)

The sconce in Figure 5-7B is the simplest of all. It's an earring finding, minus the bead trim; the hinge part just wraps around the candle.

The style in Figure 5-7C is a gold cuff link separated from the back piece. The candleholder is a necklace clasp and bead or bell cap.

Making the sconce in (D) is a bit more work, but worth it. Cut a ¹/₁₆″ wooden back piece with curved top. Stain. Cut a half circle for stand and a quarter round for support (see side view). Glue mirror into place (I used two small squares from craft store or you can cut one piece to size). Make a little outside frame (from quarter round) for mirror. Glue into place. Glue stained stand in place. Glue a filigree piece on stand and, lastly, ampule and candle in place.

A copper sconce (E) is cut from copper scrap. The bottom strip is rolled up and glued onto back piece which has been edged with a nail design (point of nail hammered all along top edge for indentation). Glue extra rounded piece on top of curl to hold candle.

Fig. 5-7   Floor lamps, Tiffany lamp and sconces.

Roll-on ball or glass bead is glued to a metal piece, which is glued to a cut wooden block (F).

Two belt tips glued to a back piece become a spotlight sconce (G).

CANDLESTICK HOLDERS

A piece of jewelry chain (or jump ring) "handle" is attached to a grommet (H). Ampule and candle fit nicely onto top.

The holders shown in Figure 5-7 I and J are made mostly from heavy aluminum, cut and glued together. Washer and beads are added to (J).

Two different size washers are glued together with a strip of shaped aluminum handle glued on (K).

A necklace clasp has two convenient places on top for candles to be inserted (L).

How to Make Chandeliers and Table Lamps

The projects in this section are shown in Figure 5-8.

HANGING HALL CHANDELIER

Materials: Thin, pliable acetate; two bell caps; two crystal beads; two washers, 1½″ and ⅜″; gold flexible trim or gold paper; straight metal trim rods (large paper clips painted gold); toothpick; fine chain; two jewelry fastenings.

Directions:

1. Glue two washers together.

2. Wrap acetate around (for fit) on outside of washers; glue acetate sides together.

3. Glue gold trim around top and bottom of acetate.

4. Paint toothpick white and glue into center of washers.

5. Now glue fitted acetate around washers.

6. Glue metal trim rods (cut to fit) at three equidistant points about acetate.

7. With fastening pins, attach glass beads to bell caps and glue to top and bottom of acetate (Fig. 5-8A).

8. Add chain to top for hanging.

HANGING GLOBES

Materials: Large square (or round, if you prefer) filigree ornament (B); five deodorant roll-on balls; five filigree bell caps to fit balls; five pieces of chain; five eye pins.

Directions:

1. Pierce one hole in each of the roll-on balls with a heated drapery hook.

2. Apply small amount of glue in and around each hole. Affix a bell cap to each ball and insert a shortened eye pin in each hole. Allow to dry.

3. Attach each chain to an eye pin and opposite ends of chain to filigree ornament top at four corners and center. Set the center globe lower than the corner globes.

CRYSTAL CHANDELIER

Materials: Eight teardrop crystal beads; gold filigree circle design, 1½″ diameter; small filigree circle; small filigree ball; assorted crystal beads and a pearl bead; 4″ of 18-gauge copper wire; gold chain for hanging and very fine chain to go through teardrop beads.

Directions:

1. String fine chain through each crystal bead, catching each up and securing to filigree circle, keeping beads equidistant. Glue ends of chain well.

2. Bead end of copper wire; string beads, filigree, etc., on wire as shown in (C). Cut wire ⅜″ above last bead. Insert end through chain and twist wire very tightly over chain to prevent limpness.

ROSEBUD LAMP

Materials: Toothpaste tube top or other small tube top; large rosebud bead (or other bead) for base; gold or silver filigree ornament for stand; long eye fastener.

Directions:

1. Glue bead onto filigree with holes in vertical position.

2. Pierce small hole through center of top. This can be done with a heated needle.

3. Secure entire lamp together with head pin fastener (D). Use bits of cotton if necessary.

Fig. 5-8 Chandeliers, table lamps and antique lamps.

ACETATE

A

B

C

CHAIN

(ASTRAL)

I

D

ANTIQUE

H

E

J

G

F

CAT LAMP

Materials: Tube top; ceramic animal; two small blocks of shaped and stained wood; round toothpick for rod; small gold bead.

Directions:

1. Prepare wooden base and provide hole in rear to insert "rod" (E).

2. Glue tube top to rod by using cotton or Styrofoam. Glue bottom of rod into base.

3. Glue animal onto base and add a small gold bead to very top of tube shade.

SEASHELL LAMP

Materials: Small piece of driftwood with flat bottom; small seashells; bottle top; large paper clip.

Directions:

For this kind of lamp the rod is glued to the back, so gouge out an area to securely insert rod against base (F). Small section of cotton will also help.

1. Glue seashells onto driftwood.

2. Insert curved part of clip to inside of tube top and glue, using cotton.

3. Glue bottom of rod to back of base.

BOTTLE LAMP

Materials: Small glass perfume bottle; paper jelly container; ruffled lace to fit around container; velvet ribbon; matchstick for rod.

Directions:

1. Glue bottom of "rod" in opening of bottle, using glue-soaked cotton to secure it in place. *Dry well.*

2. Fit a round of Styrofoam within paper container. Glue in place.

3. Glue other end of rod into center of Styrofoam (G).

4. Wrap and glue lace around shade; add ribbon to top.

TWO-WAY LAMP

Materials: Wire dress hanger; two toothpaste tube tops; something suitable for a base.

Directions:

Cut wire hanger as shown in drawing (H). Twist, then glue through and into tube top shades and to a base.

GLOBE LAMPS

Two simple modern globe lamps are shown in Figure 5-8I and J. Roll-on balls, round beads or marbles are attached to a small black cube (how about using dice?) or a black button.

ANTIQUE LAMPS

The five antique lamps are made with an assortment of collectibles: round beads, cylindrical beads, marbles, screw earrings, a grommet, paper clip, bracelet link and inside pen tubing.

Other small lamps are variations of larger ones, using buttons as bases.

Functional and Decorative
Containers

What's a container? It's something that you put something in. It can be a dish, glass, cup, bowl, vase, pot, pan, urn, basin, jug, can, mug, pitcher, carton, basket, bucket, barrel, tub, chest, tray, planter, umbrella stand, wastebasket, soap dish, napkin holder, compote, cake plate, salt cellar, epergne, magazine rack, candy dish, ashtray, canister and much, much more. Whew! Obviously, containers are indispensable. They fill everybody's needs every day.

Containers come in a variety of materials and designs (Figs. 6-1, 6-2, 6-3). Dishes, for instance, may be porcelain, pottery, glass, sterling, wood, pewter, lead, copper, aluminum, plastic or even paper. Then they can be engraved, etched, cut, pressed, hammered, painted, glazed and stenciled.

I'll let you investigate the possibilities for all the above-mentioned items, plus the teapot, coffeepot, spoonholder, punchbowl, casserole, butter dish, beaker, tea set, platter, inkwell, perfume bottle, atomizer, bank, goblet, creamer, sugar bowl, salt box, cake mold, crock, shaving mug, flask . . . whew! and it sounds like this is where I came in.

Glass creations require a special skill and unless you're a glass blower, you'll have to benefit from the manufacturers and dealers—the English imports are beautiful. Available for a reasonable facsimile are, of course, acetate and clear plastic and we should be grateful for that, but once again ingenuity will have to prevail.

The same applies to any of the metals. Brass, copper and wrought iron require the artisan's touch, so the best that can be offered in duplication is to borrow from what's available and patch, patch, patch.

Ceramic also requires a special skill for the very best results but if you don't mind compromising, you can do your thing with the help of bread dough (described in Ch. 9) or Sculpey.

Now wood! That's an altogether different story. You can cut and glue with the best and here's where your star can shine.

Helpful Hints

✔ Small glass buttons become glass dishes.
✔ Metal buttons with back attachment be-

Fig. 6-1 A wall shelf made from a ruler and slices of pine molding displays a three-piece canister set, cut-down plastic pill vials with button covers; a spoonholder—a screw-on end attachment of curtain rod; a bowl (pin finding); a pitcher (shaped .45-caliber shell); napkin holder of cut and bent filigree; covered cheese dish (acrylic round and button top); slag bowl (toothbrush container cover and bead feet); pepper mill (rice bead); decorative box (wood and filigree clasps); lollipop jar (sparkle pins, pill vial and button top). On the floor rest a platter (button covered with cutout); tall planter (cream container with whistle and silver button base); elegant planter or wastebasket (bottlecap surrounded on four sides with necklace pieces); wastebasket with four seasons of trees painted on the sides (handmade of basswood); punch bowl (plastic dome on dapped filigree); cooking pail (12-gauge shell with staple handles); tall stand (pill vial covered with bead trim); covered cake tray (cover from film container, link and bouillon cover); two umbrella stands and mugs (see Fig. 6-8).

come "pewter, copper or sterling" dishes or platters, depending upon size. Remove back fastening and carefully hammer into a flattened shape.

✔Flattened metal buttons with heraldic, eagle, profile and other designs become commemorative plates. Show a varied "collection" on the wall or in a hutch.

✔Depressed metal buttons with two holes showing can still be used, with an extra effort. Cut a circle of card to fit and glue down, covering holes. With gold or silver paint to match rest of button, cover over. When dry, add extra coloration of black or sepia and shade with acrylic, if necessary. Apply lacquer.

✔Cover a plain, shallow metal button,

1½″ diameter, with dish cutouts from department store catalogues—beautiful platters or trays.

✔Supermarket meat packaging uses clear plastic trays. Cut out the very center of tray carefully, allowing for the rounded lip, to make perfect little round dishes. These can be rimmed or decorated with permanent marking pens. Painted silver, they resemble sterling.

✔Bullet shells come in assorted sizes: .22 caliber short makes fine beakers or mugs with a "link" handle attached; also usable as a small vase with two link handles added. The .45 caliber shell becomes a larger vase or a small wastecan. Pretty little designs can be painted on

Fig. 6-2 An assortment of trays, dishes and serving pieces are made mostly from scraps and discarded objects. Directions are supplied in the How-to section of this chapter.

surfaces. A 12-gauge shotgun shell becomes a wastecan or, with handles added, turns into a good implement for kitchen use. Add a little dappled blacking around bottom area to show use.

✔Handles for many containers can be made from cut, curved ends of paper clips, cut pieces of filigree, bracelet links and costume chain necklaces, small

copper staples, hooks and eyes and hairpins.

✔Model shops have eyelets of various small sizes—good for the tiniest of candlestick holders. They can be useful for legs or other supportive features.

✔Large eyelets used for attaching grippers in clothing make good bases for containers. Grommets are also good.

✔Antique salt cellars become fruit bowls,

Fig. 6-3 A plastic sewing bobbin, seashells, beads, filigree and other doodads combine to produce some small, interesting articles for serving and other uses (see How-to section).

Fig. 6-4 With four screw-on soda bottletops, you can acquire four different containers, depending upon where you cut, for a large pan, deep dish pie plate, pie plate and dinner plate. The inner plastic insert can also be used for a plate. Local brand inserts are often plain white and resemble porcelain. The national brands can be covered over with plastic paint; brand names on metal can be sanded off.

punch bowls and other bowls if the glass isn't too thick.

✔A dapped pin finding, minus the jewels, sometimes resembles a bowl.

✔Modern bowls can be contrived from bottle caps. Paint if needed, then add a base and handles.

Fig. 6-5 Every household needs a tray. The top one is made from a pendant finding. The Chippendale and Queen Anne shapes are metal, purchased, but with hand-painted designs. The lower tray is dry pressed flowers under acetate, framed. Go ahead—make one!

✔Clear rectangular covers from toothbrush containers can be dressed up. Find one that's a nice shape for a casserole dish; just add handles and filigree feet.

✔Filigree comes into the limelight. Bell caps are naturals for bowls; other pieces can be glued together, too—experiment.

✔Metal round bottom on small bouillon-cube packaging is a good tin tray or platter. Leave it plain or paint and decorate it. This would also make a good pizza pie platter. The plastic top can also be useful.

✔Metal jewelry frame with four prongs (for legs) becomes a tray. Add something flat and interesting for the center section.

✔Old-fashioned metal collar button is a cute little pedestal candy dish.

✔Covers can be made from plain and decorative buttons (see directions for Fig. 6-8). Cake covers originate with other bottle covers, but watch the sizes in height and width. Fake dome-shaped covers can be the plastic dome-shaped buttons; just glue something on top for a handle and place on a dish. Plastic covers from pill containers can be painted silver. Add a handle to top or a long handle off to the side.

✔Extra-large filigree rounds (2″) can be bent into U shapes. Add some feet and a wire handle and it's a magazine rack (Fig. 6-6).

✔Filigree rounds or squares of ½″, also

Fig. 6-6 Filigree can boast of being a most useful material. It steps out in style, becoming a punch bowl base, candlestick holder, wall planter, candy dish, epergne, soap dish, log holder, napkin ring, napkin or letter holder, cake stand, pastry holder, bowl, bookends and box.

bent into U shapes, become letter and napkin holders.

✔Ashtray and cigarette: cut the prongs off very small dapped nailheads. Stiffen white button thread with craft glue. Cut small piece for cigarette, add red tip and glue onto ashtray.

✔Picnickers need paper plates. Cut out circle bottoms of papier mâché egg cartons. Strip off a few layers of paper to obtain a thinner plate.

✔Faceted sequins become tiny candy dishes or ashtrays.

✔Metal tips at ends of colored pencils can be pulled off; add a handle for a mug. Add two for a vase.

How to Make Trays, Mugs, Canisters and Other Containers

Figure 6-7 illustrates a variety of trays and containers for which the construction details are given below.

DRIED PRESSED FLOWER TRAY

1. Construct a frame from thin molding (described in Ch. 3). Insert and glue thin acrylic to fit.

2. Cover thin cardboard (also to fit under glass) with velour paper, satin material or anything thin.

3. Place dried, pressed miniature flowers in an arrangement on background. Tack flowers in place with glue.

4. Glue cardboard and flowers into place under acrylic.

5. Finish off background with plain paper.

6. Add two cut pieces of filigree to sides for handles. Bend and glue.

PIN TRAY

1. Select an appropriate jewelry pin or pendant finding. Some pendants have four metal extensions that are ready made legs.

2. Cut off any hinges.

3. Cut a piece of balsa wood $1/16''$ thick to fit within oval—some will be fitted on top, others fit best from the bottom.

4. Paint wood gold and add painted artwork. This tray features a lotus petal design finished with acrylic paint.

5. Glue into position.

WOODEN TRAY

1. Cut a piece of $1/16''$ thick walnut wood into an oval $1 1/8'' \times 1 3/4''$.

PLASTIC BOBBIN

CASSEROLE

CAKE

ATOMIZERS

COOKIE TRAY

TRAYS

CORNER

(SIDE) (BACK)

PITCHER

CANISTERS

CUT 4

MUGS

2. Around the outside, add a flexible wood trim of $1/8''$ depth.

3. The handles are small copper staples shaped and glued on.

PAINTED TINWARE TRAY

This tray starts out as the humble cocoa can cover. It's been painted light yellow and the design is red flowers and trim and green leaves. Easy.

CHIPPENDALE AND QUEEN ANNE TRAYS

These beauties are obtainable through a dealer (see Sources of Supply) or perhaps one of your local craft shops carries them. Copy these designs in acrylic, accented with gold, or dream up your own. Other tray designs and even smaller sizes are also available.

MUGS ON BOARD

Materials: Cedar from cigar box or any hardwood $1/16''$ thick; four ends of toothpicks $1/4''$ long; four used bullet shells.

Directions:

1. Round four corners of wood with sandpaper and smooth all areas.

2. Drill into wood four places, indicated by dots (Fig. 6-7).

3. Apply small amounts of glue to holes and tips of toothpicks. Insert the stained toothpicks into holes, slanting the picks upward. Dry well.

4. Glue bracelet links, staples or whatever to shells for handles. Hang on pegs.

EPERGNE

One side of a plastic sewing machine bobbin is the plate. A short fastening pin is pushed through a bell cap, bobbin and filigree round for base. All are glued together with the extra use of a little cotton.

CAKE CONTAINER

The metal top from a film container is placed on top of a semiflat plastic top from bouillon package. Add a link for handle.

PUNCH BOWL

The clear round plastic bowl is the top from a toiletries Love spray bottle, mounted on a dapped filigree base.

BRASS PITCHER

The pitcher is a used .45 caliber shell with a metal link for handle. With diagonal cutter, trim and shape as shown in Figure 6-7. Shape a handle out of a piece of costume jewelry chain or large link and glue to back.

CANISTERS

See-through canisters start as plastic pill containers in different sizes. Or they can be cut down to graduated sizes, too. (Use a heated paring knife and quickly slice through the plastic. The process will be repeated until the cut-through is complete.) Tops are made with two buttons. One button is the same size as container; a second button is smaller and is glued onto first or top button (this prevents top from rolling off container). Be sure to line up the holes because the rounded end of a paper clip is cut and glued through the holes to become the handle. A simple flower and leaf design is painted on the sides with permanent felt-tipped pens. Fill the canisters with whatever you like.

SQUARE CASSEROLE

The top from a toothbrush package is fitted onto a bent metal decoration. Curved metal links are placed under four corners and small metal handles added.

PERFUME BOTTLES AND ATOMIZERS

Small, clear cut-glass beads topped with tiny round gold beads—or just the opposite, gold triangular or round beads topped with crystal—become elegant bottles. Keep them small.

For an atomizer, glue the top bead on so the holes are horizontal. String a round gold bead (about $1/8''$) onto gold $1/2''$ head pin, glue in place; push pin through holes. Glue to keep secure.

Fig. 6-7 Trays, mugs, epergne, cake container, punchbowl, brass pitcher, canister set, casserole and other serving pieces, perfume bottles and atomizers.

Place the bottles on a gold metal insert obtained at some craft stores.

For a spray can, select a cylindrical bead and top with an exact size silver or gold bead.

SALT SHAKERS

Follow the directions for perfume bottles but use the tiniest beads and filigree and your salt shakers will be ready for the table.

SHELL SERVING PIECE

Three small scallop seashells are glued to 3/8" bead cap. Eye pin (5/8") is inserted through the center and glued to become tall handle. (A small bit of cotton will help hold everything together at site of base.)

HANDLED BOWL

It's just a little gold metal top with two shaped handles added.

COOKIE TRAY

Cut out of heavy aluminum dinner plate. Cut larger and cut corners as shown in Figure 6-7. Roll each side inward over paper clip to form sides, then remove the clips.

Fig. 6-8   Covered service piece, dishes, platters, containers, umbrella stand and large jewelry box.

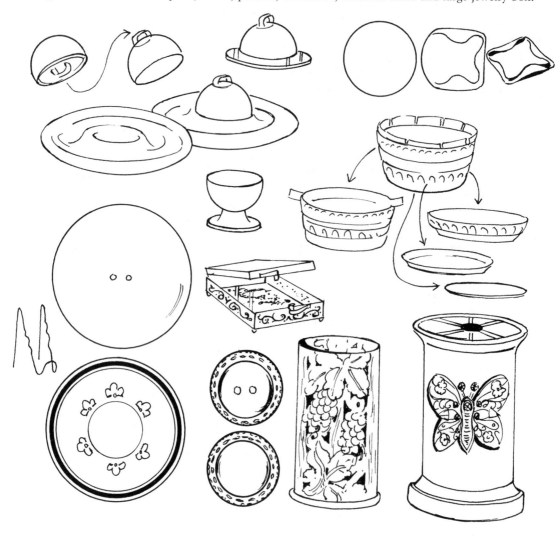

Other containers at bottom are made from toothpaste tube top, 12-gauge shell, rice bead and curtain rod holder.

How to Make Assorted Dishes and Platters, Umbrella Stand and Jewelry Box

Instructions are for the assortment of containers shown in Figure 6-8.

COVERED SERVICE PIECE

Domed metal buttons can be transformed into covers or bowls. For the covered platter, shank is removed from bottom and transferred to top. The cover becomes part of a service piece, which was cut out of the center round portion of plastic meat container from supermarket. This was painted silver.

With shank completely removed, the button can be glued onto grommet for pedestal bowl.

CLAY DISH

Thin round of modeling compound is pulled up on four sides. When dried, color with brown and rust tones for clay appearance.

BOTTLETOP CONTAINERS

By noting where each soda bottletop is cut (Fig. 6-8), you can acquire four different kinds of containers (see Fig. 6-4).

UMBRELLA STAND

This project is made from an empty gold spool 1¾" high. Remove the paper from both ends of spool, revealing a subdivided interior—a natural for holding umbrellas and canes. Mount the spool on a wooden button for base. Add a decoration to front: this one has a gold filigree butterfly, enhanced with tiny red rhinestones.

Another stand starts out with an empty plastic pill container. Gold decorative paper is glued to the surface and the see-through effect is very pretty. Gold braid is added around the bottom to effect a base.

ROUND PLATTERS

Luckily, I "found" some plain metal buttons, shallow in depth. Cut out some dishes from a store's direct-mail advertising booklet and glue them to the buttons. Squeeze out excess bubbles. Add a couple more coats of diluted white glue for gloss. Fill up back holes with thick glue. Look for the buttons; they make elegant, large platters. Stand the platters up on black hairpin plate stands.

LARGE JEWELRY BOX

The smallest of the covered plastic containers is decorated with paint or trim, mounted on gold bead feet and filled with miniature trinkets.

Boxes and Bags

How would we ever get along without boxes and bags? They, too, are an indispensable part of everyday life.

Out of the past we are charmed by the notable bandbox, which was used for travel or as a container for ladies' or gentlemen's finery. The lightweight construction of thin wood was usually covered with wallpaper or paper which sported block-printed designs. Add one of these to your antique house and you will have another eye-catching accessory. Don't forget to put something inside the box, too.

The Shakers meticulously crafted simple round or oval boxes. Complete with cover, they were made in graduated sizes for convenient stacking and were used for storing many household items for kitchen or personal use.

Let's include a trunk which, after all, is square with a cover. The original trunk was used for travel, but today these collectible old "giant size boxes" are acceptable and sought after for storage in many parts of the house (Fig. 7-1).

But getting down to the nitty gritty of boxes, they serve dozens of purposes and hold zillions of things. It's all a question of what *you* want to put in one—perhaps candy, cookies, cheese, stationery, games, tissues, soap, shoes, matches, books, cigars, hat, yarn, flowers (long-stemmed roses, of course) and much, much more.

The crate is a box and whether it's holding oranges, grapefruit or some store product, it's an easy accessory to make.

Bags are relatives to boxes and perhaps the most notorious of the family is the carpetbag, introduced at the end of the Civil War. These were traveling bags made out of carpet scraps and durable they were.

Bags are used for carrying store purchases of one kind or another, and you can make your own in the paper of your choice. But the one that really looks intriguing is the plain brown grocery bag filled with foodstuffs and household necessities.

The gunnysack, long known for its commercial value in packaging, becomes the added accessory in the old-time grocery store.

Did you know that shopping bags have become a collectible? If your mood is contemporary, let's add some of those to your household or shop. Select a simple bag of a favorite shop, then scale down the design to your bag size. Since shopping bag designs feature a flat color, rendering the appropriate colors is easy with

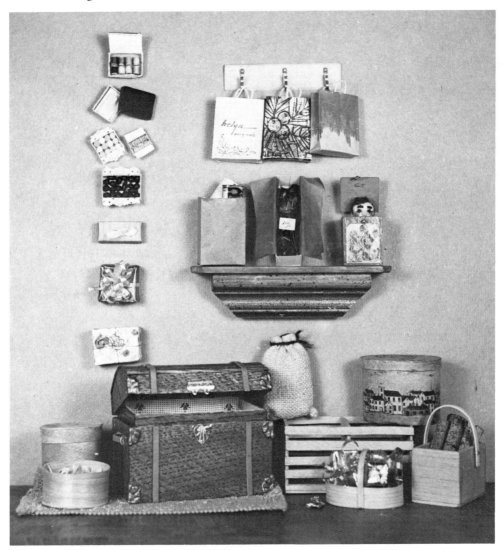

Fig. 7-1 *At left,* a small assortment of boxes hug the wall, displaying thread, stationery, candies, tissues and gift wrapping. Along the floor are a Shaker box, spit box (complete with wood shavings), trunk, gunnysack, crate, bandbox, carrier and log holder. *At top right* are three shopping bags, a grocery bag, a florist's box with red roses and a jack-in-box who sneaked in from the toy chapter. Trunk shown is the one described in the How-to section (Fig. 7-3).

felt-tipped pens, colored drawing inks or acrylic paint.

As long as you're updating bags, include the tote. This is made of material, either plain or decorated. It's an over-the-arm carrier, with a one or two-strap handle.

Maybe you'll even have a place for a "doggy" bag.

Helpful Hints

✔Wrap small block pieces of balsa wood in gift wrap paper and bow tie.
✔Use brown wrapping paper for another packaged look. Tie up with black or white button thread, add an address and "stamp."
✔Colored foil papers make the best gift

Fig. 7-2 Gifts should be wrapped in their prettiest paper and set off with colorful bows, so tie them up and set them under the Christmas tree, of course.

wrapping cover and these can be decorated in a variety of ways.

✔ Curling ribbon can be slit to a very narrow width and tied with full rolling bows.

✔ For a very tiny tie, use gold or silver beading wire. Using tweezers, fold the ends around each other over and over, and they resemble lots of bows.

✔ Gold filigree paper trims are useful as decorations. Cut out the smallest and glue in place.

✔ Paper doilies can also be cut apart in small sections and glued down.

✔ Add the tiniest rhinestones for very special holiday trim.

✔ Make a tote out of felt and glue felt design onto top.

✔ Crochet or knit a tiny bag out of colored string or crochet yarn.

✔ Make a sack out of orange nylon net and fill it with oranges.

✔ For design motif on shopping bag, copy a design from greeting cards, stationery or catalogues.

✔ For an all-over design, cut the bag pattern out of gift wrap paper featuring a small stripe or tiny design.

How to Make a Trunk

Full-size pattern parts are supplied in Figure 7-3.

Materials: Oak for cutting pattern parts, $1/16''$ thick; small-patterned material for lining; thin leather for trim; two small hinges; metal trim for corners.

Directions:

1. Glue pieces (A) and (B) together; fit sides (C) and glue.

2. Glue pieces (D) and (E) together.

3. Starting at top of arch (D), glue sections of (F) snugly together. When thoroughly dry, sand top for smooth curvature.

4. Glue tray pieces (G) and (H) together; fit and glue (I).

5. Cut lining material to fit tray and box and glue to interior of each piece.

6. Decide where tray will be placed in interior. Glue strips of wood to four sides

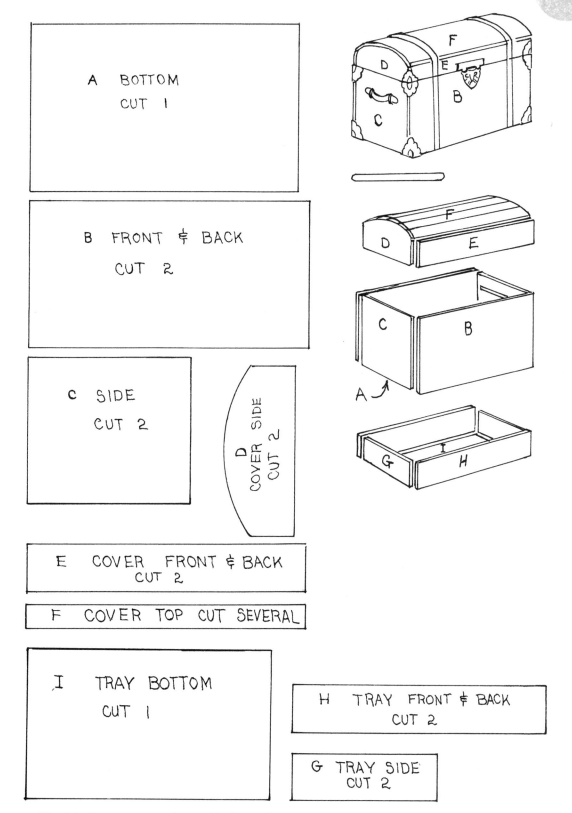

A BOTTOM
CUT 1

B FRONT & BACK
CUT 2

C SIDE
CUT 2

D COVER SIDE
CUT 2

E COVER FRONT & BACK
CUT 2

F COVER TOP CUT SEVERAL

I TRAY BOTTOM
CUT 1

H TRAY FRONT & BACK
CUT 2

G TRAY SIDE
CUT 2

Fig. 7-3 Pattern parts and assembly for trunk.

73

of inside of trunk to provide "rest" supports for tray.

7. Glue two hinges to outside cover and back of trunk. Add leather handles to sides.

8. Leave trunk plain or add strips of leather trim. Add metal corner pieces, if desired.

9. Add a lock to front.

How to Make Boxes, Crates and Bags

An assortment of useful and decorative boxes and bags is shown in Figure 7-4 and instructions are given in this section for each.

BOX CONSTRUCTION

When making a box, a $3'' \times 5''$ ruled index card helps maintain straight, even lines when folding edges. Using the lines on the card, make four creases one way and two creases the opposite way, determining your own box size. By creasing on one, two, three or even one-half lines, you can have boxes galore in all and any shapes. A box can be precovered before creasing with a pretty paper and "instant gift wrapping" will be accomplished. If the box tends to collapse, stuff it with cotton.

To construct a box with its own *lift-up cover,* follow the layout pattern of the drawing in Figure 7-4. Size can be enlarged or reduced, according to your own need. These are good for boxes in shops.

TISSUE BOX

Cut out pattern for box (Fig. 7-4). Cut out oval opening. Cover with colored or print paper (or you could have started with a design-printed card). Cut slits in the top, glue together, add extra design if desired and finally stuff small piece of tissue through opening.

CANDY BOX

Prepare box; add cut pieces of straight lace paper doily to two sides of box. Add small pieces of chocolate, bonbons (see Ch. 9) or mints (sequin cake decorations). Glue into position, Make special occasion holiday candy boxes in Valentine shape, complete with red bow; don't forget Christmas, or Easter candies shaped into eggs and decorated.

STATIONERY BOX

Prepare box: make a box cover just slightly larger and decorate cover with paper or design. Cut out several envelopes and notepaper to be placed within box. Use white or colored papers. Envelopes can be lined by gluing a second, designed or colored paper to pattern before cutting out.

CRATE

Materials: Pattern parts are all cut from $^1/_{16}''$ pine.

Directions:

1. Glue sides (A) to bottom (B).

2. Glue middle section (C) in the center, to bottom (B).

3. Space strips (D) evenly and glue five to each side of crate.

BANDBOX

Materials: Tube from plastic wrap—although thin, these seem to be sturdy and flexible; index card; scenic design paper.

Directions:

1. Cut tube $1^1/_4''$ deep and flatten round shape into an oval (A).

2. Hold oval in position on index card and pencil around shape. Cut out oval. Glue to bottom of oval tube (B). Dry well.

3. Cover bandbox with wallpaper design or, preferably, some scenic design. Reproductions of old, antique scenes are good.

4. Cut strip of card $^3/_{16}''$ wide and long enough to go around bandbox, for side of cover plus overlap. Glue overlap together (wrapped around box) so it fits.

5. Cut an oval from card for top of cover. Glue onto side area.

6. Cover top and sides of cover with matching paper or scenic design.

Fig. 7-4 General directions for box construction; tissue, candy, stationery boxes and bandbox; crate and shopping bags.

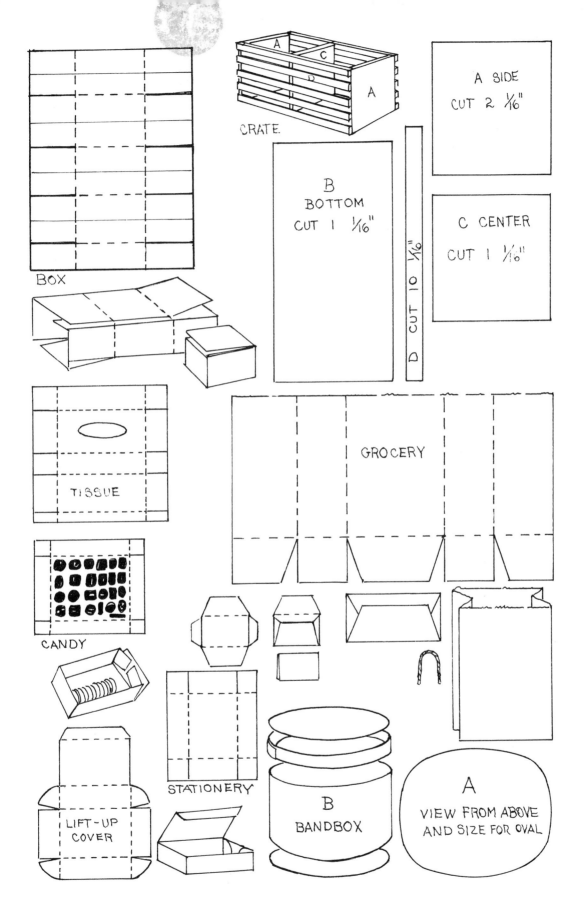

CRATE.

A SIDE
CUT 2 1/16"

B
BOTTOM
CUT 1 1/16"

C CENTER
CUT 1 1/16"

D CUT 10 1/16"

BOX

TISSUE

GROCERY

CANDY

LIFT-UP
COVER

STATIONERY

B
BANDBOX

A
VIEW FROM ABOVE
AND SIZE FOR OVAL

GROCERY BAG

Select a small brown bag which has smaller serrated edging on top than a regular grocery bag. Cut out pattern (Fig. 7-4) and proceed to glue together. Stuff with groceries and paper products.

SHOPPING BAG

This is made similar to the grocery bag. However, when drawing the pattern, make the bag shorter and wider. Attach string handles to front and back for carrying. Coat handles with glue to stiffen them.

SHAKER BOX

Flexible wood trim which comes on a roll can make a satisfactory little box (see Fig. 7-1). Whether it's the covered box, the spit box (complete with wood shavings) or some other box, follow the general instructions described for the bandbox.

Another reasonable facsimile is to make box out of card and cover with wood design contact paper.

GUNNYSACK

Use a small piece of coarse beige material. Cut $2'' \times 3''$, placing top along selvage edge. Fold material over and stitch side and bottom closed. Invert material. With thread, sew or tie off corners at bottom. Stuff the bag with cotton. With a running stitch, pull top closed and tie off with piece of brown crewel yarn.

Playthings, Games and Leisure Items

Life is not all responsibility. There must be a time for leisure, too. Toys, games and entertainment are necessary ingredients for balancing human existence, and many a reader will look back, recalling some childhood fantasy that made playtime more pleasurable.

Toys have a language of their own. There are no barriers. Hand a child a toy anywhere, anytime, and his eyes will light up. Although creativity has prompted the introduction of many new innovative toys, it's the child who ultimately decides which will endure. Many lovable toys created centuries ago, and now updated, remain desirable and popular (see color Fig. 9).

In Puritan days, nature's own products were a source of entertainment for children. Collecting seashells, leaves and pebbles filled their needs. Dolls were made from cornhusks and rags and simple toys of wood were crafted by artisans. Tin, pewter, cast iron, steel, silver, china, rubber and plastic toys followed in their order, and time will tell which will be most enduring.

Artisans of special crafts created miniature replicas which were used as toys, sales display pieces or curios in private homes. Many of these prized creations are now gracing someone's dollhouse.

The most popular toy of all times is undoubtedly the doll. The variety of dolls from earliest to later periods is highlighted by historians and writers.

The ball, antiquated and simplest of all toys, can be a great source of joy to a child. It is used in many ways, depending upon imagination and resourcefulness. Of course, the ball became a necessary factor in other games. Sometimes the size, weight and shape was changed, but croquet, cricket, baseball, basketball, football, tennis, soccer, billiards and other sports would be meaningless without it.

Toys have always imitated the grownup things in life. Hence, the sailing ship, stagecoach, naval vessel, car, truck, fire engine, circus wagon, plane and spacecraft all have something to contribute. As each was invented, the child benefited from enjoying the replica in wood, iron, tin, plastic, paper, papier mâché or other compositions.

The hobbyhorse grew into the rocking horse and there's hardly a child who hasn't yearned for one.

Fig. 8-1 Appropriately, a Christmas tree is placed next to the toys. Waiting to be discovered by a lucky boy or girl are a palette and brush, a Paris cutter sled, a dollhouse, teddy bear, battledore and shuttlecock, tennis racquet, baseball bat, paper hat, hobbyhorse, drum, jack-in-the-box, doll's bed, fluffy mouse and alphabet blocks. Since there are so many different ways to decorate a Christmas tree, this activity becomes a matter of personal taste. The simplest method is to use what is already available and yet resembles trimming. The gold twisted stretch cord used to keep gift packages together is perfect for a garland. A reasonable facsimile for Christmas balls are Bubble Bead 6mm in aurora boreal colors. They are beautiful. Apply a tiny dab of glue to the edge of the branch and slip the bead onto the branch. The star is five gummed foil stars (gold or silver). Each star is folded in half, then they are glued to each other to form a three-dimensional star. Spread out evenly and glue to top. The star can be sprinkled with glitter for extra glow. Candy canes can be cut and shaped out of red and white striped electrical wire.

Toys, the lifeblood of every child (and even of adults, who become collectors), deserve a place in your miniature world, too. Add a toy or two or three whether it's a doll, an animal, a puppet, a jack-in-the-box (Fig. 8-3), alphabet blocks, building blocks, a top, kite, hoop, tin soldier or whatever else you can find easy to make, or easier to buy.

Competition has always emerged in one way or another and is both instructive and rewarding when used in a positive way. When young, the competition of sports and games can help get on with the business of growing up.

Pitching horseshoes may not require much stamina or skill, but it helped pass the time of day and, while most sports were active and physical, there were other means of passive fun.

Before movies, radio and television became commonplace, the population depended upon games as another source of entertainment. Chess, checkers and backgammon were among the notable games of skill that come to mind, and in many an affluent home there was a permanent game table readily available in the parlor, waiting for the occasional or, more often, routine game that followed an evening meal.

Fortunately, books are also a part of the

78

Fig. 8-2 Petite "playtime" dolls, no bigger than a paper clip, are made with copper wire and dressed in a variety of ways. Sunbonnet Sue, Pantaloon Polly, Flirtatious Scarlett, Raggedy Ann and the Precious Bride all line up to display their beautiful dresses.

quest for amusement. Books and magazines provide an outlet for relaxation, whether a youngster or oldster, and reading matter is evident in every home. Books can range from sheer fantasy to factual entertainment, but certainly with present day libraries no one can deny that reading is the most economical form of amusement and education available. Even in your dollhouse a few books can be an economical accessory (Fig. 8-4).

Culturally speaking, there is always room for the artist in a little home.

Fig. 8-3 Almost without exception, the first question anyone asks is, "Does it work?" Yes, he really pops up! The box is pine and Jack is molded Sculpey attached to a spring retrieved from a used ball-point cartridge pen.

Whether it's painting or music, a palette or a musical instrument will provide additional interest.

There is great diversity in the world of entertainment. What you do with it in miniature will enhance your little home and help make your little people a better adjusted and happier family.

Helpful Hints

✔Small ball from vending machine becomes an impressive beach-size ball.

✔Furniture for dollhouse within dollhouse can be made from nail heads which come in an assortment of sizes and colors. They become tables, chairs, stools, etc. Another source of building material is H structures from model railroading (Fig. 8-5).

✔A rolling hoop can be made from a very thin bangle bracelet.

✔Do a puzzle: acquire two small exact pictures. Glue one picture onto thin card and snip the picture into small sections. Put back together within a box which you have constructed. On cover of box, glue second picture.

✔Make a pinwheel out of 1″ square colored paper. Tack together with cutoff straight pin, using applicator stick as holder.

✔Build a train out of cut rectangles of balsa wood. Use flat beads for wheels.

✔Make a kite with thin pieces of balsa for frame, tissue paper for covering, thread for tail.

✔Add a little pull wagon for your set of blocks.

Fig. 8-4 Serve your books up in many different ways. Shown here are the literary book, photograph or wedding album and autograph album. Some of the popular book selections have identifiable jacket covers, cut from advertising. Bookends, made from wood, are decorated with nailheads, blocks, filigree and shells. Oh yes, a pair of purchased antique stickpins are now minus their pins and have become *very* elegant bookends.

- Have a croquet set: the mallets are ⅛" dowel and applicator sticks, balls are made from bread dough, and wickets are curved from paper clips. Paint each set of balls and mallets a different color.
- Books can be diversified. Create scrapbooks, wedding albums and even autograph albums. Collect tiny signatures in your autograph books, reserving one each for friends, family—and VIPs, if you know any.
- Make a tiny top from a small wooden bead. Insert handle in one end of opening and toothpick, pointed tip end, in other. Paint.
- Using the pattern for doll bed, replace legs with rockers and turn it into a cradle.
- Construct a "nesting set" of four boxes from card. Glue pictures of animals, flowers, large letters, etc., onto sides. Coat all sides well with diluted white glue. Repeat a few times.
- Party favor sections in stores feature tiny pinball machine games. Mount one of these on legs and it fits into the modern game room.

Fig. 8-5 The tiniest bits of furniture, intended for a dollhouse within a dollhouse, can be made from H structures of basswood usually sold in craft and hobby shops for model railroaders. The basic shapes of cut furniture can be upholstered with small scraps of anything, painted or decorated as you wish.

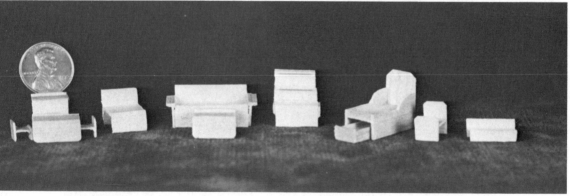

Fig. 1 Imagination can run wild with planters and plant life, both real and artificial.

Fig. 2 Tiny little Christmas arrangements inside 3″ cubes are delightful to give and a joy to receive.

Fig. 3 Miniature dolls, each no bigger than a paper clip, are easy, lovely and fun to make.

Fig. 4 A serpentine open-top corner cupboard and table-chair rest against wall covering of slipcover fabric.

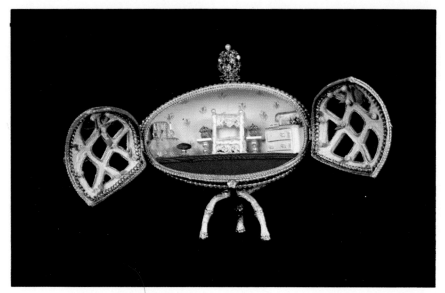

Fig. 5 Rooms are even showing up in goose eggs! This enchanting bedroom creation with tiny pink rosebuds was made by Ann Clark of Ann and Gloria's Chelsea Shop.

Fig. 6 Victorian it is! . . . with the circular conversation sofa, bentwood easel, hand-painted screen, fern planter, Austrian curtains, open-front bookcase and, of course, a parasol.

Fig. 7 Ready for a gala picnic is a selection of appetizing food made from modeling compounds, then painted.

Fig. 8 Torchere lamps are mounted on a wall paneled with Contact paper; delicate mural is framed above an eagle console table.

Fig. 9 Toys are scattered about the deacon's bench, or painted settee, and the wall decoration is needlework over a small fabric cutout. Wall covering is fabric and the carpet is an upholstery remnant.

Fig. 10 A hand-painted Oriental table is surrounded by a theme arrangement, a Bonsai tree, driftwood wall hanger, red rose corsage and Victorian dome arrangement.

Fig. 11   An assortment of formal and casual frames, handmade or contrived from miniature "finds." A variety of contents shows the resources available for decorating a wall.

Fig. 12   A lacy Victorian dressing table and bench. The rich-looking carpet is Belgian tapestry.

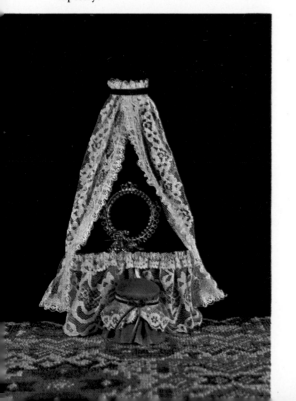

Fig. 13   An English Regency bookcase console is majestic and very impressive.

Fig. 14 A modern armless sofa is upholstered in plush material. The wall decoration is from a greeting card; the wall covering is gift wrap paper.

Fig. 15 Folding screens replace drapery and form a backdrop for various contrived planters and arrangements. The table is made of cafe curtain clips and a round of glass.

Fig. 16 A delft tile fireplace is the background for such accessories as bellows, hand screen, andirons, fireback, warming pan and log holder. The corner chair and candlestand are also handmade; the carpet is cut from upholstery.

Fig. 17 An array of decorator pillows, resting on a red afghan. Any one of these makes a small, thoughtful addition to a miniature room.

Fig. 8-6 A 1½″ Christmas tree decorated with filigree and rhinestones has two wee, well-behaved mice seated at the bottom, both contemplating how to attach the silver star at the very tip-top. One mouse holds a teeny package. Miniatures encased within cubes are adorable and loved as gifts (see color Fig. 2).

How to Make Doll's Dolls, Dollhouse and Its Furniture

This section supplies the instructions for projects shown in Figure 8-7 and color Fig. 3.

DOLL ARMATURE

When making a doll armature, the important thing to remember is to allow time for the glue to set firmly before proceeding to the next step. Since this is all very time consuming, it's advantageous to do several armatures at the same time. You can always costume the extras at your convenience.

Materials: 3/16″ round or 5mm pink wooden beads; 18-gauge copper wire; 1/2″-wide white bias tape; small piece of adhesive tape.

Directions:

1. Cut three copper wires (A).

2. Insert one wire through bead (B); use needle-nose pliers to twist and secure

wire down on top; apply a little craft glue.

3. Place second wire next to first wire (on top of sticky adhesive tape); apply small amount of craft glue (C).

4. Tightly wrap two wires within tape (D).

5. Twist third wire underneath bead for arms; clip off arms and legs to match size on drawing (E).

6. Cover arms and legs with bias tape as shown in (G) directions. Cut four pieces of bias tape to size shown in illustration; dotted lines are fold line of tape. Place each wire arm and leg onto tape. Do one at a time. Apply craft glue on tape and fold up once. Apply more craft glue and fold over once. Allow tape to dry *thoroughly.* When completely dry, cut excess tape away with cuticle scissors.

Since the body is constructed of wire, it can be bent for any position.

DRESSING THE WEE DOLL

Materials: Pantalets: straight lace; glue around waist, cut between legs. Petticoat: ruffled lace. Pantaloons: ruffled lace—wider in size. Skirt and bodice: 5/8″ satin ribbon. Hat: one daisy from length of daisy lace trim. Hair: embroidery floss, color of your choice.

Directions:

1. Wrap lace petticoat around waist area of doll and secure tightly by gluing, sewing or both. If pantaloons are made, eliminate petticoat. Pantaloons will be turned up over outside of dress.

2. Cut into bodice as shown in Figure 8-7; slip on over doll's head; glue open sides together under arms.

3. Use small stitches and gather top of skirt together; wrap around waist of doll and sew securely in place. Glue or sew back opening together.

4. Glue strands of embroidery floss for long loose hair onto head. For upswept coiffure, wind long strands of floss around and around head, gluing in spots to hold floss in place.

5. Add daisy hat on top.

6. Paint in two small black dots for eyes, small red dot for mouth and two dark spots on tips of feet for shoes.

There are many colorful and different ways to dress a doll. Ribbons do away

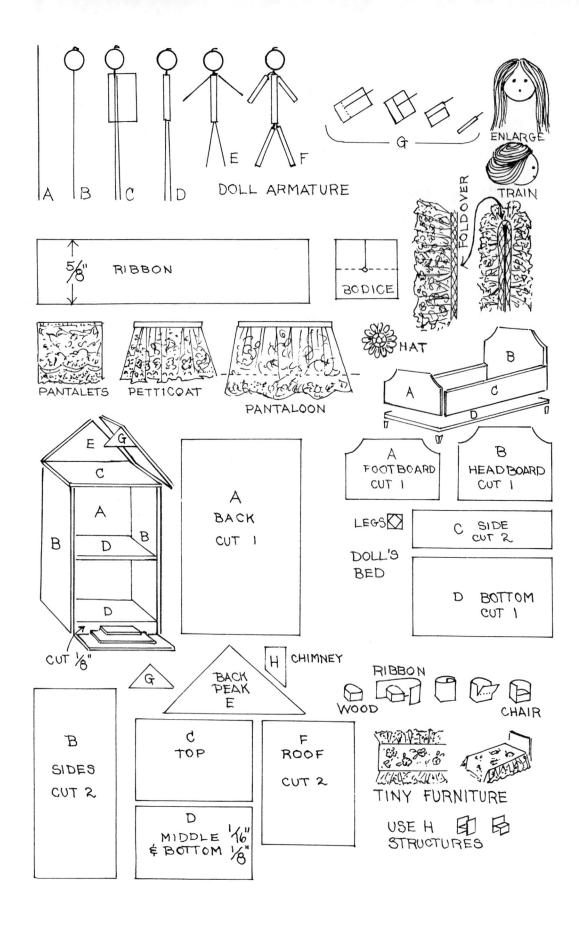

A B C D

E F

DOLL ARMATURE

G

ENLARGE

TRAIN

FOLDOVER

5/8" RIBBON

BODICE

HAT

PANTALETS PETTICOAT

PANTALOON

B

A

C

D

A FOOTBOARD CUT 1

B HEADBOARD CUT 1

LEGS

C SIDE CUT 2

DOLL'S BED

D BOTTOM CUT 1

E G
C
A
B D B
D

CUT 1/8"

A BACK CUT 1

H CHIMNEY

G

BACK PEAK E

RIBBON

WOOD

CHAIR

B SIDES CUT 2

C TOP

F ROOF CUT 2

D MIDDLE 1/16" & BOTTOM 1/8"

TINY FURNITURE

USE H STRUCTURES

with hemmed edges—but a small amount of glue glazed over the edges of other materials will prevent raveling.

P.S. This may seem irrelevant to doll-house miniaturing, but for an offbeat idea, create two miniature dolls, attach to earring findings and you'll have the sweetest attention-getting dangle earrings anywhere.

Doll's Bed

Materials: 1/16" balsa, basswood or pine.

Directions: Glue footboard (A) to sides (C). Glue headboard (B) to sides (C). Add bottom (D). Add 3/16" triangular leg at each corner. Paint brown and add some decoration on headboard if you prefer.

Note: The doll that is made in this chapter will fit within this bed, so dress a doll in nightclothes, too.

THE DOLLHOUSE'S DOLLHOUSE

Materials: 1/16" and 1/8" balsa wood; acrylic paint; inside decoration uses bits of wood, ribbon trim, beads, sequins, greenery, lace, other trim.

Directions:

1. Cut out all pattern pieces (A–H). Glue pieces together as indicated in Figure 8-7, adding (H) as a chimney.

2. Paint inside and outside to colors of your choice; or finish off interior with wallpaper (easier to do before gluing pieces together).

3. Carpet interior floors with thin tweed upholstery material or ribbon.

4. Decorate interior with tiny pieces of cut balsa wood or use "structural shapes" (see Fig. 8-5). Use any small decorative trim for coverings, pillows, upholstery; beads for light fixtures, etc.

5. Add some stairs at the front of the house.

How to Make an Assortment of Toys, Games and Books

Instructions are supplied in this section for the projects shown in Figure 8-8.

JACK-IN-THE BOX

Materials: 1/16" pine; modeling compound for head; spring from cartridge ball-point pen; paper clip; map pin (pin with ball); hinge.

Directions: This piece is prepared in stages.

1. Mold a head, following the drawing for size and shape. Before head hardens, insert one end of spring up into "neck" area. A little glue will help. Dry well. Color head a light pink (white mixed with a touch of red). Add rosy cheeks, red lips, black eyebrows and eyelashes. Two black mustard seeds or beads are glued into eye sockets. Hair is acquired by shearing small pieces of yarn or wool and applying to glued surface of head. Add red felt hat to top.

2. Cut out pattern parts (A–D) from pine. Gouge out small area in center of stand (D). Glue other end of spring into center, securing well with glued cotton. Dry well.

3. Glue four sides together (A and B). Glue on bottom (C).

4. Paint outside of box and all of cover.

5. Adhere catch (made from paper clip) to and through top of cover (C) and insert (glue) pinhead through front on (B).

6. Using a good hinge, glue to back and top cover. Make sure catch works. Dry very well.

7. Glue stand with Jack into bottom of box (Jack's head should be sticking up).

8. Add some painted decorations or decoupage a cute picture onto the front.

DRUM

Materials: 1" diameter plastic pill container; strong, glossy colored paper; thin cardboard tube, 1¼" high; gold bead wire; gold flexible trim (or substitute); parchment (or substitute); two round toothpicks.

Directions:

1. Cut pill container down to 1" height.

2. Wrap tube around container, allowing for 1/8" overlap; cut off excess.

3. Cover tube completely with paper, outside and inside; have overlap inside.

Fig. 8-7   Doll's dolls and clothing, dollhouse within the dollhouse, doll furniture.

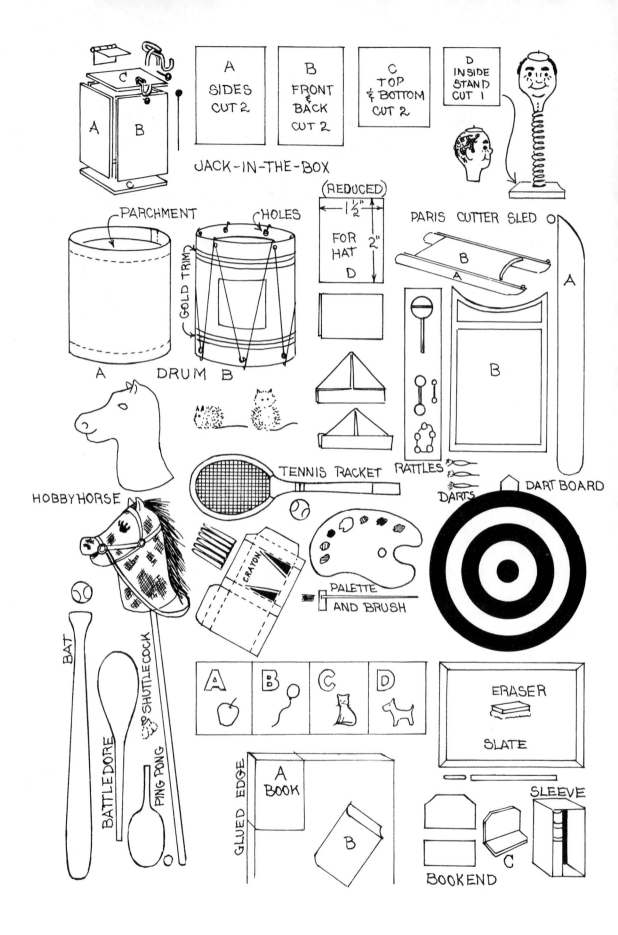

JACK-IN-THE-BOX

A SIDES CUT 2

B FRONT & BACK CUT 2

C TOP & BOTTOM CUT 2

D INSIDE STAND CUT 1

(REDUCED) 1½" 2" FOR HAT D

PARIS CUTTER SLED

PARCHMENT HOLES

GOLD TRIM

A DRUM B

RATTLES

DARTS

DART BOARD

HOBBY HORSE

TENNIS RACKET

CRAYON

PALETTE AND BRUSH

BAT

BATTLEDORE

PING PONG

SHUTTLECOCK

A ▢ B ▢ C 🐱 D 🐕

ERASER

SLATE

GLUED EDGE A BOOK

B

SLEEVE

C

BOOKEND

4. Glue covered tube to pill container. See drawing (A) for placement.

5. Cut out two rounds of parchment 1″ in diameter and glue onto container for top and bottom of drum.

6. Glue strips of gold trim around tube at top and bottom.

7. Drill six holes through top portion and six holes through bottom portion for bead wire. See drawing (B) for placement of holes.

8. Glue on an appropriate small catalogue picture.

9. Thread bead wire back and forth through holes, as shown in (B) and tie off.

10. Cut toothpicks to 1⅜″ lengths. Round the wider ends for drumsticks.

PARIS CUTTER SLED

Materials: ¹/₁₆″ pine; two small rings; string.

Directions:

1. Cut pattern parts and glue side runners (A) to top (B) as shown in drawing.

2. Paint entire sled red.

3. Paint lines on top and side design in white.

4. When dry, tie a string from ring to ring for pulling.

HOBBYHORSE

Materials: Bread dough (see Ch. 9 for recipe) or Sculpey; ¹/₁₆″ strips of thin leather or ribbon; four small jump links (cut to make smaller, if necessary); black embroidery floss; two black mustard seeds; ⅛″ dowel, 2¾″ long.

Directions:

1. Sculpture a head out of bread dough or Sculpey to size shown. Make slight depressions for eyes and nostrils. Glue stick into bottom.

2. When dry and hardened (if it's bread dough, it will require several days), paint head medium gray, eyes white and mouth red. When dry, add darker gray color for dappled effect and accent the area around eyes.

3. Glue on strips of floss for mane. Glue two seeds into eyes. Cut and fit strips of leather around head and to rings as shown in drawing. Glue into place. The rein is, of course, loose.

NEWSPAPER HAT

If you have a miniature newspaper (available at shops where miniatures are sold), use one sheet for the easy-to-make soldier's hat. Just follow the steps shown in Figure 8-8. Don't you remember making one as a child?

RATTLES

Baby's rattle can be made from painted (pink or blue) beads with handles of paper clips or slivers of wood. Decorate too.

FUZZY ANIMALS

Make the little fuzzies out of pussy willows. The mouse has ears from the tips of toothpicks (painted black), a thread tail, hair whiskers and painted-in eyes. A kitty is much the same with an added head.

DARTBOARD AND DARTS

Cut a circle out of thin cork. Fill in dark circular areas with black or red as indicated on drawing. Add paper clip end for hanging.

Darts: Shape toothpicks to size. Add pieces of straight pin at one end and tiny feathers at other end.

PALETTE AND BRUSH

Cut palette out of pine or balsa. Lacquer. Add dabs of acrylic color.

Brush: Using round toothpick for handle, paint black. Glue fine cut hairs to handle (these can be long because it will be trimmed). Tightly wrap and glue piece of heavy aluminum around both at the joint. Clip hairs short.

TENNIS RACKET

Use drawing for size and positioning. Shape white or black electrical wire into

Fig. 8-8 Jack-in-the-box, drum, hobbyhorse, Paris cutter sled, rattles, tennis racket, dartboard and darts, palette and brush, blocks, slate and eraser, books and bookends, bat, battledore and shuttlecock and table tennis set.

oval. Cut handle out of balsa or pine. Paint on stripes. Glue together and dry well. Cut piece of screen wire to fit within oval and paint it white. Glue within oval. Make a ball following one of the suggestions earlier in this chapter.

BASEBALL BAT

A bat is shaped out of $5/16''$ dowel and the ball is shaped out of bread dough.

BATTLEDORE AND SHUTTLECOCK

For a game from long ago, battledore paddles are shaped out of $1/32''$ balsa and the shuttlecock has tiny feathers glued to a cut piece of cocktail plastic straw or ink pen insertion. The other side has a white seed bead glued in place.

PING-PONG

The paddles are cut from $1/32''$ balsa. The ball is shaped or a round bead is used.

SLATE

Mount black paper on card. Add a frame. Add small extended tray area to front bottom. Make an eraser with wood top and felt bottom, and chalk from a sliver of toothpick, painted white.

BOOKS, BOOKENDS AND BLOCKS

Materials: Fine sandpaper; gold paint; white notepad, leatherette; $1/16''$ and $1/8''$ balsa wood.

Directions: Books, the elixir of learning are easy to make when you know how.

1. The glued side of a notepad (A) becomes the back binding of the book. With sharp single-edge blade and steel-edge ruler, cut through thickness of pad as indicated. Cut leatherette to fit around book. Glue binding and first and last pages to leatherette. Other sides of notepad can become binding by applying white glue to side surfaces and allowing to dry well. Repeat with second application of glue.

2. Cut piece of balsa wood to size of book for another method (B): Gently sand back of book into slight curvature and opposite side into a slight indentation. Cover with leatherette. Paint edges white or gold.

Covers can be left plain or, using gold paint, lines or other trim can be added.

3. Books need bookends. Use $1/16''$ balsa wood or another hardwood. Cut, glue, sand and decorate in your own inimitable way. A three-volume set can be housed in a boxed sleeve made out of index card. Cover or color. Two independent standing items such as ceramic owls, are the least trouble of all to use for bookends. Make bookends using a pair of pennies mounted on a stand. The proper year will help date your house.

Blocks: The children's blocks are real cute when they spell out a child's initials (see Fig. 8-4).

TEDDY BEAR

To make the bear shown in Figure 8-1, purchase a small ceramic bear. There are different coverings that can be adhered to the surface to obtain a soft fuzzy look. I have cut the surface off of a tan cashmere remnant or snipped minute pieces of fake fur. Acquire a small pile of cuttings.

Apply small amounts of glue to bear; using tweezers, pick up and apply tiny bits of cuttings onto glued areas. Push down firmly with fingers. Repeat, covering entire surface. Use paint for eyes if necessary, but try to avoid covering eyes. (Household pets can be covered in this way.)

SET OF BLOCKS

Cut several *squares* from $1/4''$ balsa wood (see Fig. 8-1). For each block, paint each side a different color: red, green, orange, yellow, blue and white. With a ball-point pen, add a variety of letters and numbers to each side of block. If background is dark, apply letters with white paint.

ALPHABET COLORING BOOK

Cut a "30-page book" (15 sheets) to size of page needed. In outline, draw alphabet letters on each page and a picture drawing for each letter. Apple, balloon, cat, dog, egg, flower, grapes, hammer, insect, etc. Create your own cover design.

BOX OF CRAYONS

Copy pattern onto orange paper. Cut out and fold. Add box design and letters in dark green. Glue box together, leaving top open. Insert different colored crayons, made of toothpicks, colored and glued together.

BLACKBOARD WITH ERASER

Cut blackboard out of black poster board and construct a fitted frame around board out of miniature frame molding or balsa wood strips. Add a ledge to bottom of board. Cut small rectangle of wood for eraser. Sand and shape and glue piece of black felt to bottom.

Food, Clothing and Jewelry

My own philosophy about food is "eat to live," not "live to eat"; yet, ironically, if someone were to ask "what is most enjoyable to make in miniature?" I just might reply, "food." Modeling this commodity and watching it take shape is thrilling, adding the color and seeing everything come alive is a very fulfilling accomplishment (see color Fig. 7).

Food doesn't have to be limited to the kitchen or dining room in a dollhouse. Introduce it throughout the house in a casual way. Show a plate of hors d'oeuvres sitting on a living room table, cookies and pastry ready to be devoured by expected guests. A bowlful of fruit or even a single piece of fruit (apple, orange or banana) resting near an open book suggests someone is going to both read and appease his appetite. There are any number of ways to show food, natural or cooked, and observation will serve you best in this respect.

If food creation becomes an all-consuming factor, you can indulge your desires by becoming a miniature shop owner: a mall of food shops devoted to bakery (Fig. 9-2), candy, cheese, delicatessen, ice cream, and grocery would really delight the food faddists.

Clothing is another commodity that brings "instant life" to a dollhouse and, while I both admire and hate the neat-as-a-pin housekeeper, it's nevertheless quite charming to see an occasional piece of clothing casually lying around. A hat on a hat box, a dress strewn across the bed, a petite shawl here and slippers there—it all adds up to the lived-in look.

I'm not going to delve into much about clothing. There's such a vast history of styles and periods, and even sex and age differences create more diversity and discussion. Clothing could really take up a whole book in itself, but I want to include a nibble, so that everyone who is nimble with the needle will look into the potentials of clothing her dollhouse family.

There have been tiny hats fashioned into pins and there might be some small doll hats in the toy fashion world—but don't wait to find them, get out your needles and knit, crochet, cut, sew or even glue a miniature chapeau to completion. Inspiration can originate anywhere. I was recently dining in a famous New Jersey restaurant where all the waitresses were wearing little white colonial caps. Naturally, I went home and made one.

The smallest of small items must be jewelry, the darling of all personal adorn-

88

Fig. 9-1 Food may be difficult to visualize from this bizarre view but, believe me, it will look good gracing any dollhouse table. To whet your appetite, here's a basket of red apples, a bowl of assorted fruit, a basket of eggs, a chocolate-topped bundt cake, a strawberry frosted birthday cake, roast chicken, eclairs and black and white cookies, a gingerbread man, healthy carrots, tomatoes and a head of lettuce, roast beef, hard rolls, fish, loaf of bread, jam and peanut butter sandwiches, hamburger and french fries, a sandwich, grapes, hot dog in roll, a wedge of cheese, a fried egg and brownie à la mode. (*Jack Ruthberg, photograph*)

ment. Nothing much is really new in jewelry. There are only variations. After all, this ornamentation goes back for centuries, having been retrieved from the tombs of Egyptian monarchs.

While most jewelry is for self-gratification, the timepiece—pocket watch or wristwatch—comes to the fore as a tiny necessity.

Necklaces, pendants, bracelets, pins, rings and earrings are personal adornments that may not show up too prominently in miniature but are nice to include. In fact, my pocket watch gets more acclaim than a larger, more noticeable ob-

ject. So display your little "pretties" in a see-through jewelry box, on top of a dresser or even on the person of a little figure that lives in your little house.

Helpful Hints for Making Food

- ✔ Study the structure and actual coloring of food.
- ✔ Keep the proper size scale in mind and refrain from overemphasizing size.
- ✔ Use photos in magazines and cookbooks for good reference material.
- ✔ If you need ice for a shrimp bowl, or

Fig. 9-2　Typifying the specialty shop is the bakery. This one was made by Sally and Wayne Lasch of SHAKER MINIATURES. Wayne crafted the furnishings and the bakery cases are made from Plexiglas and wood. Sally made the food and it's very tempting. (*Wayne Lasch, photograph*)

something else, use candy rock crystal.

✔Crumpled Styrofoam makes good popcorn. Add a little yellow in spots for buttered effect and heap in a bowl.

✔For a glazed frosting on cake and one that dribbles down the sides, (bundt cake) mix color with white glue. For a thicker frosting mix, color with craft glue. Swirl it around when it begins to harden.

✔Use nonpareils and sequin cake decorations for candies.

✔For spaghetti, cut many pieces of white *button* thread of various lengths (¼″ up to ¾″). Swirl the pieces around in white glue with a dot of ochre for off-white color. Curl them up on a plate to dry. Add brown meatballs. When dry, swirl a rust-colored glue sauce over all.

✔Sauces can be applied over other foods. White paint mixed with white glue is cream sauce and yellow-orange color is cheese sauce.

✔Smallest pearls or beads are made into clusters of grapes and cherries.

✔Save the pits of fruit and color them for miniature fruit. Cherry pits become peaches and plums.

✔Air fern substitutes for greenery on carrot tops.

✔All-day lollipops are made from sparkle pins. Stems are removed and tiny wooden sticks are inserted and glued into the colorful round balls, which come in all the favorite flavors.

✔Use pieces of corn broom or whisk broom for handle of candy apple on stick. Submerge round bead (apple size) in "red glue" mixture, or sculpture your own apples. Lacquer for shine.

✔When you have used up a small Cake Mate decorating tube, clean it out and insert your own *thick*, colored glue solution for miniature decorating —puffed potatoes, cake frills, whipped cream.

✔Sugar crystals on cake decoration are grated Styrofoam.

✔Fine sawdust wood shavings make coconut.

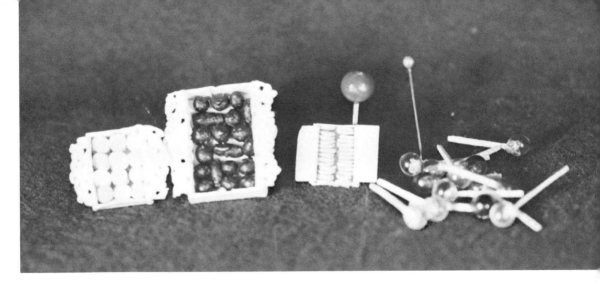

Fig. 9-3 Any child will tell you that candy is food. Have some boxed mints (sequin cake decorations), assorted chocolates (molded bread dough), a candied apple on a stick (red colored bead) and different flavored lollipops (sparkle pins). (*Jack Ruthberg, photograph*)

- Color sawdust pieces green for shredded lettuce or chicory.
- Slice ¼″ dowel sticks thin for slices of bologna and salami. Paint brown, rust, etc. Use large dowels for cakes; sand top edge rounder; frost.
- For grill marks across steak or ham slices, dip a straight string in thick black paint and quickly, gently, press down on "meat" surface.
- Skewers are fastening pins with small round of card inserted for guard.

BREAD DOUGH RECIPE

The art of working with bread dough has been revived along with many crafts of years gone by and much to our benefit. Bread dough is made with a chunk of bread and a dash of glue. Of course, the ingredients are a bit more exacting than that but the method for making this modeling compound to create yummy food is unbelievably easy.

  3 slices of regular white bread (5–7 days old)
  3 tablespoons of white glue
  3 drops of lemon juice

If you wish, you may double the recipe. The dough can be kept in a small airtight plastic bag in refrigerator for a few weeks.

Note: Bread dough can also be used in making other products and appliances.

Directions: Cut off crusts. Place small pieces of bread in palms of hands and, with circular motion, shred the bread into a pie pan. Repeat until all bread has been shredded. Transfer bread crumbs to a small bowl. Add the glue and lemon juice and mix with a fork until glue is absorbed. Place the mixture in the palm of your hand and, using both hands, knead dough. The dough will at first seem gritty, but it will soon become smoother. Continue the kneading process for about 10 minutes.

If dough is left exposed to air, it will dry out; so break off amount that you intend to work with for your project. Place the rest in a small airtight plastic bag and steal a snitch from the bag whenever you start to shape a new food creation.

A second useful composition and one that is more suited to my use is Sculpey, a modeling plastic. This soft, workable compound can be easily shaped, baked in the oven to become hard and can be cut and painted. This is available in some art shops, but the toy departments also feature a boxed assortment for the benefit of the kiddies.

MODELING BREAD DOUGH

There are certain implements that can aid you in making food. A paring knife with a pointed blade tip is used for cutting, indenting and helping to shape the object. The side of the knife blade is also used for flattening the dough. A Bic ball-

91

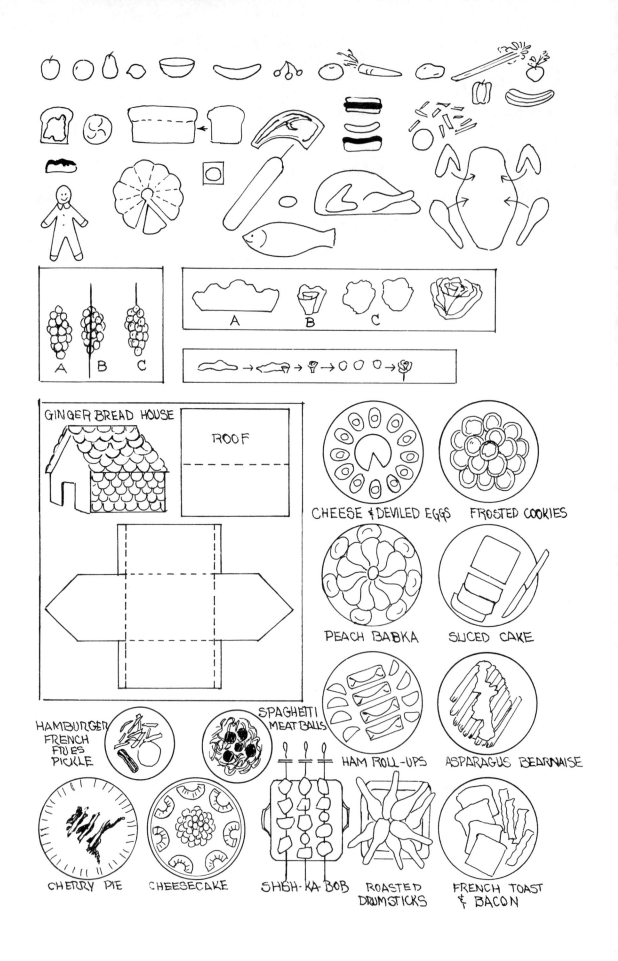

GINGER BREAD HOUSE

ROOF

CHEESE & DEVILED EGGS   FROSTED COOKIES

PEACH BABKA   SLICED CAKE

HAMBURGER
FRENCH
FRIES
PICKLE

SPAGHETTI
MEATBALLS

HAM ROLL-UPS   ASPARAGUS BEARNAISE

CHERRY PIE   CHEESECAKE   SHISH-KA-BOB   ROASTED
DRUMSTICKS   FRENCH TOAST
& BACON

point pen makes use of both ends: the plastic cover on the tip is used for punching holes into dough and this rounded contour is also helpful in shaping food, rolling and smoothing a surface. Top of pen can also punch into dough for larger hole. Rounded tips from brush handles and round toothpick tips are also serviceable.

Work your projects on a generous sheet of waxed paper which resists sticking. When the food is completed, place the bread dough creations in a square Styrofoam container from the food market; allow to dry thoroughly for several days. Small pieces, like cookies of course, dry quicker than a generous size cake, so use good judgment for drying time. Sculpey, on the other hand, can be hard baked and ready for coloring the same day.

After food is thoroughly dried, use acrylic paint to color or you can color the dough ahead, using a bit of acrylic before you begin your food modeling. Several colored portions of dough can be completed, depending upon your choice of food selection. Assuming you have your base coat applied, you will sometimes need to acquire shading (variable colored apples, specks on bananas and pears, roasted chicken, baked ham, browned toast). The easiest method is to apply small amounts of needed color on a fingertip and gently dab at the food. When the paint has dried, give the food a quick spray of sealer or lacquer. The food can then be lightly adhered to a dish or platter, which you have either acquired, purchased or handmade yourself. Don't forget to place some pretty paper or lace doilies under the pastries (cut from larger doilies). One last word of warning: your food will look so good that you must take care that the ants don't come and carry it away.

How to Make a Variety of Food

Suggested sizes and step-by-step procedures for making foodstuffs are shown in Figure 9-4.

GRAPES

Paint tiny pearls the color of grapes (roll pearls around in a puddle of paint that has been mixed with white glue). Arrange pearls (A) on waxed paper. Dry well. Turn over and glue brown button thread down center (B) and add more "colored-glue" pearls on top (C). Dry well. Cut off bottom of thread.

LETTUCE

This resembles Boston lettuce. Flatten a thin piece of modeling compound (A). Roll up (B). Flatten a few very thin pieces (C) and continue to wrap and press around outside area, building it up. When dry, color with two mixtures of green paint.

Note: White and purple cabbage can be made the same way, but shape a more rounded formation.

ROSES

Apply same principle for forming lettuce to make roses used to decorate cakes, only work much smaller. It's advisable to color the mixture first.

GINGERBREAD HOUSE

Cut out pattern (Fig. 9-4) from card and glue together. Using white glue, apply layers of sequin cake decorations. Create your own pattern or just use multicolors haphazardly. Allow for a door and a window or two. Add a chimney. When finished, quickly brush a light application of white glue over the entire surface. Dry well.

Fig. 9-4 Drawings at top show sizes for various kinds of food. Middle drawings show working procedure for making grapes, lettuce and roses. The remaining drawings show food suggestions discussed in the Helpful Hints section.

Fig. 9-5   Hats of different eras are all brought together for one grand showing. Mother wears her "basic" dress with a lace shawl added for warmth, and daughter wears her cape. Along with the red suspenders and leather vest, all apparel is described with directions for Figures 9-12 and 9-13.

Fig. 9-6   A dollhouse often has "little people" residing within. This is a copy of a dollhouse doll, probably German, from around the turn of the century. It is made of porcelain bisque, with cloth body, molded hair and shoes. She is dressed in the fashion of the time. (*Courtesy of Dolls by Faith*)

Helpful Hints for Making Clothing

✔Hang up an apron on a wall rack in the kitchen or place it nonchalantly over a chair back.

✔Glue a slipper into the mouth of a little doggy.

✔Fashion a small headstand out of bread dough (or use a bead) and place a hat on it.

✔Place a coat hanger in a hallway and, trying not to hide the hanger, suspend a coat from it.

✔Crochet a lacy shawl and casually place it somewhere.

✔Fold some tiny handkerchiefs and stack them on a dresser top.

✔Tiny feathers attached to a wide-brimmed hat will really draw sighs. Obtain feathers from pet bird department. If parakeets are in homes that are hot and dry, they conveniently molt all year.

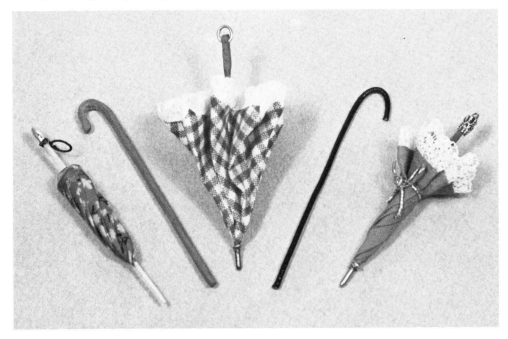

Fig. 9-7   Parasols used to be very much a part of ladies' attire and the cane enhanced men's fashions of the time. The cane on the left is cut out of walnut wood and sanded round. But the one on the right is black electrical wire, bent to shape. Two styles of parasols are described in the How-to section.

Fig. 9-8   Hats of felt can be fashioned for different occasions and eras, as shown by brimmed flower creations, the jockey hat, skull hat (which can be trimmed), the tri-corner hat and even a Mouseketeer hat for the contemporary younger set.

✔Show a wardrobe of dresses on hangers in a wardrobe chest.

✔A tiny scrap of mink or mouse fur can make an elegant muff or hat.

How to Make Hats and Parasols

Head coverings from many eras can be made easily, with a parasol or cane added to the costume for charm (Fig. 9-12).

FELT HATS

Felt, which comes in a fine array of colors, makes an excellent beginning for a hat. It is easily shaped in the following way.

Cut a 2″ square of felt; soak material in water, squeeze out excess moisture; wrap material tightly stretching it around deodorant ball or bead; place this in bottle cap until dry.

A variety of hats can be cut from this mold, each one different in style, period and use (see drawings):

1. The *brimmed hat* has a ruffled effect when completed, and I like it that way, but if you prefer, the ruffle can be ironed out. Decorate with fabric flowers, ribbon, tiny bows, lace, tiny beads or whatever.

2. The *skull cap* is cut completely around at the base of the shaped area. Decorate with lace trim, veiling or braid. For the younger generation, include a *Mouseketeer hat,* destined to become a "classic." Add two big mouse ears to the top of a black skull shell and cut out a circled capital M from a magazine and paste on the front.

3. The *cap* is also cut around the base line, but leave an area of material for the peak. Add a band around edge (I cut the thin edge of lace from hem lace). Add a small jump link to front.

Fig. 9-9   Compared to the ring outside the frame, the tiny ring at bottom right is undeniably small. Other precious pretties are pendants, necklaces, watches, bracelets and pins. Oops! I forgot the earrings. (*Jack Ruthberg, photograph*)

Fig. 9-10 Half of a lace cuff becomes a lined cape. Just cut holes for hands to come through and your doll is ready to go out in style.

4. The pattern for a *Colonial hat* is cut before stretching procedure. After it's dry, iron out any ruffles; add white military braid trim to edge, pull up brim at three points and tack-stitch to top.

COLONIAL CAP

1. Cut circle pattern from fine-textured white handkerchief.
2. Cut thin strips from lace, enough to go around the circle; glue or sew lace strip all around edge.
3. With needle and thread take small stitches along the line; gather together enough to allow cap to fit on top of doll's head. Tie off. Leave plain or trim with a little ribbon.

PURITAN CAP

1. Cut out pattern from handkerchief; glue sides inward.
2. Glue small edging of anything delicate to front part of bottom, placing wrong sides together. When dry, turn right side out and flatten back.
3. With needle and thread, take small stitches to gather together the back hem-stitched area very tightly; tie off.

4. Add tiny strips of lace edge for ribbon tie.

SCARLET O'HARA HAT

1. Cut out oval pattern from sturdy material.
2. Press folds on each side for turn downs.
3. Add lace edge ties, feather on side and a narrow braid trim along the edge.

LACE HAT

1. Cut about 3″ of delicate lace edging.
2. Glue sides together to fit doll's head.
3. Cut a round section to fit within top area and glue together.
4. Add trim of braided embroidery floss around top.

PARASOL

Materials: Walnut rod, 1/16″ square, 2½″ long, shaped to point (use hardwood for rod); lining or cotton blend fabric; lace trim; ball-point pen tip; handle trim.
Directions:
1. Shape wooden rod as shown in drawing.

Fig. 9-11 Daughter can team up with mother for a matching outfit, too. Half of a lace cuff is lined and holes made for arms.

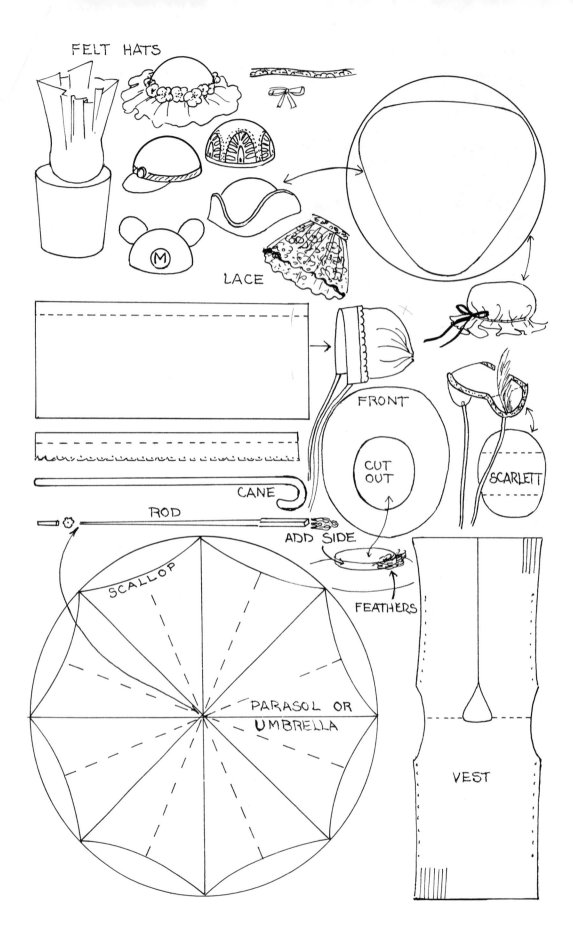

FELT HATS

LACE

FRONT

CUT OUT

SCARLETT

CANE

ROD

ADD SIDE

FEATHERS

SCALLOP

PARASOL OR UMBRELLA

VEST

2. Draw pattern circle 3¾″ diameter, and trace off onto material.

3. With finger, lightly apply glue around cutting edge.

4. When dry, cut out pattern of scallops.

5. Glue delicate straight edging of lace to inside area of parasol material along scalloped edge.

6. Iron folds into pattern: short area (dotted lines) to fold out; longer area (straight lines) to fold inward.

7. Through pinpoint hole in center of material, gently push bottom of wooden rod.

8. To prevent slipping, glue one long side of material to stick. Dry.

9. Twirl material gently around stick.

10. Secure in place with gold covered wire; simulate bow.

11. At bottom of stick, glue on a very tiny filigree bead cap (leave a point showing) and squeeze around material.

12. At tip, glue on the metal tip of a used ball-point pen (be sure it is free of old ink).

13. Decorate handle with ¼″ filigree bell cap.

Variation: Instead of twirling material, catch each end with needle and thread, pull tightly and secure with a few stitches.

MAN'S BLACK UMBRELLA

Rod will be in shape of cane; covering is black cotton material. The cane is cut out of ⅛″ thick walnut. All edges are sanded round and smooth until *you* are satisfied that it's a worthy stick. Follow pattern and instructions for Parasol.

VEST

1. Cut vest out of suede or leather, following pattern in Figure 9-12.

2. Fold over at shoulder; cut fringe trim at bottom.

3. With matching color embroidery floss, lash two sides together and tie off just above fringe. Tiny bead trim can be added or hand paint a design on front.

How to Make Clothing and Accessories

Instructions are given in this section for garments and accessories shown in Figure 9-13.

RED SUSPENDERS

Materials: Red hem tape; kid leather; three lengths of black elastic cording; two silver hairpins; aluminum from disposable plate.

Directions:

1. Glue both pieces (A) to (B), connected with leather pieces (D) on each side.

2. Wrap piece (C) around elastic cord and glue to (B).

3. Fold piece (A) over flat part of hook end (hairpin) and return, gluing onto same material.

4. Wrap piece (E) over rounded part of hook, catching elastic cord; glue.

5. Fold around and glue down small aluminum cut pieces as shown in drawing.

6. Cut ends of elastic cord to length shown in drawing.

SCUFFS AND SLIPPERS

For scuffs, cut out soles and (A) parts; for slippers add (B) parts. Glue (A) to front section and (B) to back. Use felt, leather or any sturdy material. If using satin, glue material to a slightly firmer piece first, then proceed. Trim if you like.

CHILD'S CAPE

Soft fabric that *doesn't ravel* is preferable (flannel or nylon acetate).

1. Right sides together, stitch top of cape together. Turn.

2. Using yarn, make running stitches at neck for gathering. Leave enough yarn at both ends for bow tie.

3. Slash for arm openings.

LADY'S BASIC DRESS

1. Bodice: sew darts and sew seams of

Fig. 9-12   Patterns and instructions for making an assortment of hats, umbrellas, a cane and a vest.

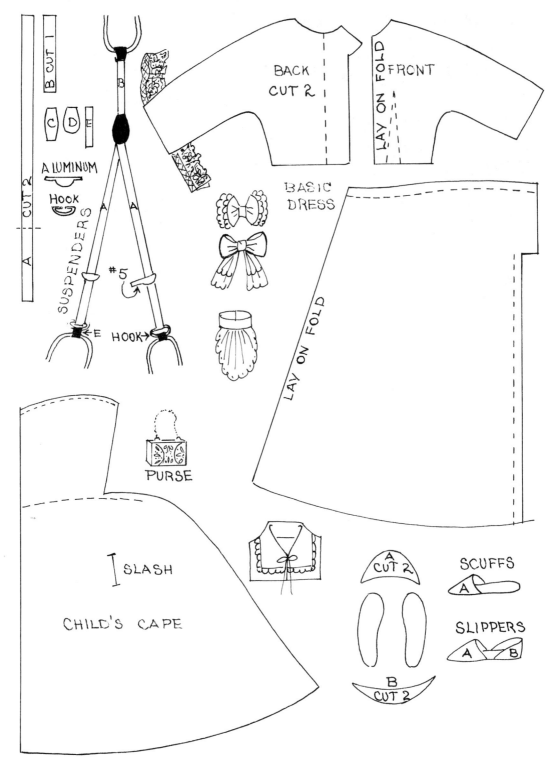

Fig. 9-13 Patterns and instructions for doll's dress, cape, slippers, suspenders, purse and other accessories.

sleeves and sides of front and back together.

2. Skirt: sew back seam closed. With running stitch, gather material at waist.

3. Adjust bodice and skirt to doll's body. With right sides together, stitch bodice to skirt.

4. Finish any decorating with belts, bows, peplums, swags, lace or buttons (seed beads). Lace, added to sleeve edge, should be sewed on *before* stitching *underarm* seam.

How to Make Jewelry

The crafting of these tiny accessories really requires the smallest of everything. Use jeweler's chain and bead wire, tiny rhinestones and cut pieces of filigree.

Necklaces: String rocaille beads, bugle beads and tiny pearls.

Pendants: Cut pieces from larger pieces of jewelry; cut piece of filigree with something mounted on top—rhinestone, gemstone, seashell. Attach to fine chain.

Bracelets: Cut filigree and shape into oval for wrist, add an accent piece; shape links (wide bands). Several narrow assorted links become bangle bracelets.

Pins: Bead caps are decorated with a rhinestone. One section, cut, becomes a bar pin.

Rings: Wrap bead wire together (two times) around short area of toothpick. Slip off, cut off excess wire and glue on the tiniest colored rhinestone, diamond chip or a ruby from old watch works.

Wristwatch: Cut a strap out of leather or use decorative chain from a chain necklace (length from 6″–7″). For a fancy watch, center and glue a filigree bead cap; add a 1/16″ paper circle to center. Add spots for numerals and hands.

Evening Purse: For the box style purse in Figure 9-13, use a box filigree necklace fastener 3/8″ or 1/4″. Remove connecting clasp. Attach jewelers chain to two hooks for handle. Pull chain through holes and glue to itself.

10

Plants, Flowers and Planters

Plants are individuals . . . in fact, much is being written about their sensitive feelings and reactions to various stimuli. Luckily, you don't have to possess a green thumb to keep your miniature greenery responsive. Plan it well and it will continue giving you and your dollhouse family pleasure, indefinitely (see color Fig. 1).

Plants and flowers are one of nature's great gifts and perceptive people have realized the vast business potential in their existence. England and the Netherlands were notable for such enterprises as early as the sixteenth century. The gardens of the early royal Governor's Palaces, best exemplified by Williamsburg, speak much for this ability.

During the eighteenth century, bough pots and crocus pots were designed and used to force bloom of crocus and blossoms of forsythia, pussywillows and other boughs.

Although gardening and flower arranging were enjoyed in early pioneer days, it wasn't until the early nineteenth century that floriculture became impressive. A notable fad was the use of special glass hyacinth vases to promote the full growth of this flower in water. Many vases and jardinieres were imported and were made of pottery, parian, majolica, pewter, brass

and cast iron. American factories produced their share of glass vases—cut, pressed and other styles. The miniature glass conservatory (Wardian case) added its personal touch, but the ferneries, flower and plant stands, bracket stands, flower urns, pots and baskets proliferated. They were constructed of wire, brass, cast iron, wrought iron, wicker and wood.

The Victorian era was immersed in feathery ferns as the popular plant, but the twentieth century plays no favorites. Plants of various botanical strains are prominent in many homes as individual guests or united in groupings with a variety of assorted species.

Every miniature home should have some plants and floral arrangements. They breath life into the tiny structure.

PLANTERS

Now it's decisions, decisions, decisions! You are wondering if you should use a certain top upside down or downside up. Tops are so versatile that, hopefully, if you have several of the same design, your choice of how to use that "special one" becomes uncomplicated. So always duplicate your findings and keep any and all tops in reserve (Figs. 10-1 and 10-2).

When you have acquired a box full,

you'll soon find that some will fit together in multiple ways; many combinations become highly sophisticated and attractive planters.

Since tops, which are mostly plastic, come in a variety of finishes, including gold, silver, transparent, colored and indispensable white, you may often be able to use the top as it is.

Tops can be decorated, added to, mounted on pedestals or feet and changed about in a conglomeration of ways. They can become planters for tabletops, shelves, floors, walls, entrances and for hanging. Size will determine the best placement and use (Fig. 10-3).

PLANTS AND FLOWERS

When you have an assortment of planters available, they are ready to be filled. Your choice of fillers can range from the natural to the unnatural.

Baby's tears are lovely, delicate plants with multitudinous leaves and small root systems. They'll grow naturally in diminutive containers.

There's a variety of small plastic leaves and flowers available in the flower shop sections of variety stores, and many garden or flower shops and supermarkets feature dried flowers, too. The tiny star flower, which is multicolored, is a gem to work with and there are other small dried-out varieties waiting for you to choose. Boutique and craft shops, can often provide petite flowers that are made of fabric, in addition to the dried variety.

The more resourceful person can readily dry out her own flowers when the spring and summer season is in full bloom, and this is probably the most gratifying of all. The most popular small flowers that adapt themselves to drying are baby's breath and alyssum (white and purple). You might also try tiny red rosebuds and coral bells. There are other flowers which seem to be large in appearance, but in reality are made up of clusters of smaller flowers: these small stems, when dried, can be broken apart and grouped together singly or with other flowers or plants. Scotch heather produces a small budlike flower, and one tip-top spike looks stately in a bud vase; or use several

pieces branching out, along with another flower or two for accent.

I have even dried the large stamens of rhododendron and their slim, curly appearance adds another interesting dimension to arrangements.

Dried grasses and weeds (the small variety, of course) provide interesting shapes, but you'll just have to *bend* and bring your eyes down to meet Mother Earth to realize all the great possibilities there are. Get out into the country, too, where wildflowers and grasses are abundant. And while you're looking and picking, also keep in mind the possibility of dry pressing some of nature's wonders for pressed flower arrangements under glass or acetate to help decorate your walls or a tray (see Ch. 4).

There are a few selective methods for drying out the flowers. Silica gel, a moisture-removing chemical, can be purchased at flower departments. Clean, unsalted sand is usable and, although I have never tried it, borax and kitty litter have also been recommended. There are some small flowers that just seem to dry naturally by themselves. Trial and error will sometimes suffice, but use an airtight container with a cover and gently cover over your blossom with one of the suggested ingredients.

During the summer season, there are rock garden plants; their availability can open up a whole new world for you in planting arrangements. Sedum and other succulents can be put into a little oasis—or can rest within a small container of water. Plastic pill containers are useful, for they can also be set inside another, more decorative unit. But even if these plants aren't in anything aqueous, it's amazing how long they will last with just a smidgen of water dashed onto them once a week. You might even try drying some sedum. When it's in bloom, its yellow flowers fit into most any vase. So pick, pick, pick and you will smile at your new floral arrangements.

Helpful Hints

✔ If you have any plastic pill vials, which come in assorted sizes and in clear or

Fig. 10-1 Hanging planters start with bottletops, pill containers, miniature bottles and seashells. Add twine, floss, chain, string or strips of leather for hanging. Finish off with trim or painted designs and add natural or artificial plant life. *At bottom,* a black egg holder is the base for an Oriental display of a beautiful twisted "tree limb," a sculptured man, a rock and gravel. The floor planter with dried fern tips and the standing terrarium are described in detail with how-to direc-

brown color, these can be cut down in size and used in different ways. Heat is the only way to cut through plastic without cracking it so, using a small straight-edge paring knife, heat it well over a gas burner and when very hot, quickly slice into the plastic and through the area you wish to sever. You will have to repeat this process a few times (reheating each time) before complete severance is accomplished. There will be some rough edges which can be carefully clipped away using your parrot-nose diagonal cutter.

- Clear plastic containers are great for table terrariums, hanging planters, large and small terrariums.
- They can become water-holding containers within other containers that can't ordinarily hold a liquid, such as straw baskets.
- Toothpaste tube tops are most useful as small pots. Arrange several "pots" in a grouping, using different plants and flowers.
- Teeny metal caps from sample perfume bottles make the smallest of all planters.
- Insert a plant in the opening of a one-inch univalve seashell.
- Use filigree bell caps or other curved pieces: mount on base of your choice. Leave gold or silver or paint black or another color.
- Look for glass beads that resemble a cut-glass vase.
- Beads from India and wooden macrame beads offer other possibilities.
- Glue several jump links together for a single-stem bud vase, then mount on small button base for support.
- Small salt shakers can make a unique jardiniere.
- A dollhouse pitcher becomes a charming holder for your flowers or plants; a pitcher with matching bowl will be twice as attractive.
- Hollow out a small piece of driftwood and place plant material inside.

Fig. 10-2 Let's go ornamental with a planting arrangement. A small narrow box, covered with Weldwood flexible wood trim or veneer, becomes the base for plant containers (bottletops) and assorted plants (plastic, dried, or fabric); add small white pebbles to top. The background screen is the box from a bottle of cologne and the sculptured ivory decoration is a discarded lamp finial. At the base of the modern bottletop table rests a small ceramic frog, guarding his domain. The finely finished brass container is a purchase. Pale blue wallpaper is from a sample book and carpet is textured beige material.

- Cut ½" to 1" off bottom of plastic bottles that are oblong in shape. Cover plastic with decorative braid that resembles woven material or use other trim. These become long, narrow planters.
- A perforated salt shaker top becomes a flower arranger in a container.
- Small incense burners produce some very exotic planters.
- Egg stands are large and impressive. Add a top or settle some container within the hole area.
- Fill a miniature basket with greenery and hang it up.

tions in this chapter. A saucer-shaped button on a fancy bottletop and different heights of cut twig are bases for matching toothpaste tube top pots. Other "vases" are more tops, beads, a large finger ring, straw basket and button. There's all manner of plants and flowers from plastic to dried beauties.

Fig. 10-3 The popular display of plant life under glass can be imaginatively accomplished with a dome top from a vending machine or Love spray bottle. Tiny little plastic stem glasses can hold the smallest of plant life and display some sand art, too. You might also try a terrarium table, using a large clear pill container, cut down to size needed.

Fig. 10-4 The smallest of flower and plant achievements is a wee bonsai tree, complete with bridge and little figurine. A small piece of driftwood with a ready made opening, courtesy of Mother Nature, accepts a bit of dried plant and looks quite comfortable hanging on the screen. The corsage is real dried red rosebuds nestled with some tiny white flowers and green dried grasses, accented with full rolling bows of ribbon. The Victorian dome-topped flower arrangement is dried alyssum, and I couldn't resist adding the transparent glass bead as a bowllike vase. In case you're interested, the table on the left is a decorated bottletop and the white square one is also a top. The screen is a sample of slatted window shade, (see color Fig. 10).

Fig. 10-5 Three pink roses are made from bread dough or Sculpey. Of course, they can be painted any color and can be made into centerpiece arrangements or used in other ways. Or, if you prefer nature in the raw miniature, dried rosebuds are placed within a vase. (*Jack Ruthberg, photograph*)

✔Small sample perfume bottles become glass vases.
✔Everybody loves straw flowers; they're small, attractive, colorful and reasonably sturdy. They're pretty in a cluster as part of an arrangement and lovely under a glass dome.
✔Air fern, although greener than most of nature's plant life, is a terrific solution for many problem spots. It is feathery, light and especially adaptable for the smallest arrangements.
✔Dry the tips of ferns; you can't get more "real" than that, especially for Victorian.
✔Keep the little dried-out pieces in empty plastic pill containers to prevent breaking, until ready to use.
✔Roses and other flowers and plants can be sculptured out of bread dough.

How to Make Hanging and Standing Planters

A wide assortment of planters to hang, to use on table surfaces or as standing floor planters is shown in Figure 10-6.

FIVE HANGING PLANTERS

One method for achieving a hanging planter is to use small chains (A). By attaching chains to top of container at three equidistant points, catching the three chains together at a center area above plants with another single chain, you have a planter which can be attached to ceiling of room. There is an easy method to hook the chain to the plastic. Punch a hole through the plastic, using the heated tip of a sharp-pointed object. An ice pick, poultry skewer or large needle serves this purpose well. Insert a jump link through the hole and connect up with the chain. Use another jump link to catch the three chains together at junction point.

If chain is unavailable, you can use string (B). Knot lengths of string near the ends to make a tassel and feed it through the hole and up. Knot three strings together to join above the pot or they can be collected together with a bead. Use a little glue to keep bead from slipping out of place.

A curved bottle top is perfect for a Mexican planter (C). Add zigzag design in red. Use thin plastic straps, knotted on the inside of planter, for hanging.

Upholstery trim is all ready to be glued into place on a top (D). Add a tassel to the bottom, securing well with eye pin through bottom hole and with jump rings make a matching color hanging on top.

Select a univalve seashell and glue plastic strips, strings or whatever onto shell as shown in (E).

MACRAME PLANTERS

The art of macrame is an admirable and beautiful old craft and, with a little effort, you can simulate a macrame plant hanger for pot, seashell or bottle (F and G).

1. Start with sixteen 6" colored strings (crochet string or string art string) and knot all together for (F).

2. Separate into four sets of four strings each; pull four ways; knot each set.

3. Separate two strings from each set and return to meet other two strings and knot.

4. Repeat separation process again.

5. Bring four sections of strings up to common center area and knot.

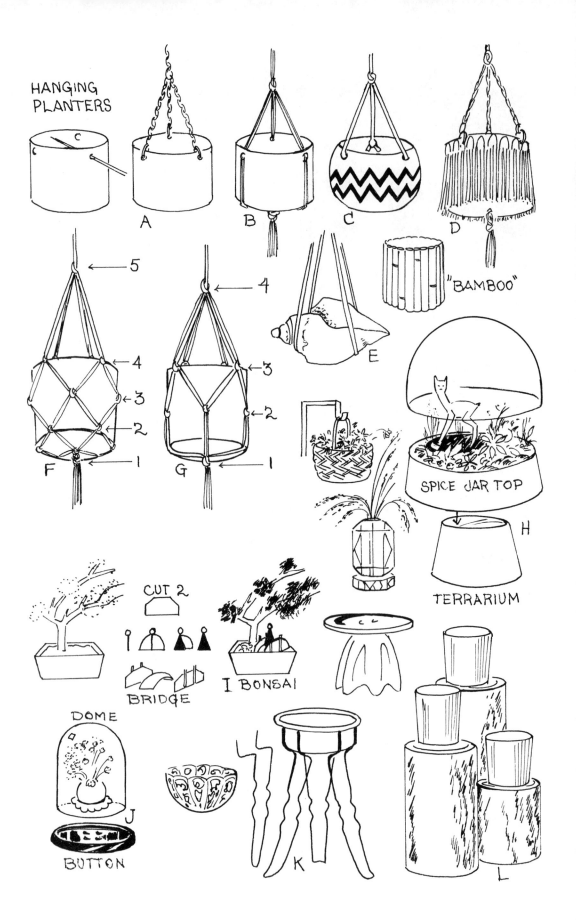

HANGING
PLANTERS

A

B

C

D

"BAMBOO"

5

4

4

3

3

2

2

F 1

G 1

E

SPICE JAR TOP

TERRARIUM

H

CUT 2

BRIDGE

I BONSAI

DOME

J

BUTTON

K

L

Directions:

1. Knot eight 6″ lengths of cord or string for planter shown in (G).

2. Catch sets of two together with small beads, then glue or knot.

3. Each two-string set separates to knot with other string set.

4. All are brought together at center point and knotted.

STANDING TERRARIUM

Materials: Transparent top from cosmetic product (Love); top from spice jar; top from bottle; very tiny animal (deer); small flat stone; plant life—real or plastic.

Directions:

1. Glue *base* of bottletop onto *top* of spice jar top.

2. Glue animal onto stone and glue into top; fill top with ozite and moisten. Set animal and stone on top and arrange plants within top opening.

3. Carefully fit transparent lid over all. Other tops (although smaller or larger) can be transparent plastic domes from vending machines or plastic jelly containers.

Note: Plant suggestions are sedum, buds from pachysandra, fern. Flower suggestions are alyssum, coral bells, yarrow. A beautiful *terrarium table* can be made using a large clear plastic pill container. Cut container shorter. Fill with plants. Add a glass cover to top (or small plastic cover from cheese package).

Extra Note: For a very special effect, add *sand art* to the bottom for a contemporary look.

BONSAI TREE

Bonsai is the exquisite Oriental art of dwarfing trees (I).

Materials: Container for base; small twigs; HO tree or greenery (lichen) from model hobby shop; flexible wood trim for bridge or Contact paper glued to index card; white bead, scrap of red material; craft glue; cotton.

Directions: Unless you're lucky enough to find a twig already preshaped by nature, glue tiny branches of twigs together to resemble illustration. Glue small pieces of lichen (greenery) onto twigs. Soak lots of cotton in glue, wrap around bottom stem of tree and set into container. Dry thoroughly overnight.

Figurine: Glue white bead onto tip of toothpick. Wrap half circle of material around glued toothpick and overlap. Apply glue to top and back portion of bead, dip into tiny cut pieces of clipped wool, fake fur or thread to acquire hair.

Bridge: Construct bridge from flexible wood trim or balsa wood as shown in illustration (I). Glue figurine onto bridge. Paint dried cotton "terrain" green. Glue bridge and figure onto top of terrain.

VICTORIAN DOME

Materials: Clear plastic dome from vending machine; black button that fits under dome; one daisy embroidery; very pretty small bead for vase; dried white and purple alyssum.

Directions: Glue embroidery (doily) over button holes and glue bead on top. Glue flowers into place, then glue dome over all onto button (J). Although the delicate alyssum is preferred, other flowers can be used: straw, bread dough roses, grasses.

FLOOR PLANTER

Materials: Chrome or gold cabinet door pull; black hairpins.

Directions: Bend three hairpins as shown in (K) and glue to underside of door pull. A large filigree bead cap or other containerlike item can be used as a container.

LOG PLANTERS

Bring the outside in. Cut a dried, seasoned twig to three different heights and glue together as shown (L). Glue three toothpaste tube tops on for pots.

Other planters show basket hung on copper staple hanger, a glass faceted bead on glass button, saucer button on bottle cap and a bamboo-style planter made from cut antiseptic sticks glued to a cylinder made from card.

Fig. 10-6   An assortment of planters and terrariums for hanging or standing on various surfaces.

✧ 11 ✧

Fireplaces and Hearthside Equipment

Every dollhouse should boast at least one fireplace. But if your choice of furnishings is related to an era of the past, then fireplaces are not just a charming addition to the decor, but a necessity to the way of life that existed. Since there were no central heating systems, fireplaces provided necessary warmth for comfort.

In the evening, families gathered around the fireplace, which also provided light. There was much togetherness as father read, often aloud, women caught up on their mending or embroidery and children studied their lessons.

In early Colonial days the fireplace was the improvised stove, used for cooking, baking, making soap, boiling water for baths or for whatever needs a fire could satisfy.

Fireplaces are fun pieces to make because they are flat surfaced, easy to cover, and offer a variety of finishes and styles, from primitive stone to modern mirror.

You will find satisfaction in using veneer woods for finishing your fireplaces. A vast selection is available and some wood sources even provide tiny strips of inlaid wood; others provide tiny scale moldings which produce a fine finished piece of work.

Delft tile fireplaces were very popular in the nineteenth century (Fig. 11-1). The tiles were usually decorated in blue painted designs and indeed they presented a most attractive front. Small tiles that are commonly used for ashtrays (usually sold in craft stores) can be glued into position on the face of your cardboard shape. The front and sides can be further decorated with wood of your choice. A tiny red or blue design is added to each tile with a permanent felt-tipped marking pen or with acrylic paint (see color Fig. 16).

Marble front fireplaces can be achieved with the use of Contact paper (Fig. 11-2). A coat of polyurethane or a spray of lacquer will provide the gloss. Combined with wood, this also produces a charming and elegant effect. A gem and mineral shop may be able to cut marble to your specifications.

The charm of an old, old fireplace can be duplicated by using small pebbles. Off-white stones are usually sold at florist and gardening establishments or tropical fish stores. With careful and patient scrutiny,

110

you can collect small stones from your yard. Don't forget to smear the stones and inside of fireplace with darkening to give an effect of soot (Fig. 11-3). Soft carbon pencil, soft charcoal or burnt matches work well, or you may solve this in some other way.

Mirror-faced fireplaces are for the modern minded and can be designed and

Fig. 11-1 Individual red urns in different styles are hand-painted on each tile to present a distinguished front. The fireback, made from a daguerreotype case, is an added feature.

Fig. 11-2 A marble-front fireplace is made from Contact paper, and wood veneer finishes off the top, sides and mantel. The andirons and fireguard are made from gold embossed paper. Both are glued to acetate for extra firmness.

Fig. 11-3   The stone fireplace is made with garden stones, but pebbles could also be used. There's a foot warmer on the left and a log box is on the right. Andirons are bent copper staples, painted black; the powder horn is the tip of a King Crab claw. A hearth broom rests against the stone front. The delft tile fireplace has bellows hung up on the left and a warming pan leans against the right side. The daguerreotype case fireback silhouettes the strung-bead andirons. On the mantel is a hand screen, used to protect the face from excessive heat.

mirrors cut with a glass cutter to suit your needs. I luckily came across some small mirrors in a craft shop already cut to the small square size of ½″, in continuous lengths (Fig. 11-4). I also found some smaller squares of ⅛″ mirror for other purposes. Keep looking and, eventually, something that you need turns up.

The accessories for a fireplace are varied, purposeful and oftentimes beautiful.

The firedog or andiron provided support for burning wood in a fireplace. Made of different materials—wrought iron, cast iron, steel, brass and cast brass—firedogs were either very simple for unpretentious homes or elaborately adorned for the elite clientele (Fig. 11-5). There were various designs, among which were examples of figures and birds. In many contemporary fireplaces, the andiron has been forsaken for the simple iron basket—not very decorative, but functional.

Fire screens, too, were either simple or elaborately trimmed. Not just ornaments, they were well-intentioned pieces designed to keep sparks and ashes in their proper place.

Portable fire screens, often embellished with lavish needlework, were adjustable panels mounted on poles. They were necessarily used to avoid the direct heat of fire.

Hand screens were dainty fans held by the ladies to protect their faces from excessive heat. There were usually a pair resting atop the mantel.

Bellows were the necessary tool for helping to get a fire started. Other necessities—shovels, tongs and brooms—played their role in fire control and hearth cleanliness.

Fenders, decorative low brass fences, were another protective device and were usually set in front of the andirons, extending from side to side of the opening.

Special heating equipment devised to make life more bearable was comprised of the warming pan, used to warm up the

cold covers of a bed, and the foot stove which contained hot coals, helping to bring comfort to many cold feet.

Firebacks, made of iron, copper and bronze, were decorated flat pieces that were placed in the back of the fireplace. Used as a radiant reflector, it helped produce more heat.

The Colonial fireplace had character of individual distinction. Designed for the necessities of life, it contained a long fireplace crane necessary to hold iron pots for cooking. The peel, a flat shovel attached to an extra-long handle, was used in handling baked bread.

Log containers, coal scuttles and decorative fans all add their signature to fireplace accessories.

Several of these items are described within this chapter and, whether purposeful or decorative, fireplace accessories are necessary to complete the "fireplace look."

Helpful Hints

✔A nice stone fireplace can be carved out of a mixture of plaster and papier mâché. The latter keeps the plaster from cracking.

Fig. 11-4 Small craft mirrors and cut portions of picture-frame molding team up for the front of a fireplace. Plastic owls are made into andirons and two metal doodads become a fender guard.

Fig. 11-5 This proud array of andirons indicates a variety of origins. On the left is a pair made from decorative gold embossed paper, next are strung beads, followed by large bent copper staples, plastic owls and, lastly, a pair of abalone earrings.

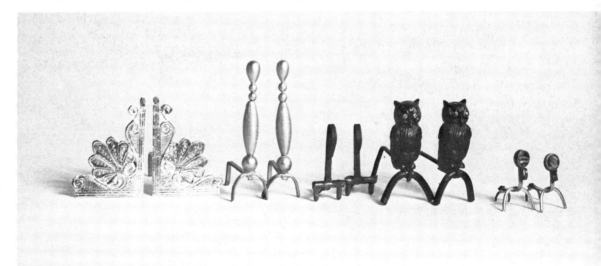

✔Frame moldings about ½″ to 1″ in size can be mitered and three sides fitted together for handsome fireplaces—but be careful not to make these too deep.

✔Molded sheets of miniature bricks are available from dealers. Have the face of a fireplace covered with bricks and use these for the inside, too.

✔Pocketbook handles can start you off with a very modern approach to a front (Fig. 11-6).

✔The hearth of a fireplace can be made in different ways: with a piece of marble, slate, marble-pattern stained glass, or Contact paper resembling pebbles. For the more ambitious, tiny flat stones can be laid into plaster; wood brick pat-terns are available from dealers; for a "cement" hearth, keep your eyes open for a plastic sealer (used to cover merchandise), rectangular in shape. Fill the rectangle with plaster about ⅛″ in depth. When hardened, cut away side of plastic and set onto floor.

✔A large copper staple can be bent into a snake shape for the old Colonial style andiron. Paint black.

✔Small chess pieces are potential andirons. Paint black, gold or silver.

✔Don't overlook lamp finials for solid brass andirons.

✔For a screen, cut actual fine screen to sizes needed. Insert and glue into strips of ⅛″ window sash. This is made like a picture frame. Make one screen or a three-panel screen. Paint black.

✔For a rounded top surface on screen, use black electrical wire for outer edging.

✔A 2½″-high scallop shell, painted gold and mounted on a base or attached to staples for support, is a beautiful front piece.

✔Round 2″ filigree decoration, cut in half, becomes a fireplace screen. Attach supports.

✔Gold embossed paper border becomes a fender in front of fireplace. Glue to thin acetate for support and bend two sides back for standing.

✔A square gold filigree is shaped into a U. Add legs to the bottom and wire handle to the top for a handsome log container.

✔Using plastic bag ties, weave a pattern, rectangular in shape and large enough to curve into a U for another log holder. Add thin strips of wood or card to top for strengthening—also around curve. Glue on a handle and legs. Brush a couple coats of glue or gesso over woven surface for stiffening. Paint holder black, brown or gold.

✔A small white cream container from restaurant, painted black and with an added wire handle, becomes a coal scuttle.

✔Obtain a small amount of aquarium gravel or gardening gravel and paint black for coal.

✔Round earring finding (with cluster of beads removed) becomes a warming

Fig. 11-6 A metal pocketbook handle becomes the opening for a modern fireplace. It's backed with a scrap of birchwood. The gilt accordion-pleated fan and gold Buddah are decorative torches and the log holder is bent filigree.

pan. Attach applicator stick for handle or, even better, shape a ⅛" dowel stick. ✔Twigs broken into small pieces add a bit of authenticity as logs. Stack and glue several together in a pile and place behind andirons in fireplace. Stack some extra logs in a holder by side of fireplace.

How to Make a Fireplace and Hearthside Accessories

Pattern parts and assembly instructions for the red delft tile fireplace and variations, along with a set of fireside accessories, are shown in Figure 11-7.

DELFT TILE FIREPLACE

1. Draw outline for fireplace background on illustration board after transferring to 1" graph paper. Cut out on solid lines. Fold on dotted lines. To make fold, use ruler and sharp blade. Gently make cut into board and fold away from you (#1).
2. Glue (B) to (A) as indicated in (#2). Finish off inside of fireplace with brick paper or brick-wood composition and color rust. Dirty it a little so it looks used.
3. Glue tiles to outside area of fireplace opening (#3).
4. Cut ¹⁄₃₂" or ¹⁄₁₆" thick wood to fit areas on front and sides. Miter corners leading into top tiles (see #4). Stain and glue to cardboard surface.
5. Cut a molding trim of matching wood to fit around and next to tiles. Miter corners to fit (#5). Sand and round outer edges or use quarter-round strips. Stain and glue.
6. Cut a mantel from ⅛" thick wood, making it larger to allow for overhang. Bevel three sides (#6). Glue on top.
7. Paint urn designs onto tiles with red acrylic.
8. Select a hearth for fireplace to stand on and allow hearth to come forward at least one inch.

Note: If you can't locate ceramic tiles at your craft store, make them out of a modeling compound. Make a long strip for each side and, when hard, sand away grooves to complete the look of individual squares. Paint white. When design is added and well dried, apply clear acrylic or clear nail lacquer. Illustration board can also be cut into squares, mitered, glued and painted.

FIREBACK

A fireback can be made from the outer embossed covering of a daguerreotype case. Soak in hot water until covering is sufficiently loose to peel off. Dry. Cut out a shape to fit back of fireplace and glue onto piece of bristol board. Attach to back. (Note: The case designs with a circle are best, but other designs can be used.)

SET OF HEARTHSIDE TOOLS

Tools: All handles are ⅛" dowel, made with slight turnings at top and bottom. Stems are cut paper clips glued to bottoms. *Tongs* are a cut large paper clip. *Brush* is end of a paintbrush cut from its handle. *Shovel* is a shape cut out of "curved corner" of aluminum frozen dinner plate—the "corner" is the top part of shovel.

Stand: Base is a button. Top is cut out of heavy aluminum: tilt edges upward. Attach to a dowel handle, which is attached to button base. Make some turnings on the handle-post before attaching. Paint utensils black, except handles and base.

How to Make Fireside Accessories

This section provides instructions for making the woodbox, foot-warmer stove, andirons and other items shown in Figure 11-8.

LOG WOODBOX

Cut pattern parts out of ¹⁄₁₆" thick balsa wood. Stain or leave plain. Glue box parts together as shown in drawing. Handle (¹⁄₃₂" thick) is bent (see Helpful Hints, Ch. 2) and glued to sides. Cut pieces of straight pins; glue and push through handles and box.

FOOT-WARMER STOVE

Cut piece of aluminum from baking container measuring 1" × 3⅝". Cut two

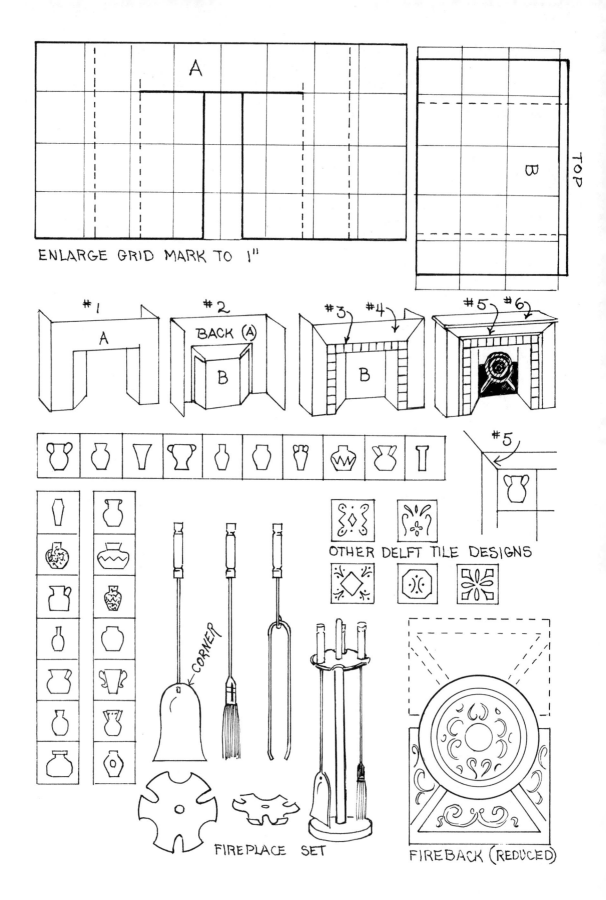

ENLARGE GRID MARK TO 1"

TOP

#1 A

#2 BACK (A) B

#3 #4 B

#5 #6

#5

CORNER

OTHER DELFT TILE DESIGNS

FIREPLACE SET

FIREBACK (REDUCED)

pieces of wood for top and bottom (A). In one piece (B) cut out center square section as shown.

1. Bevel and round for sides of both top and bottom pieces. Round inside area of cut-out square, too.

2. Fold aluminum (C) so that each side measures ¾" high and ⅞" wide. There should be an overlap at both top and bottom and closure. Cut to fold line and fold in. This part of aluminum will be glued to top and bottom wooden bases.

3. Aluminum slide top (D) is cut and square end is rolled forward over itself. This will slide in and out between top and box stove.

4. With compass point, puncture holes in aluminum as shown in drawing.

5. Add four pinheads to each corner, drill, glue and insert.

6. Add some black coals to the inside (black-painted aquarium gravel, chipped charcoal, painted tiny stones) and slide the top back over them.

BELLOWS

Cut two bellows pieces (A) out of 1/16" thick wood (walnut, cherry, balsa). Cut gusset (B) out of *very thin* leather (pattern is laid on fold). Cut piece (C) out of same leather. The tip is from a used ball-point pen.

1. Drill hole through each handle of bellows, as shown.

2. Stain wood.

3. Glue gusset onto edges of both sides of bellows. Trim edges neatly, if necessary. Dry well.

4. Fit and glue tip up over pointed end of bellows.

5. Wrap and glue piece (C) around both tip and bellows, securing both together.

6. In center of bellows add a circular metal decoration, or paint a design or decoupage a picture.

To hang bellows up by fireplace, cut ⅜" piece of sturdy wire, shape into L, drill hole into fireplace at the side or front and glue L piece into hole.

GOLD ACCORDION FAN

Cut piece of gold foil paper to size, 1½" wide × 6" long.

1. Glue both sides back ⅛". Fold back and forth ⅛", accordion pleating the entire length of gold paper.

2. Curve folded paper into fan shape (see drawing). Apply thick white glue to pivot area; hold together until glue "takes." Glue small round gold ornament to pivot area.

3. Cut 1/16" piece of balsa to size, ¼" × 3". Glue underside of fan to balsa wood strip for support and stand.

HAND SCREENS

Cut pattern out of two-ply bristol board: make either style—or both. Cut 1" length from round toothpick.

1. Paint screen a pastel color. When dry, glue on very tiny paper cutouts of flowers, birds or anything pretty. Add a few coats of diluted white glue for decoupage effect.

2. Carve a turned effect on toothpick as drawing shows. Gently slice down into toothpick from top, thicker end. Paint handle gold. When dry, glue handle up and over fan.

Note: Outline of fan can be cut in other designs, too.

HEARTH BROOM

This broom starts with a chunk of multicolored bristles cut from a paintbrush. They are glued around the end of a turned ⅛" dowel stick, stained or painted. Lightly wrap string or twine around bristles, gluing into place. Drill small hole at top of handle and insert jump link.

BED WARMER

To make this warming pan, select an old earring that has clusters of beads on it. Remove beads and back hinge. Cut ⅛" dowel stick to size shown, make turnings as indicated and stain wood. Insert dowel into side protrusion (left over from hinge)

Fig. 11-7 Pattern parts for red delft tile fireplace and hearthside accessories.

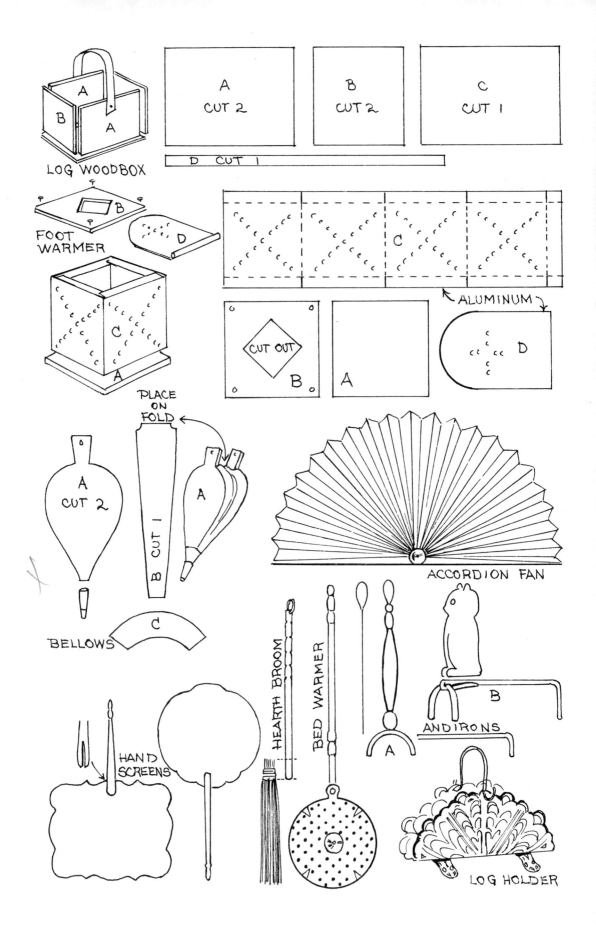

LOG WOODBOX

A CUT 2

B CUT 2

C CUT 1

D CUT 1

FOOT WARMER

C

ALUMINUM

CUT OUT B

A

D

PLACE ON FOLD

A CUT 2

B CUT 1

A

BELLOWS

C

ACCORDION FAN

HEARTH BROOM

BED WARMER

A

ANDIRONS

B

HAND SCREENS

LOG HOLDER

and wrap metal around stick. Add a circular, designed bauble to center area if you have one.

ANDIRONS

Hat pins or corsage pins still make a good beginning for conventional andirons (A). You may copy the beads that are shown here or select your own variety for a built-up design of strung beads. Large copper staples from corrugated packaging are used for supports. Drawing shows shaping and size. Glue everything together, including beads so they don't slip. Paint everything gold.

The owl andirons are two plastic owls painted black (B). Glue amber or green rocaille beads to eyes. Front rounded support is black electrical wire. Back support is large copper staple, shaped and painted black. Glue everything together (note that staple is curved around wire and returned). Retouch black paint, if necessary.

GOLD LOG HOLDER

Bend a gold 2″ round filigree decoration into a U shape. Bend a fastening pin and attach to each side at top. Cut two filigree pieces that are oval shaped and bend for feet. Glue onto bottom for supports.

Fig. 11-8   Parts and assembly for woodbox, foot warmer, accordion fan, andirons, log holder, hand screens, bellows and other fireside accessories.

✤12✤

Window Treatments

Mix-mix, match-match, mix-match, match-mix. This is the situation that develops when you begin to get involved with windows. Fashion may vary from room to room, certainly from house to house and, naturally, from era to era. Since some windows use curtains, some use drapes and others use both—and don't forget shades—there are many alternatives.

The curtain of an early settler was one simple piece of muslin, held by a rod at the top and drawn back for daylight. Curtains then advanced to the "pair," simply made, with top loops added and perhaps a little ruffled valance. As homes became less primitive and more gracious, window coverings became quite fashionable. Cornices, swags and jabots became popular and, during the eighteenth century, the curtains were matched to the curtains and valance of the tester bed. All of these structural elements were used either singly or together, depending upon the taste of the household, be it simple or lavish.

The nineteenth century home often had decorated window shades, which were either painted by manufacturers or home do-it-yourselfers. Shutters, blinds and venetian blinds all fall into their niche for total concealment.

Stained-glass windows of the nineteenth century are becoming a popular late twentieth-century attraction; this same latter day era also sees a return of the bead motif in some small measure. Creating your appropriate miniature window may take a bit of research and that's a small price to pay for a beautiful effect.

Keep your curtain treatment suitable in style (Fig. 12-1). A formal room requires formal drapery and fabric, so think velvet, taffeta, silk, lace, damask satin and moiré. The informal room is comfortable with linen, chintz and cotton; the casual mood is best exemplified with gingham, seersucker, denim, muslin and corduroy. Watch the textures and patterns on some of these fabrics—they can be tricky with $1/12$ scale. Since styling is variable, it's best to view real rooms that meet your approval for miniature duplications and make notes of the window treatment.

The next time you pass by the handkerchief counter in a store, stop and take a discerning look at the many kinds of designs and consider all the possibilities for some very beautiful curtains. This is undeniably the easiest and fastest way to provide a good-looking window covering and, since the material is lightweight and sheer, this is an asset.

Any lightweight material can be easily incorporated into attractive curtains and drapes. Heavy material such as velvet has been utilized, but be advised that it is more difficult to keep self-contained. While scouting for materials, be alert for petite designs, tiny checks or any small patterns that will remain in scale with the rest of your furnishings. Of course, solid colors are always a good choice, especially if your walls are patterned.

While you have fabrics on your mind, take note of some of the clothing that may be destined for rummage and decide whether anything can be salvaged for miniature use.

When you visit the fabric department, remember to scout for lace tidbits, too. Narrow lace or wide bands up to 3" width can be adapted for many uses (Fig. 12-2).

If you know anyone who's a sewer, she'll be glad to share her scraps of material with you. And fabric outlets very often provide small bags containing odds and ends of trimmings; these offer many possibilities for windows and other decorating schemes.

If you want to view a landscape scene through your window, keep an eye open for a greeting card that depicts an attractive scene and adhere this to a window under glass or clear acetate which simulates glass. The latter, being lightweight, adheres to the wall more easily. The acetate can be found on boxtops of stationery, packaged greeting cards or cosmetic products. Acrylic can be purchased at glass dealers and good art stores. If portions of the window on the top, bottom or sides are going to be visible, be professional and add some strips of balsa wood or special wood moldings around the window to simulate framework, sills, windowpanes or any other effects of sectioned glass that you wish to portray. Paint or stain wood before attaching to window area. I personally love to see a window with diamond designs on it, and couldn't you imagine this with stained glass or a reasonable facsimile?

Now that I've mentioned staining, there's much that can be done with this, too. Stained-glass windows which were long associated with period architecture are enjoying a revival in new homes and, as a decorator touch, they are exciting. You can render a window with a conservative design of the past or go quite modern with your own imagination. If you happen to have a stain-glass paint set (individual jars of color can be purchased) the colors can easily be applied to glass cut to the size of your desired window. If you prefer, heavy acetate is also serviceable. A good substitute for the stain paint is to use permanent color felt marking pens, or permanent colored ink. Whichever you use, section each color with a black line to simulate leading. This type of coloring is effective if you have a see-through window in the wall of your room. If your furnishings are in a bookcase or box room, you can again place a greeting card landscape scene in back of the stained glass for special effect.

Your curtains and drapery, which have been mounted on rods of some kind, can also be glued to the top of the window frame. However, if you're a fastidious housekeeper and expect to wash your curtains, we'll make them detachable. Take two small eye screws—you will have to use your judgment as to size, depending upon size of rods. Using your clippers, cut out a small area of circle on top. Screw the rest into wall and slip ends of rods into the open ends of eyes.

Although I offer different suggestions for rods, the one that I prefer for practicality, size and sturdiness is a cut wire hanger. Much can be done with this: if you choose to arch a curtain forward or back for a bay window effect, the metal can be bent.

For best appearance, curtain and drapery should be contained in place. It has been said that Mrs. James Ward Thorne, renowned for her fabulous miniature rooms, actually glued some of her folded curtains to the wall itself. Of course, that was before hairsprays were available. Plan your window treatment and lay it out on a

Fig. 12-2 Availability of a variety of laces can be helpful for numerous projects in this book. Large panels make exquisite curtains and other narrow designs become trim and edgings.

large piece of corrugated cardboard. It is easy to push pins into this. Construct your folds, swags and jabots by holding each piece in place with straight pins. When the arrangement pleases you, spray the entire set up with hairspray lacquer. Repeat, if it is necessary. When dry, the stiffened structure can be spot glued to your window.

Helpful Hints

- ✔Cut shape for valance out of sturdy cardboard. Allow extra area on sides for turnback to wall.
- ✔Consider using felt for covering a valance and, if valance has scalloped edges, felt is especially accommodating. It cuts clean and lays nice and flat.

Fig. 12-1 Windows can be big, short, stained or tall, wide, narrow, curved or small and, necessarily, they do vary in treatment. The sash curtain is panel lace and embroidery trim. The cafe set is red and white plaid with tiny lace edging, sewed to jump-link curtain rings. The elegant white lace-trimmed curtain is a hankie with white tassels added on each side. The small window, allowing the outside to invade the room, has a fabric cornice and a shirred lace half-curtain. The bottom stained-glass window needs an extra touch of "something" and a ruffled edging of lace just does the trick. Elegance and formality are evidenced by lace panel curtains plus drapery, swag, jabots and a cornice of gold-painted wood and trim; tiebacks are cut curtain rings. The Austrian curtain easily started with a lemon-yellow shirred material edged with ball trim; the top swag, held in place by cut filigree, is white cotton damask. The diamond-shaped window panes, carefully "stained glass" colored, started as a supermarket food container and are painted brown. A wooden strip is added at bottom for molding and bleakness avoided with the addition of an edging of thin embroidery trim. Tiebacks are filigree, ear clips, package twine, tassels, chains, trim, beads; rods are dress hanger wire and shaped dowel stick with filigree bead caps and beads attached to ends.

✔Pad a valance with thin cotton padding before covering with choice of material.

✔For a straight valance, use embroidery tape in an appropriate design and color. It comes in a variety of widths, designs and colors.

✔If valance and drapery are of solid color, glue on one or two miniature embroidered "sew-ons."

✔For thin curtain rods, use cut wire from dress hangers, an applicator stick or a round toothpick for very tiny windows. Wire hanger makes a good rod for shower curtain in bathroom.

✔For thicker rods use pencils and plastic straws which can be painted with acrylic. Dowel sticks can be painted or stained.

✔Use jewelry jump links for rings on rods. The size is determined by size of rod. Sew links to top of finished curtain or drapery, whether pleated or scalloped.

✔Place glued beads or a decorative piece at both ends of rod. This helps keep curtain intact.

✔Tie-backs for curtains and drapes can be self-material, thin embroidery tape, ribbon (flat or bows), tasseled cords, gold and silver tie cord, rickrack, string beading, tiny chains, clip-on earrings, bent filigree, bracelet links, etc.

✔Upholstery tacks, although large, can hold the tie-backs securely in place; two inexpensive tie tacks are perfect, too.

✔If all else fails, hammer two small nails right through everything and glue a small attractive bead on head of each nail.

✔Plan material to be twice or thrice the width of the area to be covered. Remember to allow extra material all around so there is a sufficient amount for hemming on sides and bottom, and for casing and/or heading at top. Excess material can always be cut away and it's easier to handle if there is a generous amount to work with.

Fig. 12-3   Patterns for stained-glass window design, swag and jabot.

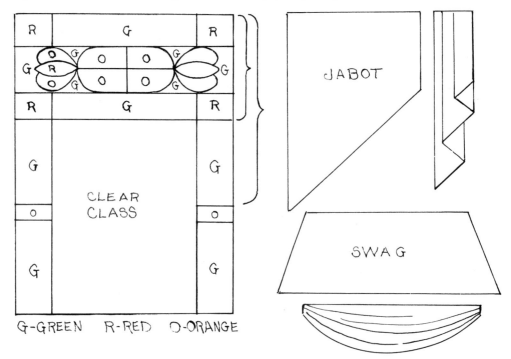

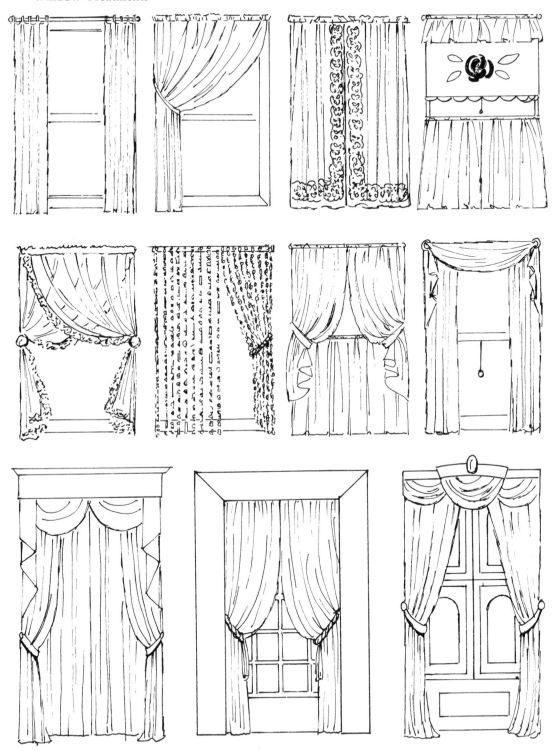

Fig. 12-4   From informal to formal, different window treatments are offered.

Fig. 12-5 Cornices can be used as simple wooden pieces, painted or upholstered. Fringes, decorations and other attractive doodads make them more elaborate. Swags, jabots and combinations of both are other ways of finishing off the top of a window.

✔A unique, small stained-glass window uses a color transparency slide, 2¼ × 2¼ preferred. Take a picture of an actual stained-glass window or color a picture in a children's coloring book and photograph that. When processed, cut out the area needed and mount within molding, etc.

✔Make a small stained-glass arrangement and suspend it from chains in front of a window. This is the modern approach.

✔Construct venetian blinds with thinly cut balsa wood 1/32″ thick or use index card.

✔Open lacework with a large pattern can be gesso painted, sprayed black, stiffened with hairspray and used for ironwork outside of window.

✔Last but not least, consult home and decorating magazines for ideas and designs for curtains and drapery. Countless photographs will provide numerous suggestions and will keep you happily occupied with needle and thread by the "minute."

How to Make Stained-Glass Windows and Window Accessories

Figure 12-3 provides pattern parts for the stained-glass window shown in Figure 12-1, as well as patterns for a swag and jabot to get you started. Figures 12-4 and 12-5 provide graphic suggestions for all manner of window treatments, from the elaborately formal eighteenth-century drawing room style to the current vogue in lightly dressed windows that let the sun shine in.

STAINED-GLASS WINDOW

1. Using 1/8″ balsa, cut strips to sufficient lengths to border glass window as a frame; or use commercial window frame molding. Following the pattern, outline design in black acrylic paint.

2. Fill in areas with color, using special glass stain paint, available at crafts stores. Colored transparent inks can also be used, or permanent marking pens, which give a limited color selection.

Note: If used in a shadowbox, a greeting card landscape scene can be placed on the back to give an outside view.

❈13❈

Table Linens, Decorator Pillows and Bedding

Homespun flax and sheared wools, spun into woolen yarn, sparked the first textile products. Later, cotton, cotton-wool and cotton-linen blends became accessible for textile use. Handwoven sheets, bedcovers, blankets and coverlets were part of the pioneer way of life. Quilts were exquisitely all-white creations or appliqued and pieced. Using unbleached cotton, coverlets were boldly stenciled in bright colors of green, yellow and orange. Cotton tablecloths were also stenciled using other colors. Imported textiles from France and England were elaborate taffetas, silks, moirés, damasks and others. Bed hangings were necessary and popular, ranging from simple to elaborate material and enhanced by intricate needlework.

The next time you complain about an uncomfortable mattress, consider that things could be worse. There were actually *mattresses* filled with straw, oak leaves and beech tree leaves, twig shavings from the witch hazel bark, palm leaf fillings and Spanish moss. And of course, there were feather-filled mattresses, which must have frustrated the allergic individual. Today there are spring mattresses, latex foam rubber and water beds.

Practically speaking, the easiest way to create a mattress for your miniature bed is to cut a piece of ½″ to ¾″-thick foam rubber to the size that is needed. Another alternative is to purchase a soft household sponge. Either can be covered with cotton ticking or a fancier material, cut to fit and stitched together by machine or by hand.

Although *sheets* and *pillowcases* are

Fig. 13-1 At the top is a crocheted spread made from ready-made crochet trim, sewed together. A bolster and two sachet pillows are highlighted near a handmade crochet spread. On the left are a red hand-knitted afghan, a small quilt, and two bed pillows with cases made from handkerchiefs. The petite print cotton spread, trimmed with baby rickrack, is surrounded top and bottom with an assortment of decorator pillows made from cotton checks and prints, felt with fruit designs and appliqued lace, novelty and woven. Lastly, a nylon acetate blanket is bordered with satin ribbon. The red afghan was knitted by Helen Suresky and the crocheted fringe spread was made by Mleta Mullenix.

usually covered with a spread, it's nevertheless with special pride that you grandly pull back the top cover to show off the bed's lingerie.

With printed linens in vogue, you might even consider a very, very tiny percale print for your sheets and pillowcases. But for the more traditional or period type home, there's nothing that makes a better sheet or pillowcase than a sheer white hankie. The already finished edging which comes in a variety of ways provides a beautiful effect.

Bed pillows are simply made by cutting rectangles of material. Sew three sides together, turn inside out. Stuff pillow with shredded foam or cotton and hand stitch the fourth side closed.

Decorator pillows are fun pieces to make (Fig. 13-2). There is such a variety of ways to add a personal touch to this mini product that, once you start, it's going to be very difficult to stop. Pillows come in an assortment of shapes and you can decide whether you prefer round, square, oblong or triangular (see color Fig. 17). There are also bolsters and bigger sizes for floor sitters. Just about

any material can be used for this effort, except that heavy fabrics will be bulky to handle. If your pillow doesn't have a previously planned or executed design and you wish to add something, you can decorate by gluing on appliques, lace cutouts and other trim. This can be experimental. Or just leave the pillow unadorned.

Blankets, too, should give a realistic effect without being seemingly heavy. Cotton flannel and nylon acetate are excellent for this purpose: both cut nicely, leaving clean edges which require no hemming. Use either solid colors or small prints. Remember to stitch a tiny satin ribbon ½″ wide on top and bottom, folded over the edge for a finished effect. Very early blankets were woven and some fine, thin woven materials are often available at fabric counters or even in discarded clothing.

The bed's *top covering* again will depend upon your whim and the period of your furnishings.

Perhaps the most appealing bed accessory is the dust ruffle, topped with either a matching cover or a contrasting print, color or fabric. If you use a printed dust

Fig. 13-2   An assortment of pillows shows what can be done in the making of this small article. Use felt, embroidered ribbon trim, appliques, laces, sachets, ribbons, tassels, crochet work or anything delightful enough to enhance a pillow.

ruffle, you might even consider making a matching quilt, selecting additional colors to harmonize with your print.

A quilt can be produced by joining together small 1″ squares of contrasting patterns of material. Make the second side with a solid color, creating a reversible effect. Using a very thin layer of cotton batting between the two materials, stitch the layered pieces together following the block stitching or some other design of your choice. Instead of stitching, you can acquire a softer effect by catching the quilt together through to the other side with a series of little tie knots, regularly repeated throughout the pattern. French knots are another excellent way to secure your quilt.

Free-falling *coverlets* seem to be the most popular of all spreads today, but remember, if fabrics are too heavy they will not fall gracefully on the sides of the bed, so select a sheer, lightweight fabric for best results. But, then, remember that you can spray the folds into position. Sheer polyesters are especially good and, again, make use of the many-faceted hankie. If you prefer to make a fitted or boxed bedspread, this will allow for a slightly heavier fabric.

Appliqued patterns of flowers, leaves, trees, animals or whatever also give a distinctive note. The most authentic looking and notable of all covers are those that employ needlework. This is probably due to the appreciable amount of time necessary for completion of one of these darlings.

A crocheted spread using regular crochet string is excellent, but don't overlook the colored strings that are being used in string art today. The colorful fingering yarns, which are slightly heavier in weight will produce beautiful *afghans*. Tiny granny squares fitted together will also make an afghan.

No doubt, the most charming of all needlework is the spread that is decorated

Fig. 13-3 Two fabric designs with a conveniently "built-in" square pattern simplify the procedure for a quilt. Add cotton batting and contrasting material for back, stitch together in the conventional squared method, and you "have it made."

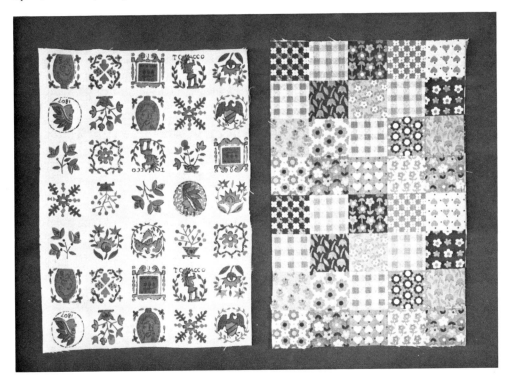

with crewel embroidery. A design can be boldly done or intricately and minutely executed (depending upon your patience) with one strand of embroidery yarn or cotton thread. If your room boasts a theme, embroider a matching subject and, while you're at it, remember to initial your work and add the year. Several years later you'll be glad you did and so will the lucky heirs who inherit your heirloom.

Does one of your little beds cry out for a lacy-looking bedspread? If you crochet, then you can personally whip up a little creation of your own. If you don't crochet but have a friend who does, you are fortunate. However, if you have neither benefit, you can still acquire a crocheted spread and canopy, too, with the purchase of two yards of crochet trim, needle and thread and a bit of "flim-flam." Merely join together panels of lace that resemble

Fig. 13-4 Precious little crocheted doilies (no bigger than a pin) were made by Mleta Mullenix. They can be transformed into darling pillows, or several of the same design, stitched together, would complete a most beautiful bedspread or afghan.

Fig. 13-5 It looks as though hours of work were spent making the crocheted bedspread and canopy, but with a little flim-flam, a selection of crochet trim and needle and thread, you can produce an exquisite creation guaranteed to fool most anyone.

crochet work (Figs. 13-5 and 13-6). The sewn together areas won't even show and you will be pleased and proud of the finished, impressive piece of work.

Table linens can be carried out in a variety of ways, too; essentially, only the very finest, lightweight material is recommended for full coverage. Again make use of the lace-edged hankie for square cloths or add your own choice of tiny lace to your material. Prints, stripes and colors can offer lots of possibilities and match up those cloths with teensy napkins, too.

If you intend to embroider a cloth, be careful where you add the stitching. Because embroidery will prevent anything resting on the tabletop from sitting flat, confine the trim to edging—more or less. You might consider a chain stitch, a simple floral or even a minute initial in the corner of your cloth or on the napkins.

Miniature place mats can offer additional choice and, since they do lie flat, a firmer, woven material can also be used in addition to the dainty fabrics. A woven fabric enables you to fringe the edges by pulling out some of the threads along two or four sides of the mat. But mats can be most anything in paper, fabric or plastic.

Fig. 13-6 A few examples of lace crochet edging are shown. These would make up into a completed spread by sewing bands of same edging together.

A very popular and decorative table covering is the long-skirted cloth used in living rooms, bedrooms or other rooms of choice. This can be neatly carried out by covering an empty thread spool—the size should be determined by your need. Ordinarily, the larger spool is favored for necessary height, but if you want a smaller diameter for a table, glue a couple of small spools together.

Your material will be cut out as a full circle and should hang just a "mite" above floor. If your material is very sheer, presenting a see-through problem, then cut another lightweight solid material to same size and gently spot tack two pieces along inner edges with craft glue. Take advantage of the wonderful varieties of trim that are available.

Usually, a table skirt tends to expand out at the sides and needs to be self-contained so that it hangs nicely. You can manage this by gluing a swath of cotton around center of spool (Fig. 13-8). Apply glue to top of spool and place about six or seven small dabs of craft glue around center areas of cotton. Center the circle of material on spool and catch the skirt at these points of sticky contact.

Helpful Hints

✔ If you have a down-filled pillow, snitch a few feathers for a feather-bed mattress.

✔ For a modern boxspread, stitch wide embroidery trim together in panels and

Fig. 13-7 Lace and velvet trim become a table runner and two strips of lace edging are joined together to be used as a bureau scarf. An odd assortment of mats and doilies are produced from woven materials, ribbon, lace and daisy trims. At *top left*, red and white plaid tablecloth is enhanced with extra embroidery and the bottom red check has a baby fringe edging. The sheer white

Fig. 13-8 There's more than one way to secure a long skirt. The tall table has three paper cups stacked together and a round of cardboard glued to top. Around the cups is a generous amount of cotton, glued to side. On top is double-stick masking tape (placed back to back). The outer sticky side will catch the skirt when it's pressed against the tape. The short table is much simpler, using a large spool and dabs of craft glue placed regularly around sides to hold the skirt in place.

extend same trim around three sides of bed.

✔ Use ruffled lace for a dust ruffle, adding a colored material underneath.

✔ An acrylic pile spread looks plush and modern.

✔ Use a lace-bordered batiste handkerchief for a tablecloth. Adjustment to size is usually necessary. Cut one or two sides shorter and restitch lace to new edges.

✔ A tablecloth will look better if the corners are held firm and sprayed with hairspray.

✔ Your all-lace tablecloth should be a very fine, small design. Chapel head coverings are sometimes suitable for round tables.

✔ Old-fashioned doilies will sometimes be very appropriate for cloths.

✔ Napkins can be cut from material (apply glue to edges) or paper napkins for the picnic crowd. Roll and place within napkin rings or fold several and insert in napkin holders (see Ch. 16).

✔ For place mats, use embroidery tape that can be cut apart, showing individual designs for each mat.

✔ For webbed mat, use red and white striped plastic bag ties. As you crisscross the strips, keep stripes connected and a design will result. Glue patterned pieces to card and cut out the mat. Weave ribbon strips or cut paper strips for other webbed effects.

✔ For small pillow embroidery, use corner designs on handkerchiefs. Cut out enough of the material around design, plus extra for work and stitching area.

✔ Initials on handkerchiefs offer other embroidery possibilities.

✔ Purchase tiny appliques from fabric department and glue onto a finished pillow.

✔ Small embroidered sachets (imported from Switzerland and available at cosmetic counters) are sweetly delicate and make large pillows.

✔ Make a bolster by rolling art foam until you have the desired thickness—about ¾″. Predetermine width ahead or cut

lace-edged cloth is a hankie and the elegant lace cloth is a cutting of sheer lace with an edging added. The larger skirted table is dark green velvet topped with an old fashioned lace doily and the skirted side table is a pretty floral print edged with lace. Napkins are small cut squares of material and lace.

through thickness. Glue with rubber cement. Cover ends of bolster first with material, bringing it up over edges. Then cover rolled area.

✔ Coordinate your bathroom with a matching set for rug, seat cover and trash can.

✔ Make tiny ½″ square or round potholders. Attach a small jump link or thread at corner for holder.

How to Make Decorator Pillows

An assortment of tiny pillows is shown in Figure 13-9, along with instructions for mitering corners and making tassels.

WEBBED PILLOW

1. Cut twelve strips of ribbon or trim (six each of two colors) to make the webbed pillow shown in (A).

Fig. 13-9 An assortment of decorator pillows, easily made. To miter a corner with ribbon or trim, place two pieces with right sides together. Sew and cut at 45° angle, then straighten out. To make a tassel, use a curved paper clip to aid in pulling ends through opening.

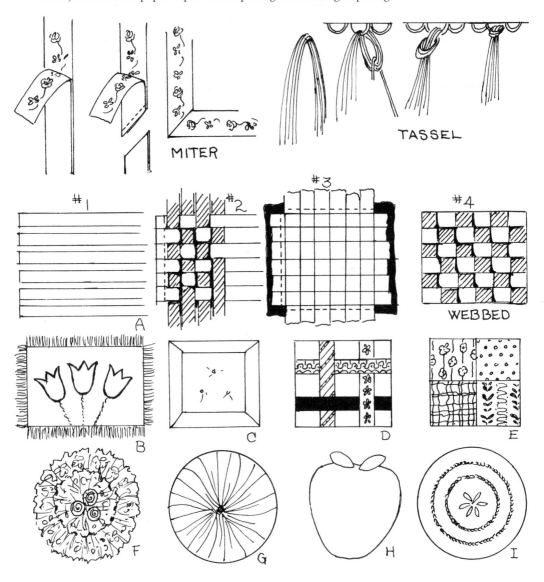

2. Sew together one set of six strips across one end, as shown by dotted line in (#2). Weave the second set of six strips across the first set, gluing in spots to hold in position.

3. Stitch or hand sew three sides of the webbing to a felt backing (#3). Trim away excess. Turn and stuff with cotton.

4. Trim fourth side. Turn in seams and hand sew last side closed.

TULIP PILLOW

To make the floral pillow shown in (B), simply cut the tulips out of three colors of felt and glue onto white pillow. The stems are stitched on with crewel yarn.

TAILORED PILLOW

Make a pillow from two squares of felt (C). After stuffing, catch through with French knots.

CRISS-CROSS PILLOW

Work four different ribbons or bits of trim onto top of a completed pillow in a criss-cross design (D).

PATCHWORK PILLOW

Use four squares of fabric in different designs to make a patchwork (E).

LACE PILLOW

Make a small round pillow. Glue two or three rows of straight or ruffled lace around and around as shown in (F). Glue an applique into the center.

GATHERED SPIRAL

Two strips of material are sewn together and joined at ends. Each edging is gathered together tightly to become the center of the pillow (G). Stuff, then sew opening closed.

APPLE PILLOW

The procedure for making any "fruit" pillow is simple. Cut the shape (H) and backing out of the appropriate color felt. Stitch three quarters of the way around your fruit shape, turn and stuff the pillow with cotton. Then finish off the opening edges. For the apple, add leaves of green felt after closure.

EMBROIDERED PILLOW

Embroider chain-stitch circles on pillow front. Use a different color for each circle and finish with a lazy daisy center stitch (I).

14

Floor Coverings

Give a little thought to your floors and what you want to do about them. Do you want to cover them completely or just add charming accents here and there? You may wish to adhere to the styling of the room or you may boldly blend period with modern. At any rate you do have a good opportunity to create mood and to exercise choice in this area, depending upon your period of furnishing.

Prior to the manufacturing of rugs, which gained momentum about 1850, floor coverings were executed in a variety of ways by hand. Needlework rugs were designed and created by use of a stitch that resembled chain stitch. They were either small in size or several squares were joined to complete a large carpet. Turkey work rugs appeared to have a thick pile achieved by strands of wool stitched through, then puffed and clipped on the surface. These were imitations of eastern knotted carpets. Applique rugs from brightly colored materials made interesting patterns which were adhered to cloth

foundations with the buttonhole stitch. There were even rugs worked with cross stitching on canvas.

Eventually needlework rugs were replaced by hooked rugs, which were completed more quickly. Oriental and Persian carpets were imported from Asia by well-to-do colonists. About 1760 there were English factory-made Wiltons and Axministers, as well as tapestry and needlework rugs. But for the most part, home-woven rugs covered the floor, which in some instances did go bare. If bare, however, an attempt was oftentimes made to avoid austerity by using stencil designs.

Some contemporary floors remain bare by choice, exposing beautiful hardwood, tile, marble, slate, linoleum or brick.

A wooden floor, if not varnished, can be painted a solid color, spattered with paint, or even have painted-on designs through stenciling or direct brush painting.

When it comes to coverings, floors dictate whatever is fashionable at the time. A

Fig. 14-1 A section of Belgian tapestry is carefully cut out; ends are fringed and sides are glued under, unveiling a beautiful little rug with no fuss or bother. Other sections can be cut to smaller or larger sizes; long narrow areas can be cut for hall runners. Wall tapestries can also be provided and a carpetbag can even be sewn together. You can get much "mileage" out of a small piece of tapestry.

138

Fig. 14-2 Rugs for miniature rooms make their appearance in unexpected ways, as evidenced by this selection. The large floral, hooked in appearance, is cut from a tapestry shoebag. Both the wool three-color pastel braided rug and dark green crochet rug are handmade. The small Oriental was a cigarette giveaway. The round "hooked" rug was purchased as a coaster. The small mat is baby rickrack that's been braided. Across the bottom, the "lollipop" flower rug is made with strands of crewel yarn glued to a backing to form the pattern (see Fig. 14-4). The small throw rug is a cut piece of ribbon trim with edges fringed. The plush Oriental is cut from tapestry material (see Fig. 14-1) and the last throw rug is embroidery trim with baby fringe added to each end. The braided and crocheted rugs were made by Kathryn Krogh.

floor may be completely carpeted, semi-covered with a room-size rug or dotted with accent rugs.

Fashions and color schemes come and go but your choice of miniature floor coverings can demonstrate your love for simplicity or intricate detail as evidenced by your selection or even hard work. Some very ambitious miniaturists are creating carpets of needlepoint. This can be time consuming, but the long involvement is rewarded with a truly beautiful finished piece of art—and I do mean *art*.

A mini-hooker is also available, en-abling you to complete your own little hooked rug creation.

Recall the giveaways that came with cigarette and cigar packages many years back? These were small pieces of material that resembled tiny Oriental rugs and they look perfectly at home in a dollhouse. I must confess that at an antique show, this was the very first purchase that started my journey into miniaturing. They are usually found in antique shops or at shows; luck or perseverance will eventually produce some for your use. That starts us off on helpful hints, so here goes.

Helpful Hints

- Beware! If rugs are too thick it makes everything look awkward in scale, so unless commercial carpeting is very thin, avoid the temptation to use actual scraps of carpeting.
- Keep a watchful eye out for rectangular Oriental antique tapestries that were used on tables. These come in various sizes and designs.
- An old tote shoebag that has a tapestry design can be cut into a large oval rug. Add fringe.
- Imported Belgian tapestries, sold in fabric departments, are lush with beautiful rich designs and velvet texture.
- Other tapestries, resembling hooked rugs, are available in fabric departments.
- Upholstery material of flat, woven, tweedy appearance is good for casual rugs.
- Woven place mats make good rugs.
- Nonshiny place mats can become rugs; shiny ones substitute for shiny linoleum floors.
- Use thin washcloths or guest towels, with or without fringe. Velours are especially soft looking.
- Bright acrylic pile material produces a fabulous plush effect. Velvet is good, too.
- Real linoleum can be cut to room size.
- Contact paper that resembles wood can be laid on a cardboard backing. Add thin dark-brown lines to simulate planks or indicate pegging with small circles.
- Thin vinyl tile can be cut down to size and pattern (imagine a miniature checkerboard floor—beautiful!). If you decide to do this, glue down the design on a thin piece of cardboard cut to size of room and then place entire floor into position in house.
- Braid a rug: use very thin strips of rag, lightweight acrylic, wool yarn, thin shoestrings or nylon hosiery. Cut strips 1/4" wide or less, depending upon thickness of material.
- Rugs can be knitted and crocheted and are most charming in circles and ovals. Use solid color or multicolored yarn.

Fig. 14-3 The softness of a polar bear rug especially delights the youngsters and is easy to make with white acrylic pile (see Fig. 14-4). (*Jack Ruthberg, photograph*)

- Felt material can be cut and shaped. Embroidery can be added to edge. Fringe can be applied to edge. Decorative tape can be purchased and glued to edging. Miter corners of tape for best effect.
- Cut a large felt rug in shape of circle, oval and octagonal, as well as rectangle. Use plain or glue cutout designs to top.
- Glue crewel yarn to a backing. Create a design and cover entire area.
- Make a floor of cork and create your own overall pattern.
- Take acrylic material with a plaid appearance and pull stitches away from material around four edges. Fold gauze backing back and glue. The stitches on two ends of rug can be pulled to resemble fringe.
- Wooden floors can be made from mail-order wooden planks.
- Popsicle sticks with the ends cut straight can be laid end to end, staggering them.
- Stairways and halls can be carpeted with wide velvet ribbon, wide embroidery trim, grosgrain ribbon.

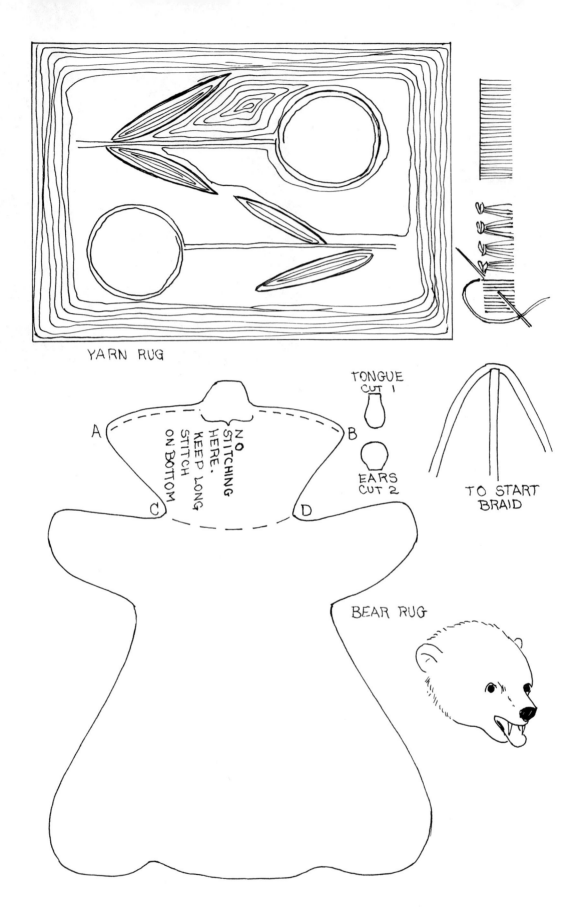

YARN RUG

A

NO
STITCHING
HERE.
KEEP LONG
STITCH
ON BOTTOM

B

C

D

TONGUE
CUT 1

EARS
CUT 2

TO START
BRAID

BEAR RUG

✔Baby fringe, which is very fine, is useful for finishing off edges of rugs.

✔Select dried-out twigs (1″ diameter). Cut or slice several ¹/₁₆″ thick; these become a natural wooden patio floor or can be used as a pathway in a garden. How about a Japanese garden?

✔Paint an Oriental design on velvet material.

How to Make Area Rugs

Pattern parts and techniques are illustrated in Figure 14-4 for making the three types of rugs detailed in this section.

YARN RUG

This rug (3″ × 4″ plus fringe), is made by gluing strands of colored crewel yarn onto a neutral woven background. Draw pattern onto background. Glue on yarn for stems and leaves (dark green). Glue yarn for outer edges of flower (two rows of dark red). Glue "around" inside, rest of flower (rose red). Glue background (light gray-green).

Start background along four outer edges, continuing around until blocked by the design. Then begin to fill in center areas. Add light gray-green fringe edging to ends of rug (see Fig. 14-4).

BRAIDED RUG

If using a fabric, the material should be cut on the bias in ⅛″ wide strips. Hosiery which is thin and flexible can be cut wider.

1. Start three strips each of different color at one point (see Fig. 14-4) and tightly anchor the strands to a firm object.

2. Begin braiding and keep the work even. When you've finished a certain amount, flatten it down on a table, coil the braid and slipstitch into an oval or a round. Complete more braiding, if necessary.

3. Finish off ends by poking them through outer round. Steam press the finished rug.

BEAR RUG

1. Trace the pattern onto back of white acrylic pile material. Short pile is best, but higher pile can be sheared shorter, if necessary.

2. Cut material ¼″ larger than indicated in pattern. Now, cut away pattern only from *underside* (knit side)—*not* through entire surface—so that acrylic pile doesn't look chopped square. Practice on a small piece first.

3. Take small running stitches from (A) to (B), except in center area. Pull thread tightly together, rounding the head and producing a snout. Tie off.

4. With cuticle scissors, clip pile closer to head around nose and eye areas. Observing bear head drawing, sew black seed bead eyes into place and sew on a black nose by overlapping black embroidery thread. Glue two white ears into place and glue a red or pink felt tongue through opening below nose.

5. Slightly gather head from (C) to (D) with *long* running stitches. To stuff, glue some cotton into head cavity and sew a lining on bottom of head to keep cotton intact—or you may wish to line entire rug.

6. Lastly, glue two white painted tips of toothpicks into upper opening for eye teeth.

Fig. 14-4   Yarn rug, braided rug and bear rug.

15

Wall Coverings

Covering a wall is like gift wrapping a package in reverse. The contents are exposed, but the background in its subtle way holds everything together.

Walls do vary from the austere stone-walled domicile to the richly paneled, flock-papered domain. Early interior walls consisted of a rough type of plaster, later giving way to a finer grade. Plaster walls were whitewashed and, if there was simple paneling, this was usually stained or painted gray-blue. Along with the improvement in plaster, about 1700, paint colors and hues in greater variety provided a welcome change and French and English wallpapers appeared on the scene. Wood paneling with carved ornamentation added more elegance to the finer homes and this new late-seventeenth-century elegance was further enhanced by the use of flocked wall covering.

Stenciling, a substitute for expensive paper, was often applied to plaster and wooden walls in the late eighteenth century.

Dado walls were in prominent use during early times and were either stained or painted.

Chinese painted paper topped a dado of mahogany or other wood and later the Oriental papers were replaced by block-printed wallpapers.

Stucco ornamentation on both walls and ceilings was an elaborate feature which enhanced the lavish homes of the nineteenth century. But mansions of special wealth and design boasted painted designs, murals and rococo trim far beyond the dreams of the average citizen.

The twentieth century saw a prevalence of wallpaper and paneling as popular choices but many rooms also boast a simpler background as beautiful colors hold forth. Noticeable in contemporary homes is the innovative way of sometimes bringing the "outside, inside" and entire wall areas of a room may be distinguished with brick, stone or shingles.

As a miniaturist you will no doubt prefer to use a design. There's something so delicious about a delicate wallpaper that serves as background for furniture and a few interesting accents. There are adorable mini wallpapers available from the dealers, but if you're curious about additional sources, then let me add some special suggestions.

Keep an eye open for gift wrapping paper that has any miniature patterns and

Fig. 15-1 A paneled wall can start out similar to another and end up quite different in concept. Made with Contact paper and strips of balsa wood, the first wall is decorated with an eagle console table, matted black and white Williamsburg notepaper and earring sconces. The two porcelain vases were a gift from a friend and the carpeting is an upholstery remnant.

always purchase good quality paper. Some of the papers may feature a flocked surface. Others have elegant gold imprints.

Regular wallpapers with small patterns and solids are still another source and there are textures and more textures. You might be able to acquire an outdated sample book from a store . . . *if* you're lucky!

If you are an individual and dare to resist the conventional use of paper, you can substitute fabric for a background. Some of the teeny tiny patterns available in cotton materials are mouth-watering and colorful (Fig. 15-4). An additional advantage is being able to also use the same fabric for bedspreads, drapery, chair covers, long-skirted table covers or pillows. No one can devise better coordination than that.

MURALS

Rembrandt or not, if you feel dexterous with a paintbrush, it can be a challenge to paint your own mural. There are many sources of artwork to use for copy material or you may bravely create your own design. Modern rooms would even welcome a smart photograph as a mural, but remember to reproduce with a flat, not glossy, finish (see color Figs. 8 and 14).

If you don't have artistic talent but crave a mural background, there is a solu-

Fig. 15-2 The second panel wall is formal, with Victorian overtones. A semicircular sofa sits beneath a lovely print (from Handicraft store). Two bold sconces are made from metal nameplates, craft mirrors, bead caps and filigree. The air fern rests in planters which were once part of a necklace and the carpet is an upholstery remnant.

tion. Some of the pictorial motifs on regular wallpaper can be cut apart and they lend themselves beautifully to such a background. Usually these printed patterns are accompanied by a paper which is simple in color and can serve as the wall covering for the rest of the room. It's all coordinated, well planned and accessible at your local wallpaper shop—so keep alert for their sale days and share papers with other miniaturists.

Another fine source for a mural effect is a greeting card. Although smaller in size, cards provide an excellent source of inspiration. Flat painted landscapes, pictorial or modern designs can all be used. Well-designed and versatile, the larger cards can enhance any decor. Border the card with balsa wood trim so the effect looks finished, not incidental.

If the wall mural is not covering the en-

tire wall but is going to share it with a dado, this can be even more interesting. Wood veneers, splendid in variety and assortment, can be ordered from a dealer. A veneer, plus a molding across top, makes a handsome finish to your room.

Rooms with wainscoting or with paneling deserve consideration, but the best advice is to notice the interior wall finish in historical homes and make use of pictorial information.

Helpful Hints

✔Contact paper that resembles wood can produce an inexpensive wood paneled effect. Add some thin vertical lines to resemble paneling.

✔Cut strips of $1/32''$ balsa wood in $1/2''$ widths. Sand edges on one side rounded

Fig. 15-3 Another panel wall, boldly modern with a strong black and white plush sofa, is accented with a sophisticated line painting of a cat. The torcheres are made of larger metal nameplates and roll-on balls are supported by protective tops from disposable syringes, glued to plate with filigree backing. The coffee table is marble-stained glass, placed on top of a plastic stand purchased at a gem and mineral show. Both pieces of handmade sculpture rest on simple stained blocks of balsa wood. The carpet is worn acrylic, which looks like shag.

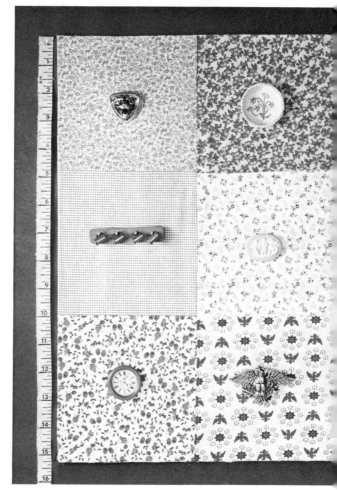

Fig. 15-4 The tape measure shows the petite size of the prints in this collection of fabric, all usable for curtains, drapery, bedspreads, quilts, pillows, table linens and, yes, even as wall covering.

Fig. 15-5 How exciting a wall can become with the rendering of a wallpaper mural! This is just a small cutout portion of a larger design; combined with a bottom wallpaper selection, added chair rail and baseboard, it's dramatic. Completing the arrangement is a purchased metal chair, a hand-painted chest of birch and walnut and tiny dried grasses, poking out of a "button-bottle cap" planter.

148

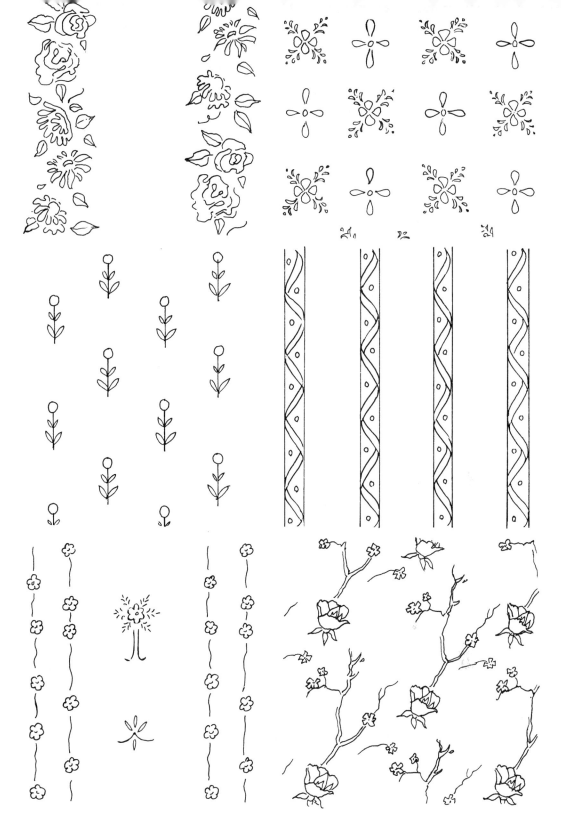

Fig. 15-6 Six designs are offered for wallpapers. Using a repeat pattern, anyone can be transferred to white drawing paper or a pastel color paper. The design can be outlined in black and filled in with color or the outlining can be eliminated. Stay with two or three colors for simplicity.

149

Fig. 15-7 Designs for wall paneling can be altered for variations, according to space and height and width of room.

and stain wood color of your choice. Glue these into position on wall for paneling.

✔Purchase miniature picture frame molding and construct square panel areas on walls. Mount flocked paper within framed panel areas or decoupage small pictures of scenic or floral patterns. Rest of wall is wood paneled.

✔Select a stencil pattern from one of the designs in Figure 3-5 and, by repeating the design, create a stenciled wall.

✔A windowless room becomes scenic by covering an entire wall with a photographic scene, either printed on paper or fabric. An outdoor scene of a forest seems to push back the wall, enlarging the appearance of the room.

✔A truly large photomural for your wall in life size costs a pretty penny, but in miniature you can highlight one of these on the wall of your choice. It can be one of your favorite photo scenes or even a big blowup of a family group portrait.

✔Copy a mural design from a decorating magazine and paint, enjoy and paint.

✔*Trompe d'oeil* (fool the eye) wallpapers can be achieved by pasting up your own designs.

✔Embossed gold paper medallions and other embossed strips can be glued to walls and ceilings. Entire areas are painted with gesso or flat latex. This will all blend together, creating a stucco effect.

Extra Extras

All the extra accessories that go into personalizing a little house or room would take much more space than this one last chapter on extras could ever divulge. They are the unaccountable bonuses that present themselves at every phase of living. The necessity of utensils, the pursuit of luxuries and the pleasure of personal triumphs are depicted in innumerable ways.

Most of these miniature extras are purchasable and are made of certain compositions that require specialized skill. Primitive pieces made of iron, copper, tin and wood are duplicated by artisans and manufacturers of today and many are perfect little replicas of items of years gone by. Other minis are inexpensively duplicated through the use of lead or plastic and these can be painted to beautifully resemble the real article.

But to craft the extra extras requires an astute eye and a steady hand because, often-times, these are the smallest of the small in miniature.

A few articles in different classifications have been created and described. These merely skim the surface, but perhaps they will inspire you to further create, devise, concoct, conceive, contrive or just plain make other little extras that may tickle your fancy.

Helpful Hints

✔Paint tiny little plastic animals completely black for "iron" door stops.
✔Soap is made from soap. When your own bar is down to a thin sliver, *then* cut your little bars. It's soft and easy to slice and shape, and it will harden again. Carve several small pieces and set inside a clear container. Small pills also look like soap.
✔Nail heads come in a variety of designs and colors—good for decorating bookends, letter holders, napkin holders or other items.
✔For large spools of thread, use ¼″ bone-shaped beads and wind thread around center.
✔Make a 1″ high megaphone for the "rah-rah" set; add a pom-pom, made with tissue paper.
✔Watch for a visiting glass blower. They usually have tiny animals and other small goodies.
✔The large acrylic boxed bottle cover within the Brut packaging is the beginning for an impressive, huge fish tank.
✔Add a teensy handle to a half-cut large silver sequin for a table crumber.
✔Visit the party favor departments of your stores. New items are always

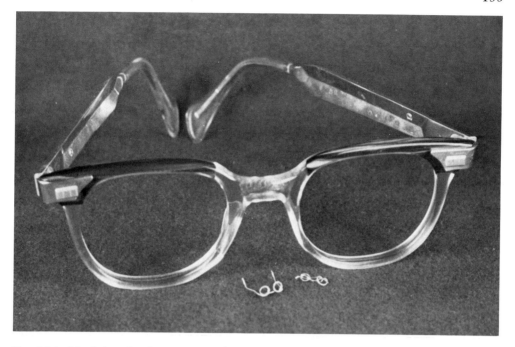

Fig. 16-1 Nestled under the nosepiece of eyeglasses are miniature spectacles, necessary for the near-sighted dollhouse doll.

being introduced and many are adaptable for mini use.

✔For a clear paperweight (¼″ or less), drop some quick-setting epoxy from tip of toothpick onto a flower, colored seed bead or colored rhinestone, forming a small round mound of glue.

✔Clear plastic pill capsules of assorted sizes become domes, vases, hurricane lamps, flashlight frontal pieces, pack-

Fig. 16-2 The most delicate sword is possible, starting with the hand of a clock. Join the eggers, too! You can either shape your own and decorate them or purchase beautiful oval beads from India. (*Jack Ruthberg, photograph*)

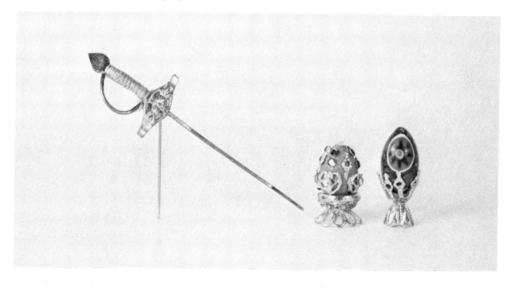

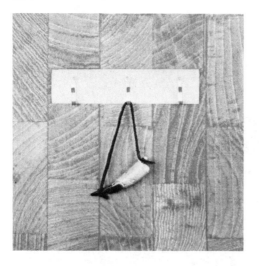

Fig. 16-3 The slightly curved tip of a king crab claw is retrieved for a powder horn (even garbage can be useful). Add a cover and a strap for easy carrying.

Fig. 16-4 Desk blotters are finished off with photo corner holders, or leatherette or embroidery side trim. Penholders, hand blotter, letter holder, ruler and notepaper are useful for a dollhouse desk.

aging for store items, small "glass" bowls. The colored capsules can be used in additional ways, too.

How to Make Those Tiny Household Extras

Instructions are given in this section for making the wide assortment of extra extras illustrated in Figures 16-11, 16-12 and 16-13.

EYEGLASSES

The spectacles in Figure 16-11 are made from a single strand of picture wire or bead wire, 3″ long.

Place halves of three round toothpicks together as shown in (A) to make a mold for bending wire. Bind together with tape (B). Wrap one strand of wire around sticks as shown (C). Pull tightly. Apply tiny dab of glue where wires cross (D). Allow to dry for several hours.

Bend wires back. Cut off tips. Gently push off from toothpicks (E). Cut tiny rounds of acetate and glue to round areas for "glass."

POWDER HORN

Make a tiny powder horn from the tip of a king crab claw. Clip claw immediately after boiling (less tendency to crack). Clean out inside. Make a cover from modeling compound to fit within hole. Add a thin leather strap or button thread, tied to each end.

WIRE HANGER

Use a 1¼″ paper clip. Bend the ends (A) and (B) into position as shown. Twist end (A) around center piece and clip end (B) as shown.

BATHROOM FIXTURES

All the items shown are made from metal filigree, necklace clasps, paper clips and beads.

DESK ACCESSORIES

Construction paper, which comes in assorted colors, makes a good *blotter*. Side areas can be leatherette, ribbon, decorative embroidery trim. *Pen or pencil holder*

Fig. 16-5 Hooks, towel holders, rods and various holders for paper, soap and spray dispensers help make the bathroom more attractive. Items are contrived from filigree, findings, chain, upholstery tacks, beads and a paper clip.

Fig. 16-6 A well-equipped kitchen needs a varied assortment of woodenware and metalware. The carved wooden pieces are a peel, bread board, rolling pin, scoops and spoons. The metal pieces represent a grater, chopping knives, cookie cutter (button) crumb scraper, wine cup, service spoons and dipper, skewer rack and three sizes of scoops, cut from three sizes of safety pins (see Fig. 6-12).

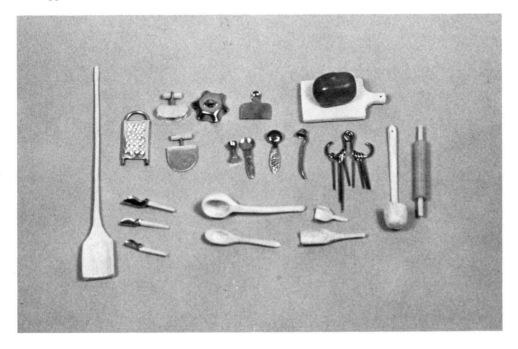

Fig. 16-7 Ready for the industrious doll are a hearth broom, pail, mop, broom, dustpan, washboard and soap, short hearth broom and lambs' wool and feather dusters.

Fig. 16-8 The little lady likes to have sewing and needlework handy. Bolts of material, trim, yarn, threads, pin cushion, embroidery and darning spool are a good beginning.

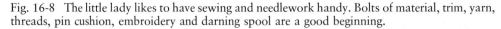

Fig. 16-9 A small plastic container complete with cover becomes an unconventional aquarium. A plastic picture frame serves as the base and the cube is filled with sand, rocks, dried sea life and plastic leaves. Mold tiny fish and set inside, using Stickum or glue.

can be a covered bullet shell or a plastic straw, covered and filled with a false bottom of round card. *Pens* are toothpicks, slimmed down, cut to size, painted in different colors and tipped with a piece of pin. The *plume pen* is a feather inserted in a bead. *Ink wells* and *ink stands* are all made from toothpicks and beads set on colored wooden bases, carved for grooves.

Letter opener with a wooden handle is cut from metal box spout. *Hand blotter* is cut from balsa wood (half circle ¼" wide). Round area is covered with construction paper; top is an ornamental paper, with a bead for handle. *Letter*

Fig. 16-10 It was easy to borrow and copy my husband's medical bag and stethoscope (see How-to section). Sitting alongside are spectacles and a pad.

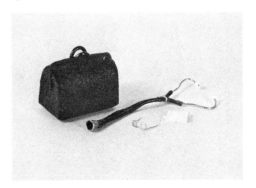

holder can be anything shaped into a U: wood, filigree, aluminum. Cover, decorate and insert some envelopes. Part of a large choker clasp (shown) is good. Add the word "Letters." A *bill holder* is a straight pin glued to head of a tack. *Ruler* has a metal edge of folded aluminum foil encased between two very thin slivers of wood. Add tiny black measurements.

SWORD

For the mini sword, you need a clock hand, fishhook clasp and paper clip. Bend paper clip as shown. Wind gray button thread around stem of clock hand, gluing to surface. Glue clip in place, then the fishhook, which has been clipped flat and away from rest of clasp.

GIFT WRAP PAPER

Select small prints from miniature wallpapers or regular gift wrap. Construct hollow tubes from card by overlapping and gluing around toothpick. Wind a few inches of gift wrap around each tube. Glue four together and cover with acetate covering.

MOUSE TRAP AND MOUSE

Cut rectangle from pine. Use spring from click-top pen and shape as shown. Glue down. Add small extension piece.

Mouse: Add hair whiskers, thread tail and toothpick ears to pussy willow. Dot in two eyes.

NEEDLEWORK ITEMS

Follow the drawings for size, as usual. *Bolt of fabric* has a base of balsa wood. Round the two long sides with sandpaper. Paint white. Cut the tiniest fabric patterns to size, allowing a white margin to show. Wind about 6" of fabric around bolt. *Spools of thread* are started with cut sections of ⅛" dowel. Sand out center area with rat-tail steel file. Wind thread of your choice around center section; start and finish with a bit of glue. A small bone bead could also be used as a spool. The *darning spool* is whittled out of ⅛" dowel. Just keep cutting and sanding.

The *pincushion* is a small flat button covered with thin "padded" material, which is all glued into a round filigree

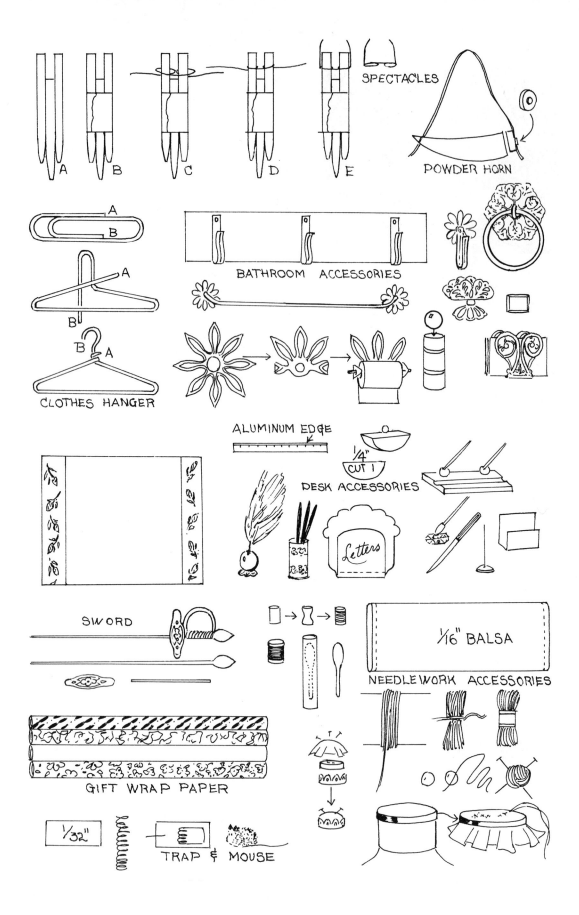

SPECTACLES

POWDER HORN

A B

BATHROOM ACCESSORIES

CLOTHES HANGER

ALUMINUM EDGE

¼"
CUT 1

DESK ACCESSORIES

Letters

SWORD

1/16" BALSA

NEEDLEWORK ACCESSORIES

GIFT WRAP PAPER

1/32"

TRAP & MOUSE

base. Add some cutoff pins. *Yarn skeins* can be made two different ways, indicated by drawings. Knitting needles can be straight pins and ends of sparkle pins.

Embroidery hoop: Fit $1/32''$ strip of card around bottletop. Glue overlapped ends together. Fit 2″ square piece of material over top and glue to card hoop. Add another card hoop (painted ochre color or silver) around material. Glue to material. Thread a tiny needle, push through top of material and clip off most of needle, leaving small section and thread intact.

SCOOPS AND SPOONS

Lengths and sizes may vary; the utensils shown in Figure 16-12 are made from $1/4''$ half rounds.

Directions: Using chisel edge from sculpture set, carefully gouge out an oval "pit" for spoon and proceed to gently whittle away rest of wood for handle. For the scoop, remove front area of wood.

The ladle is made from spruce wood, $2'' \times 3/8'' \times 3/8''$. Finished piece is $1 5/8''$ long. It is helpful to use a power tool for this work, but by careful cutting it can be accomplished with hand tools.

BREAD BOARD

Cut, shape and sand a piece of $1/32''$ pine. Drill hole in handle. This can be decorated and hung up on a wall.

SAFETY PIN SCOOPS

Cut assorted safety pins as shown in drawing (Fig. 16-12) and glue small toothpick handles in place.

SKEWER RACK

This dainty is made of 18-gauge copper wire and eye pins. Shape the copper wire as shown in drawing and string on a few eye pins of assorted lengths for skewers.

ROLLING PIN

Shape a rolling pin from $1/8''$ dowel. The pin shown at top has toothpick holders glued into gouged-out areas on ends. The pin below it has been sanded and shaped away on both ends.

CHOPPING KNIVES

The blades of both knives are cut from metal pouring spouts. The first has two blades and the second has one large chopper. Handles are toothpicks and supports are paper clips, glued as shown.

WOODEN PEEL

The peel is cut, shaped and sanded out of $1/16''$ balsa wood.

GRATER

An aluminum plate and large 2″ paper clips are needed. The aluminum is cut to wrap around the "legs" of a clipped paper clip. Gluing helps. With a nail, puncture regular holes through aluminum: rough side should show on *front* of grater.

WINE CUPS, SERVICE SPOONS, CRUMBER

These are all cut from pieces of jewelry findings. The cup is a portion of a screw earring and the spoons are straightened shapes from clip earrings. The crumber is a cut portion of clasp.

EGG

Egg #1 is modeled, colored and decorated with cut filigree and tiny rhinestones. Egg #2 is a colorful bead from India. Both are in bead-cap constructed stands.

WASHBOARD

This little extra is made from balsa wood, $1/32''$ and $1/16''$; heavy aluminum foil. Glue strips (B) and (C) onto frame (A). Fold three thicknesses of foil (3 × length) to fit within area (D). The scrub part is formed by indenting foil over a toothpick placed underneath. This is repeated for length of foil, for enough to fill area (D). Glue "ribbed" foil into position. Add a bar of soap.

DUSTPAN

The dustpan is made from two lift-off lids from cheese containers. Cut one lid to size of (A). Glue onto second lid (B). Add

Fig. 16-11 Eyeglasses, powder horn, wire hanger, bathroom fixtures, desk accessories, sword, gift wrapping, mousetrap and mouse, needlework necessities.

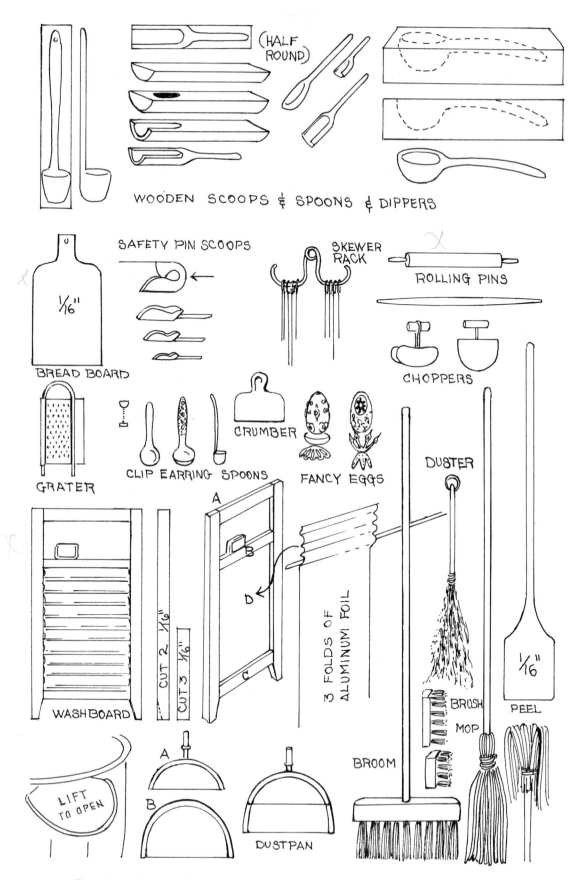

WOODEN SCOOPS & SPOONS & DIPPERS

(HALF ROUND)

SAFETY PIN SCOOPS

SKEWER RACK

ROLLING PINS

BREAD BOARD

1/16"

CHOPPERS

GRATER

CLIP EARRING SPOONS

CRUMBER

FANCY EGGS

DUSTER

WASHBOARD

CUT 2 1/16"

CUT 3 1/16"

A

B

D

3 FOLDS OF ALUMINUM FOIL

BRUSH

MOP

BROOM

PEEL

1/16"

LIFT TO OPEN

A

B

DUSTPAN

Fig. 16-12 Scoops and spoons, bread board, rolling pin, skewer rack, chopping knives, grater, wine cup, washboard, dustpan, broom and all manner of kitchen aids.

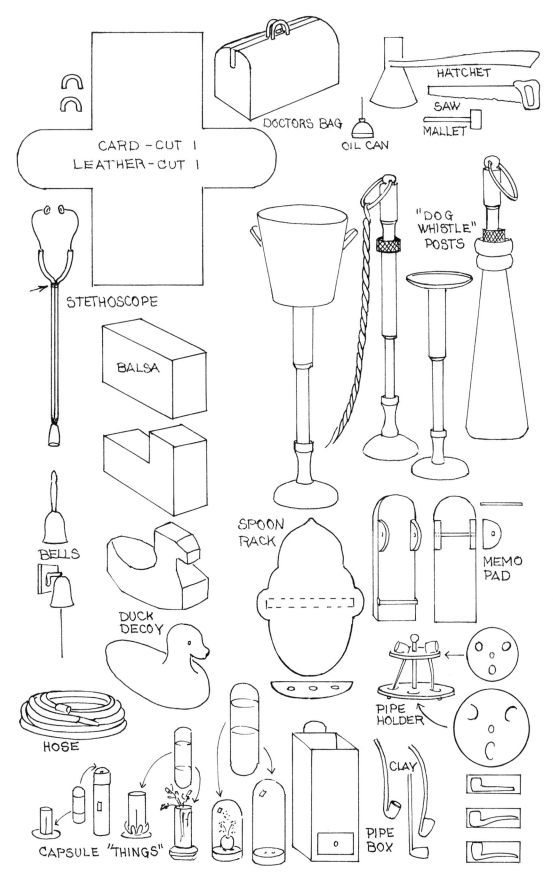

Fig. 16-13 Doctor's bag, stethoscope, posts, decoy, spoon rack, pipe rack, garden hose and other extra extras.

a handle, which is the writing tip from a ball-point pen.

BROOM

Cut through a toothbrush, leaving one layer of bristles: this requires a hot knife. Gouge a hole in center top for handle. Cover plastic top and sides with wood patterned Contact paper. Glue antiseptic stick handle into hole.

MOP

This item can be made from a white tassel or heavy white string. A handle is pushed into top of tassel and glued, or string is made into a tassel and same procedure followed. A pail (not drawn) for mop is a white cream container from a restaurant. Cut the little ridge off around top. Paint silver. Add paper clip handle with a hand holder (tubing from pen).

HEARTH BROOMS

Use bristles from large paint brushes or bristles from waxing machine, which is finer than corn broom. Glue bristles to handle and hold in place with wrapped twine. Short hearth handles, made from strips of balsa, can be turned and painted green or brown.

SCRUB BRUSH

Separate a child's toothbrush from the handle. Sand plastic smooth. Cut through bristles to shorten stem to $1/8''$ length or less.

DOCTOR'S BAG

Shown in Figure 16-13, the doctor's bag is made of thin black leather and black electrical wire. Cut pattern out of card and leather. Fold and glue into "bag position." Glue black leather to card. Glue bag edges all together. Add a thin strip of black leather from sides and over top area. Glue small piece of metal at center top for clasp. Glue two curved wire handles into place.

STETHOSCOPE

You'll need black electrical wire, tip from ball-point pen and two white seed beads.

Strip outer black covering away from wire in area of stethoscope, as shown in drawing. Add glue to prevent fraying. Strip a bit away at bottom and glue, then insert into cut opening of pen tip. Tie wire together at site of arrow with bead wire. Paint black. Glue two white seed beads at top ends for ear pieces.

POSTS

Metal dog whistles become posts using the complete whistle mounted over button base, or dismantled and used with other collectibles.

DECOY DUCK

Carve a block of balsa wood, cutting and sanding as shown. Color the duck by referring to colored picture in books or advertising.

EXTRA SUGGESTIONS

Memo pad, spoon rack, pipe racks, capsule items and garden hose are all made from either wood scraps or other items. White "clay" pipes are sculptured from Sculpey and wooden pipes from walnut. Hose is black-covered wire with ball-point pen tip "nozzle."

Part III Furniture

❉ 17 ❉

Furniture Construction

The section on furnishings, Chapters 17 through 24, will continue to dispense a "taste of this and a smell of that."

Centuries of cultural change wrought alterations in furniture styles, each bringing an imprint of individuality. Furniture not only differed in design but certain countries and periods employed different woods, constituting another aspect of history. English eighteenth-century furniture, such as Chippendale, Sheraton and Hepplewhite, was comprised of mahogany. Regency and Empire also used mahogany, enhanced with satinwood and fruitwood. Walnut was used for French eighteenth-century styles augmented with fruitwood; the early colonies used pine, cherry and maple. Early eighteenth-century colonial added the use of oak, walnut, elm, ash and red cedar—and mahogany became a major material used. (See color Fig. 9.)

Crafting with Wood

The crafting in this section offers variety and, as previously mentioned, the wood used for each piece of furniture is designated, but you may use your own selection.

The thickness of the wood may vary from $1/16''$ to $1/8''$ and this is important to note when cutting a pattern. Improper depth can throw a pattern off. Slight variations can occur when cutting, so always check your cutout pieces. Try them for fit first, before gluing them together. They may require a teensy bit more sanding in spots for better alignment. It is sometimes advisable to restrain from cutting certain pieces that require exact fit, such as bookshelves, fitted doors and drawers, until the outer shell or structure for these pieces has been finished. Then proceed to measure and cut rest of pattern, trying it in place to be sure of a proper and snug fit.

The preparation for making furniture is much the same for each piece, except for the finishing or the additional use of upholstery. To avoid repetitious instruction, I will set forth some preliminary instructions, basic for all wood construction that is to follow.

1. Place tracing paper over pattern in book and carefully trace drawing.

2. Select wood of your choice and sand surface well.

3. Using carbon paper, trace pattern onto wood (Fig. 17-1).

4. Carefully cut out pattern with jigsaw. Softer woods can be cut with an

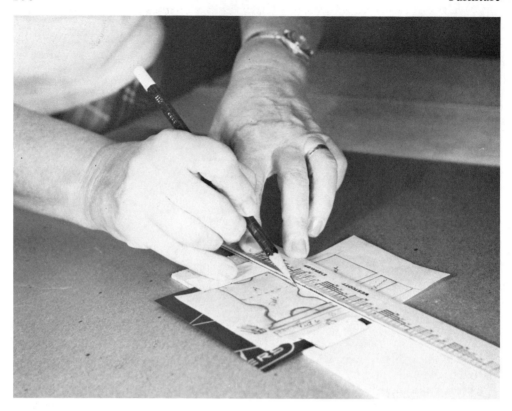

Fig. 17-1 To transfer the traced pattern onto the wood, tape both tracing paper and carbon paper to wood. This prevents shifting. Using a ruler for straight edges, redraw on pattern line with a sharp-pointed pencil. (*Jack Ruthberg, photograph*)

X-acto knife. Note: Some woods tend to split. If a pattern has a bit more intricacy in design, it's advisable to partially cut into the design, then finish off the details by using a steel file to get into delicate areas.

5. Gently sand edges of cutout pieces with fine sandpaper. If corners need rounding or edges need beveling, complete this procedure.

6. Try pieces for fit. Make adjustments if necessary.

7. If staining or shellacking furniture, do so *before* gluing.

8. If there are spindles or legs to be turned or shaped, these can be done mechanically on a lathe or by hand with the help of a diagonal cutter and steel files (Figs. 17-2 and 17-3).

Helpful Hints

✔ Always sand with the grain of the wood.

✔ Before cutting a pattern, sand surface of wood; it's easier to sand the larger piece than the small pieces.

✔ Steel files are used to smoothly sand edges of cut pieces.

✔ If both $1/16''$ and $1/8''$ thicknesses of wood are needed in a pattern but you only have the $1/16''$, don't despair! Glue two pieces of $1/16''$ wood together, place between waxed paper, lay under heavy weight (books are good) and allow to dry overnight.

✔ When shellacking or lacquering pieces, try to avoid end areas where glue will be applied. Clear, sanded wood adheres best.

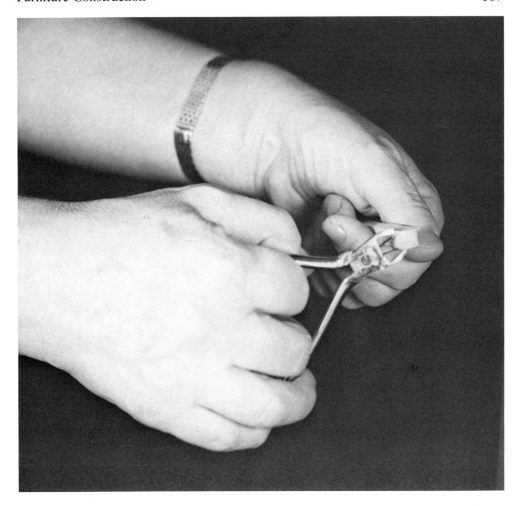

Fig. 17-2 To start simple turnings without benefit of a lathe, cut into wood with a diagonal semi-flush wire cutter. Turn strip of wood or dowel round and round to acquire even indentation. (*Jack Ruthberg, photograph*)

✔Placing a sheet of graph paper or lined notebook paper under waxed paper, which is taped in position, can help line up your pieces for 90° angles and better fit when gluing them together.

✔ If two pieces have bilateral designs with curvings or indentations, for example, chair legs, chair arms, cupboard curves, place the two pieces together and sand both at same time to acquire perfect symmetry.

✔Multicolored inlay designs are beautiful and should be considered for enhancing pieces of furniture.

✔Dowel sticks make a good beginning for many legs—short, medium and long.

✔Simple turnings on dowels and balsa wood strips can be started with a diagonal cutter. Cut into the wood and gently keep turning the stick around. When indentation has been made, further shaping is accomplished with steel needle files.

✔ If you make an error cutting a pattern and a piece is "off" about $1/16''$, glue an extra $1/16''$ length of wood against the stricken side and "set" overnight. Sand, fit and glue, then sand well again when dry. This will correct the flaw, leaving hardly a clue.

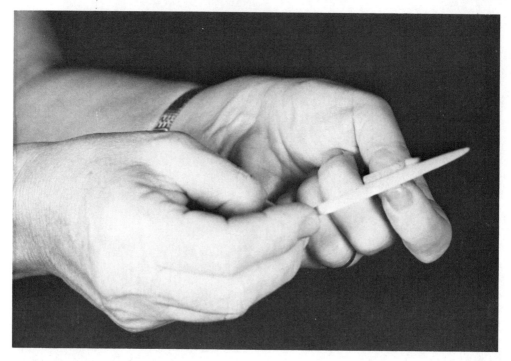

Fig. 17-3 Finish shaping the design of the turning with an assortment of steel files. (*Jack Ruthberg, photograph*)

Drawer pulls and knobs can be rendered in different ways. Drawer pulls can be stationary, using a link, shaped and glued into place; two small bead caps connected with thin wire; cut filigree for an underplate, adding the handle of hanging shaped wire; and don't overlook the possibilities of the paper clip and hooks and eyes. A working handle can be made by attaching each end of handle to the half of jump link that is glued into the drawer. Knobs can be small beads, tops of straight pins (round and regular), copper screen tacks, 3/8" escutcheon nails or even small seashells. An "apothecary" knob is a white rocaille bead with head of regular straight pin pushed through hole.

✤ 18 ✤

Sofas, Chairs and Stools

Won't you sit down? . . . Please be seated. . . . Have a chair! . . . There are various eloquent ways to proffer seating invitations; likewise, there is no limitation to the variety of furniture for this posture.

Ancient stools were the accepted form of seating and, centuries later, stools were still considered proper except for important people. Thus the Middle Ages displayed rank preference and indicated who sat on chairs, who on different types of stools, who stood. As chairs gained stature, stools obviously declined as the seat of choice, but they achieved their own niche in society, performing certain functions in different times, in different cultures and in different ways.

Sofas and chairs have run the gamut in style and reach back into time when the ancient X chair was folded and primarily carried from place to place. Although styles and designs have changed since then, the various functions of chairs offer additional testimony to their importance in furniture history (Figs. 18-1 through 18-4).

The wainscot chair, box frame in shape, was austere and uncomfortable. The advent of upholstery brought greater com-

fort and more auspicious pieces. A general rundown of the pattern of chair usage would include such varieties as chairbed, table chair, side chair, armchair, decorative chair (Hitchcock), upholstered chair (barrel, wing), dining room chair, office chair, desk chair, folding chair, writing chair, fancy chair, corner chair, rocking chair, overstuffed chair and the baby highchair.

Sofas are upholstered and accommodate two persons (love seat) or three persons, or more. Sofas have stretched out for more seating capacity, as evidenced by the sectional sofas of modern decor. Many period pieces may employ the use of carved wood along with upholstery; others are completely upholstered, minus any other trim. Backs usually run to moderate height, except for Colonial styles which are comfortably high. Extra pillows may or may not be part of the structure; sofas and chairs are offered as matching sets if this is desired. Rarely does a sofa depart in structure from the straight bench appearance, but a couple of these rarities are the vis-a-vis sofa, on which two sitters face in opposite directions, and the Victorian circular conversation sofa (Fig. 18-6). The latter was usually cen-

169

Fig. 18-1 The corner chair or roundabout is a handsome piece placed in corners or at desks. This one is made from walnut and features squared legs that are positioned one in front, one in back and two on the sides. Made during the eighteenth century, it was essentially of English and American construction. The upholstered seat is a snitched piece from the end of a maroon tie, which really provided the most suitable pattern and material.

tered in the middle of a room; perhaps some readers may recall its appearance in the lobbies of old hotels.

The settee, often called the deacon's bench, is a wooden structure, light in appearance, and is made with either two or three seats (Fig. 18-7). These charming pieces are sometimes decorated with painted designs and occasionally upholstered.

The settle is a solid all-wooden bench with a high back that may or may not feature a hood; a low arm may be part of an entire side piece or individual in shape. The lower part may sometimes be boxlike in construction, with a hinged seat as a top. The settle was often placed near a fireplace and, with its high back, offered additional protective warmth to persons using it (Fig. 18-8).

The ottoman was both a foot rest and a seat. This was quite a bit more elegant and was either matched to an armchair or remained as an entity in its own right. Sometimes used singly or in pairs, they were simply constructed and/or elaborately carved with fruit and flower medallions on sides and legs, and usually softened with an upholstered top. When the glamorous ottoman emerged with higher legs it was conveniently used as a piano stool, a dressing table bench or a window seat.

How would you like to have a bed so high that a footstool was necessary for getting in and out of your sleeping accommodations? Primarily because of drafty floors, some of the earlier beds were of such height, and that's at least one reason for the stool. Stools also kept the feet up

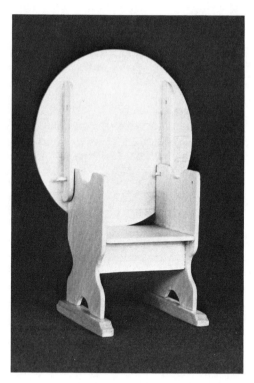

Fig. 18-2 A piece of pine furniture served the dual purpose of either chair or table. Made with a hinged back, the convertible table top was either round, square or oblong. I tossed a coin to see where the description for making this piece would be and Chapter 21, Tables, won the throw.

Fig. 18-3 The barrel chair, made from a miniature barrel, is a real cute piece for the game room, family room or patio.

off the same cold floor while a person sat before the open hearth. There are milking stools, office stools and high stools which were, in early Colonial days, the first chairs.

Most benches are differentiated from stools and ottomans by their length. Obviously, they are meant to accommodate more than one person, as exemplified by the fireside bench. There are benches for the schools, shops, churches and, yes, the street. Lest we forget, there was the occupational cobbler's bench which eventually gave way to the cobbler's table—a contemporary piece with old-time flavor.

How to Make Corner, Barrel and Colonial Tote Chairs

Pattern parts and construction sequences for the corner chair, barrel chair and Colonial tote chair are shown in Figure 18-10.

CORNER CHAIR, ca. 1760—1775

Materials: Walnut, $1/16''$ and $3/16''$; cardboard; fabric for upholstery (mine was cut from a tie).

Directions:

1. Cut and sand the wooden pieces: cut one G from $1/8''$; cut one H from $3/16''$. Center and glue (H) on top of (G). Allow to dry thoroughly overnight. With sanders (Moto-Tool) or needle files, shape a curve along front topmost area of (H). Shape curvature on right and left sides leading to rest of arm and gently round edges of arm.

2. Legs (A) remain square and straight, but uprights are shaped and have a ball turning at base (see drawing).

3. Glue three tall leg-upright pieces (A) to two side-rear pieces (B). Dry well.

4. Shape and cut out small corner area from top of front leg (D). This is to allow for snug upholstery fit.

5. Glue front-side pieces (C) and front leg (D) together and into position next to legs (A). Dry well.

6. Try uprights (A) and splats (F) for fit with curved arm. If adjustment is required, make correction with a bit of sanding. Glue splats (F) to center top area of (B) and, with slight backward tilt, glue onto the curvature (G–H).

7. On top of cardboard piece (E) place some cotton and secure material snugly over and glue to bottom of cardboard.

8. With added glue, set wooden piece (E) down, just a little, into open area. With more glue on bottom of seat and sparingly along edges of seat, set this down on top of wood (E). Press firmly together.

9. Glue four small striplings of wood (I) underneath seat and along sides for support. When finished, I gave this piece a light spraying of clear acrylic.

BARREL CHAIR

Materials: 2" high barrel; material for upholstery; thin leather for trim; straight pins for nailheads.

Directions:

1. Saw away part of barrel as shown in drawing (A). Cross section indicates how far back to cut. Sand edges and stain to match color of rest of barrel.

2. Cut two thicknesses of cotton bat-

Fig. 18-4 The Colonial tote chair was not a strong structural chair and was mostly intended for holding things. Painted black, it has a decorative backrest.

Fig. 18-6 The Victorian conversation sofa is of French origin. It was either molded as one complete piece or constructed of two parts and fitted around a centered column, which served as a
stand for a potted plant or statuary. This sofa, of two half circles, is flanked by a folding hand-
painted screen. A proud great aunt, framed and resting on a bentwood easel, complements the era.
Austrian window curtains and white damask swag are set off with filigree ornaments. A simple
floor planter with dried ferns and a delicate parasol complete the picture. The background is a
cotton fabric, and the carpet is upholstery material.

ting to fit within entire back area (B). Cut
material, plus extra 1/4″ all around, to fit
over cotton and fold extra material over.
Glue onto cotton. Glue entire back piece
onto barrel back (B).

3. Stuff open area of barrel *firmly* with
cotton to seat height.

4. Measure and cut a seat pattern out
of felt material and cover with upholstery
material, allowing extra 1/4″ all around.

Fig. 18-5 The whole world isn't period furniture, so let's include a striking and very bold armless
sofa, simply constructed out of a tie box and upholstered in a plush black and white design. The
wall tapestry is made from embroidery trim. On the left is a stand made of half a macrame bead
and round piece of wood, supporting a beautiful cast pewter sculpture. On the right is a square
"bottle top" table and a modern lamp. Wall covering is gift wrap paper and rug is plush acrylic.

Fig. 18-7 My very own painted settee provided the inspiration for crafting this bench. The miniature is made of pine and painted dark brown, and it has the delicate touch of a painted design. With patience, you too can construct a settee and add this to your collection of miniatures.

Fold under and glue back area of seat under the seat pattern. Glue entire seat into place upon firm cotton base (C). The front material overlaps, to be glued to front of barrel.

5. Cut leather to fit over areas (D) and (E) and glue down.

6. Cut heads from straight pins and insert with glue into leather for trim. Extra nailhead trim can be added to front.

7. Glue four legs (E) into a tilted position as shown.

COLONIAL TOTE CHAIR

Cut pieces from balsa as indicated by pattern in Figure 18-10. See Chapter 17 for cutting and sanding guidelines. Chair may be painted black or red.

1. Shape and round center section of legs (E) and ball the bottoms (C). Create turned effect as indicated. Sand smoothly.

2. Rout out three areas under seat (B) for legs; circles indicate placement. Since balsa is soft, this can be done by carefully pushing square end of leg into underseat, angled slightly outward.

3. Paint back and add design, using your own choice of colors.

4. Glue legs into place. Dry well. Guide for angled placement of *feet* of legs is indicated by small *x* marks outside of seat drawing.

5. Add three stretchers (D) to legs, joining them together at center. Dry well. Glue back to seat.

6. Finish painting chair.

7. Make a little round pillow for seat.

How to Make a
Victorian Round Sofa

Pattern parts and assembly sequence are shown in Figure 18-11.

Materials: Balsa wood, ½" × 4" × 12"; firm tube from plastic wrap, 3⅛" high; material for upholstery; matching embroidery floss; matching upholstery fringe; cotton batting; 1"-diameter thread spools, Velverette glue.

Directions:

1. Cut material for two seats, ½" larger all around than pattern.

2. Slice tube in half to make half circles for backrest. Cut material to cover each tube allowing extra for wraparound.

3. Cover each half tube with five thin layers of cotton batting to seat area, about 1½" from top as shown in (A). Cover over tightly with upholstery material, gluing extra side material to back of tube (B). With embroidery floss, make French knots (see drawing for placement). The needle goes through card, too, pulling material taut, creating a bit of puffing. Pull down material for coverup and glue over back surface (C).

4. Cover the two seats cut from card with five or six layers of thin cotton batting. Pull upholstery material over top and glue slightly along edge (D). Create

Fig. 18-8 For all practical purposes, the high back and side protrusions on the settle were designed to protect its seated occupants from cold drafts. It's painted a greenish-blue color which was popular in its day.

Fig. 18-9 On top are a little footstool and a simple bottle cap topped with velvet button. Below is the Victorian dressing table stool, the "spool" stool (this time a leather button), an English stool, a velvet-covered "ringbox" stool and a boudoir stool.

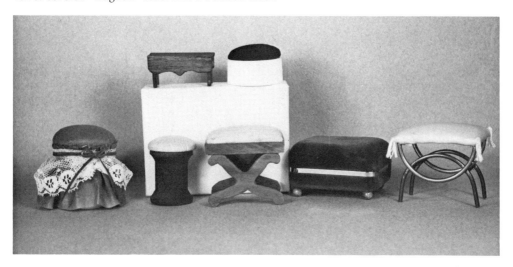

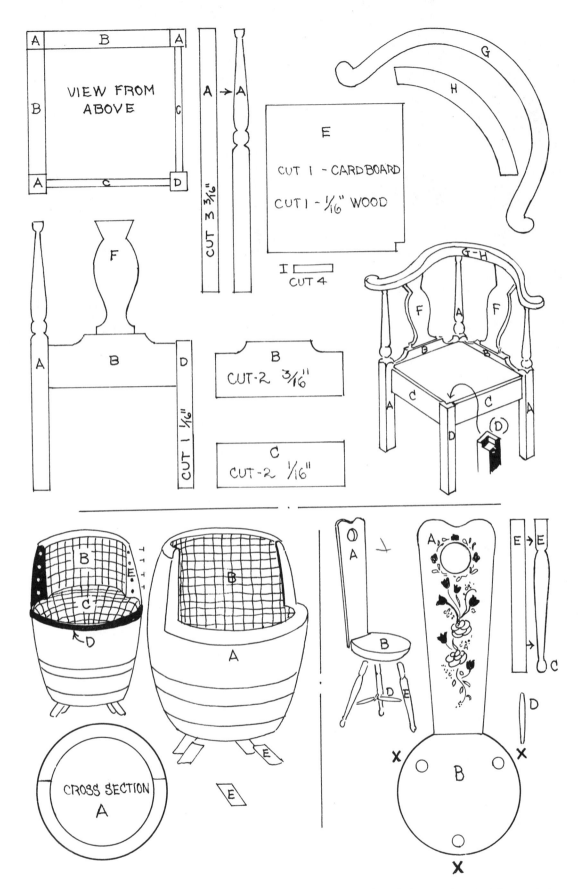

Fig. 18-10 Pattern parts and assembly for corner chair, barrel chair and Colonial tote chair.

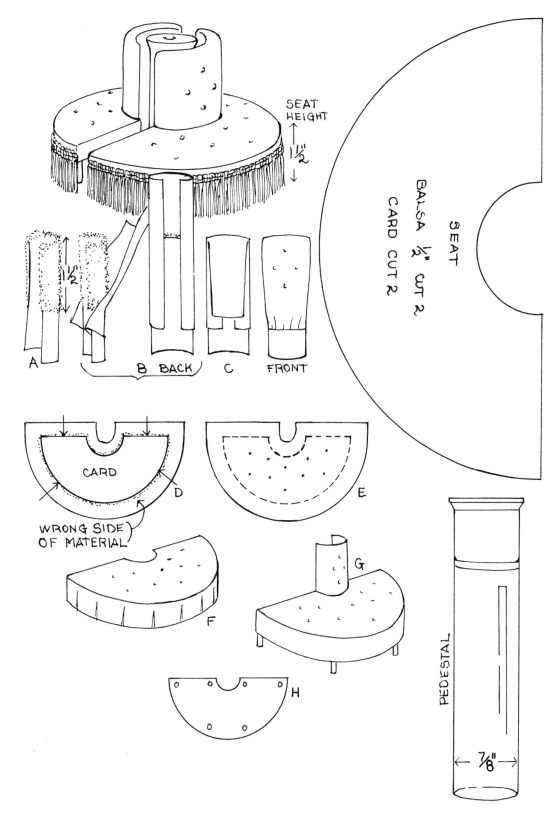

SEAT
HEIGHT
1½"

SEAT
BALSA ½" CUT 2
CARD CUT 2

A   B BACK   C   FRONT

CARD

WRONG SIDE
OF MATERIAL

D

E

F

G

H

PEDESTAL

⅞"

Fig. 18-11   Pattern parts and assembly for Victorian conversation sofa and pedestal.

puffing on seats by sewing French knots through card, cotton batting and material. See drawing (E) for placement of knots.

5. Glue upholstered pieces securely to balsa wood pieces (F). Cut notches into material if necessary for smooth fit. Finish off back with a fabric covering.

6. Glue inner curve of seat to center tube "back" of seat about 1 5/8" down (G). Glue six dowel legs to underside of *each* sofa section (H): push dowels into balsa for better grip.

7. Glue upholstery fringe to outer circular area of seats, tacking each side a bit in back.

Pedestal: The pedestal should be even with the top of the sofa backrest. Build up a pedestal to this height, using spools glued together or a thin vial container glued to half a spool on top. Curved back of sofa should fit snugly around pedestal. Paint or cover with Contact paper. On top of pedestal, place a potted plant or statuary.

How to Make a Painted Settee

Pattern parts and construction sequence for the settee are shown in Figure 18-12.

Materials: 1/8" pine wood; 1/16" pine wood; 1/8" dowel stick; 28 round toothpicks.

Note: Because there should be adequate long drying periods, this piece requires patience and days to complete. Follow guidelines in Chapter 17 for cutting pieces.

Directions:

1. Sand a curvature to front top area of seat (A).

2. Rout out eight holes for dowel legs on bottom of seat; see drawing for location of legs.

3. Drill *twenty small holes* as indicated on seat pattern; rout out *six larger holes* as indicated. Test size by inserting toothpick spindles and dowel uprights.

4. Cut toothpicks, as shown in drawing. Glue sixteen cut toothpicks into back of seat. Slant slightly backward and keep them evenly lined up. Dry very thoroughly, until good and sturdy.

5. Glue rail (B) to top of spindles. (If spindles are a bit irregular on top, even off with a sharp knife before gluing on rail.)

6. Glue two shaped end posts (D) and two shaped center posts (E) into position.

7. Glue rail (C) on top of and against posts.

8. Position arm (F); add two toothpick spindles and one dowel post to fit as indicated in drawing. Repeat for other side. Make a turned effect on each front dowel post, as shown, after checking for proper fit.

9. Glue the posts into thin holes and glue (F) on top and against back corner post (D). Repeat for the other side.

10. Sand the bottom of each leg (G) to a rounded finish. Where *toothpick stretchers* will fit, cut a wedge into *each* leg (H) for firmer fit and support. Glue legs into space provided for them underneath seat. Be sure they are straight. Allow to dry very thoroughly.

11. Cut toothpicks to fit between legs (front, back and sides) and glue into wedge-cut areas as indicated. Dry well.

12. Paint entire settee dark brown or black. Add gold or yellow ochre striping to seat, arms, legs. Paint fruit tole design on back top rail: peaches—peach or rose color; grapes—blue; plums—purple; leaves—olive green; swirls and urns—gold.

How to Make a High-Back Settle

The settle shown in Figure 18-13 is made of 1/16" balsa wood.

1. Glue seat (D) against sides (E). Dotted lines show positioning.

2. Glue back (B) into position.

3. Glue front and back skirts (C) into position.

4. Glue top (A) into position.

5. Glue back panel (F) at center of back (B).

6. Glue false drawers (G) into position. Add knobs.

7. Paint entire piece a dark green-blue color.

Fig. 18-12   Parts and construction for making the painted pine settee.

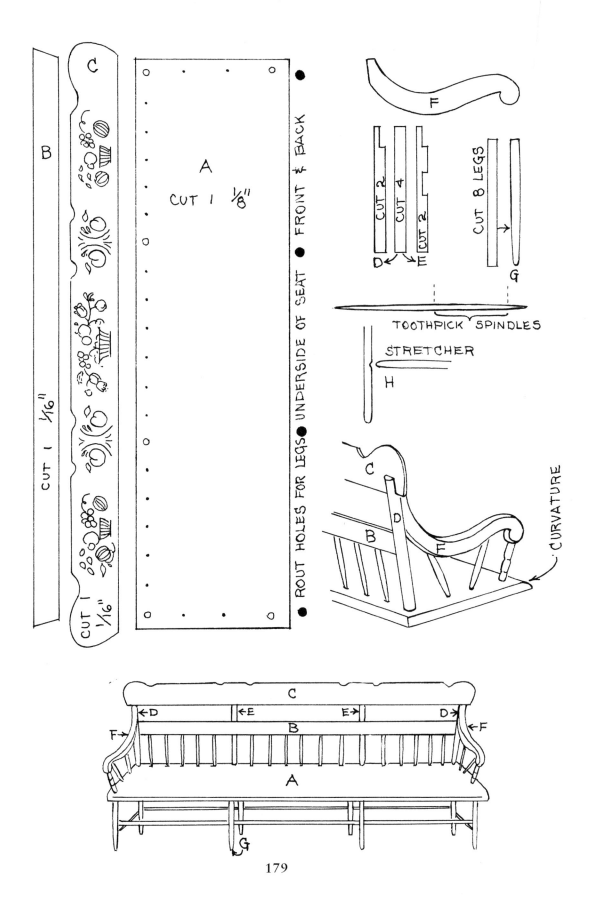

B

CUT 1 1/16"

C

CUT 1 1/16"

CUT 1 1/16"

A

CUT 1 1/8"

● ROUT HOLES FOR LEGS ● UNDERSIDE OF SEAT ● FRONT ¥ BACK ●

F

CUT 2
CUT 4
E CUT 2
D

CUT 8 LEGS
G

TOOTHPICK SPINDLES

STRETCHER
H

C
D
B
F
CURVATURE

C
←D ←E E→ D→
F B F
A
G

A TOP CUT 1

B BACK CUT 1

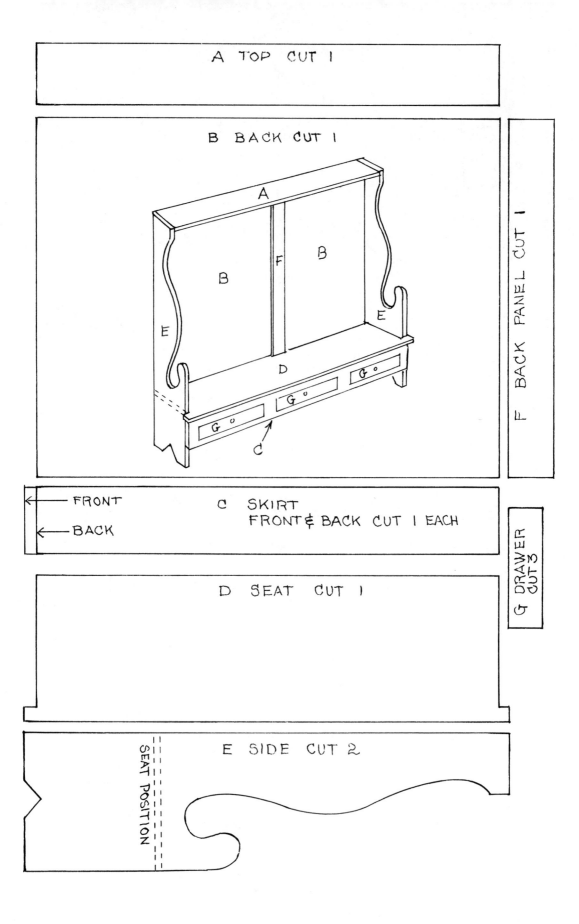

F BACK PANEL CUT 1

FRONT
BACK
C SKIRT
FRONT & BACK CUT 1 EACH

G DRAWER CUT 3

D SEAT CUT 1

E SIDE CUT 2
SEAT POSITION

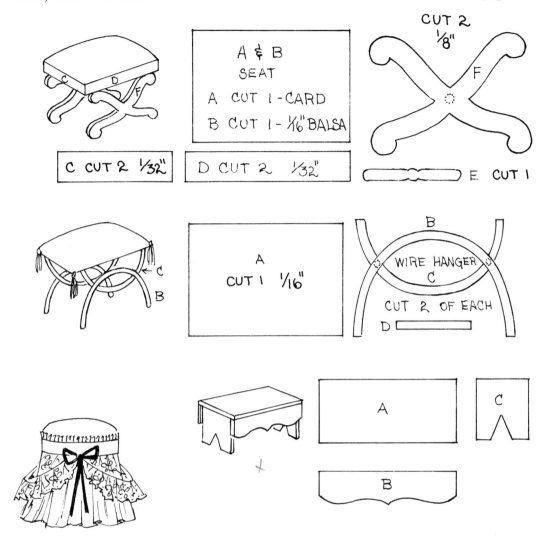

Fig. 18-14   English stool, boudoir bench, footstool and Victorian stool.

How to Make Benches and Stools

Patterns are supplied in Figure 18-14 for several small seating arrangements.

ENGLISH STOOL, ca. 1810

The original walnut stool has a carved surface.

Materials: Material for upholstery 2½″ × 3″; ⅛″, 1/16″ and 1/32″ walnut; cardboard.

Directions:

1. Cover cardboard seat (A) with four thicknesses of cotton batting. Tightly pull material over top and glue to bottom of seat.

2. Cover bottom of upholstered seat with piece (B), balsa wood.

3. Glue four side areas (C and D) in place, enclosing upholstery.

4. Round and shape 1-inch stretcher bar (E).

5. Fit and glue legs (F) to undersurface

Fig. 18-13   Pattern and assembly for building the high-back settle.

of seat and glue stretcher (E) in place, connecting center of each leg. (You may want to rout out a small area on each leg where stretcher will connect for better fit.)

BOUDOIR BENCH

Materials: Four wire dress hangers; thin material; embroidery floss; cotton padding; wood.

Directions:

1. Pad top of wooden seat (A) with cotton. Tightly pull material over top and glue to bottom of seat. Cut out rectangle of material and cover over the bottom.

2. Glue two curved pieces of wire hanger (B and C) together, as shown in drawing. Repeat for other side. Dry well.

3. Measure where legs will fit into bottom of seat. Rout out four areas for legs in the corners underneath seat. Glue legs into place.

4. Fit and glue support bars (D) into position on each side (indicated by dots), connecting the legs.

5. Make four tiny tassels from embroidery floss and sew one at each corner.

FOOT STOOL

Cut all pattern pieces from $1/32''$ balsa, following guidelines in Chapter 17 for cutting and sanding.

1. Stain wood before gluing.

2. Glue each end piece (C) to top (A), setting them in $1/16''$ from edge.

3. Glue each side piece (B) to top (A) and to end pieces (C).

VICTORIAN STOOL

Materials: Large plastic thread spool; thin material; panel lace.

Directions:

1. Cut spool to $1\frac{1}{2}''$ high.

2. Pad top with cotton and cover tightly with round piece of material, gluing to sides of spool.

3. Glue "gathered" material around sides of stool. Add lace panel on top of material and pull up in front and back for swag effect. Pin in place.

4. Add thin strip of Velverette ribbon for trim and bows.

❊ 19 ❊

Beds, Headboards and Cradles

Beds run the gamut in design from simple to elaborate or, to be specific, furniture can be country style or formal.

The simple low headboard-and-posts style used by the Pilgrims was and still is popular. It was easy to make and appropriate for low-ceilinged rooms.

The early tester beds with four high corner posts were popular and useful (Fig. 19-1). Basically similar, they are distinguished by each designer, who left their trademarks in differing styles, as exemplified by Queen Anne, Chippendale, Hepplewite, Sheraton and Empire. Tester beds complete with canopy and bed hangings of muslin or elaborate crewelwork were a purposeful style. When bed hangings were closed, they conveniently helped to seal off excess drafts in an otherwise chilly room without benefit of heat.

Similar to the tester bed was the "field bed," which had an arched top. The bed could be dismantled for use in wartime camps.

The folding bed with two tall headposts with supported frame and hanging curtains was a cleverly constructed piece that could be raised and concealed from sight behind curtains. This must have been the original hideaway bed, because this bed was usually placed in a living room to accommodate extra guests.

Posts have varied in size and structure. Posts were turned, reeded, fluted and handsomely carved—some quite elaborately. Others, modified and uncomplicated, remained plain, round and tapered. The pencil post was another simplified version, so called because it resembled a pencil with six sides.

Beds were both high posted and low posted and the Victorian period introduced the carved bed, which featured both high headboards and footboards. Other period bed styles are the Renaissance, Eastlake, sleigh bed (Fig. 19-2), spool bed and Belter bed.

The trundle bed was very much a part of early American life. Rooms were small and the extra pullout bed supplied added sleeping space for a child. The trundle is still with us, as exemplified by my own son's room, but we lovingly called this structure the bed with the giant-size drawer reserved for his giant-size friends.

But the spinoff from all past styles is beautifully incorporated in what we accept as the "Hollywood" style bed, consisting of a headboard, boxspring and mattress. Headboards are a grand selec-

Fig. 19-1 Naked and revealing is the best way to show the construction of the tester bed. The four posts are artists' paintbrush handles and, although the rest is made from balsa wood, you can select your own choice of wood. To see the bed dressed and looking its very best, refer to Figure 13-5.

tion from the old to the new. They may reach back to Early American, steal a bit from the Renaissance, take a little something from the Oriental, swipe from the French Provincial—but, whatever the style, the headboard bed sets the mood for contemporary living.

Studio beds and sofa beds suit our modern day life. Small, unobstrusive and serviceable, they fill important needs for extra guest beds, small apartments, family rooms, game rooms or whatever. They can be elaborately upholstered or simply tailored, used singly or in pairs, nestled between bookcases or built in between chests or storage units.

The day bed is the forerunner of the chaise lounge, narrow in construction and oftentimes elaborate, since this was usually found in an affluent home.

The most captivating bed is the cradle, partially because of its wee occupant. Some cradles resemble cribs with rockers added, and still other cribs are high posted, intended to support a top canopy. There are hanging cradles, box cradles and hooded cradles. The modern baby is bedded down in a bassinet, often long skirted, or a crib, but I bet if they were able to express a choice, they'd prefer the old-fashioned cradle and rock . . . rock . . . rock . . .

Fig. 19-3   A Renaissance styled bed has a headboard made from one corner metal piece of a Victorian frame, mounted atop a square of cardboard, covered with cotton-padded white moiré. The footboard is a small Victorian frame. Two matching handkerchiefs team up—one is used for curtains, accented by tassels, and the second hankie has an extra panel of lace down the center for a spread. In front of the curtains a cut detergent bottle is covered with twinelike trim and the plants are a combination of plastic and dried andromeda. Directions for the white satin bench are given in Figure 18-14. On the right side a plastic cube table adds a modern touch. On top rests a small lamp made with filigree base, silver rosebud bead and bell cap shade. The little bracket is a half oval of wood mounted on a plastic bauble and supports a porcelain vase. The background is a gray woven material and the carpet is an Oriental tapestry.

Helpful Hints

✔Chopsticks, which are tapered, can become high bedposts, and some are very elegant.

✔For a pencil-post bed, use four six-sided pencils. Sand the paint off the pencils and stain the wood.

✔Brass lamp finials make impressive bedposts. Use four across the back for real impact or station one at each of the four corners.

Fig. 19-2   The graceful curving of the sleigh bed reaches back to the Empire period. It can be displayed plain with bolstered pillows upon a matching spread, or further enhanced with extra wall drapery cascading down from a centered semicircle with an ornamental crown.

Fig. 19-4 With extreme care, a brass headboard bed can be made out of wire dress hangers. Glued together, it's not meant to take a lot of handling, but effective it is.

✔A bed can start with a box as the support for a mattress. Glove and tie boxes are good for "single" size beds, cots and sofa beds.

✔Pushpins, with the pins removed, become legs for Hollywood style bed.

✔Sometimes pretty letter files and napkin holders make good headboards or footboards. Cut away the unnecessary sides.

✔Create an upholstered headboard with a lush material. Pad with lots of cotton batting and tuft with French knots.

✔Tufting can also be done by pushing straight pins through to back and bending pins to keep in place. Cover back with protective material.

✔Put a pretty screen in back of a bed for headboard.

✔Studio beds can feature pillows that are square or wedge shaped; bolsters and coverings can be fitted with a box-shaped skirt or ruffled flounce. A simple "throw" can also be tossed over a constructed form which may consist of a box with a fitted foam seat.

How to Make a Tester Bed and Cradle

The pattern parts and assembly techniques for this bed and cradle are shown in Figure 19-6.

TESTER BED

Four artists' paintbrush handles become the corner posts. Chopsticks are another "tapered" substitute, or use dowel posts—plain, shaped or turned. Posts are 6 to 7 feet tall on the real bed.

For proper fit, cut headboard *after*

Fig. 19-5 The cherry wood grain helps beautify this hooded cradle, but the nicely curved styling would look well in any wood of your choice. Even the doll has a cradle.

posts are up, following preliminary guidelines in Chapter 17.

1. Glue boards (C) and (B) to corner posts.

2. Cut thin wood or sturdy cardboard to fit between four sideboards and glue into place *above* bottom (D). Glue four slender supports under board and against sideboards for slats.

3. Glue headboard (A) into place.

4. Top: glue two long strips (E) to top of posts. Glue two end strips (F) connecting to long strips (E). Glue two center strips (G) in place; for best fit, cut shorter strips after long strips have been glued down.

Note: To complete this bed with a handsome canopy and matching spread, see Chapter 13.

CRADLE

The cradle is made of $1/16''$ and $1/8''$ cherry, or substitute wood of your choice.

1. Cut rockers (F) out of $1/8''$ thickness wood; other pattern parts from $1/16''$ wood.

2. Glue sides (A), back (B), and front (C) to bottom (D).

3. Slightly bevel one side of right and left top pieces (E) to fit against center top. Try for fit.

4. Glue (E) parts together and to back (B) and top (A) of cradle.

5. Try rockers (F) for fit. Glue to bottom.

How to Make a Sleigh Bed

All pieces are $1/8''$ mahogany except (D), which is $1/16''$ (Fig. 19-7).

1. Glue side and base pieces (A and B) together.

2. Glue bottom front and bottom back (C) to bottom sides, indenting $1/32''$ from edges.

3. Glue on four curved corner pieces (F), simultaneously with front and back pieces (D), to base.

4. Glue two top half-curved pieces (E) to front and back.

5. Add four $1/8''$ strips of wood (G)

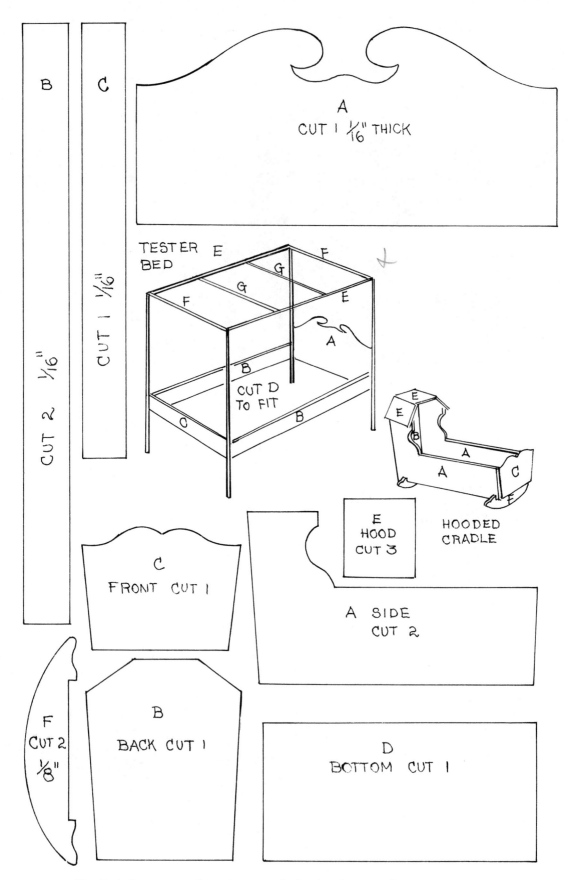

B

C

CUT 2 1/16"

CUT 1 1/16"

B
A
CUT 1 1/16" THICK

TESTER
BED
E   F
          G
F   G
          E
B
CUT D
TO FIT
C   B

A

E
E
B
A
A   C
E
HOODED
CRADLE

C
FRONT CUT 1

E
HOOD
CUT 3

A SIDE
CUT 2

F
CUT 2
1/8"

B
BACK CUT 1

D
BOTTOM CUT 1

Fig. 19-6 Pattern parts for a pine tester bed and a cherry cradle.

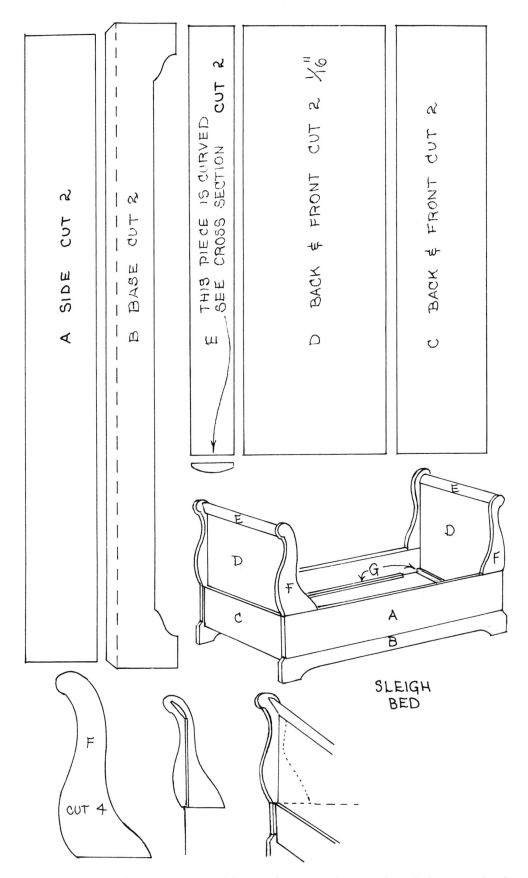

A SIDE CUT 2

B BASE CUT 2

E THIS PIECE IS CURVED
SEE CROSS SECTION CUT 2

D BACK & FRONT CUT 2 1/16"

C BACK & FRONT CUT 2

F CUT 4

SLEIGH
BED

Fig. 19-7 The sleigh bed is constructed from mahogany, or from a softwood, then stained mahogany.

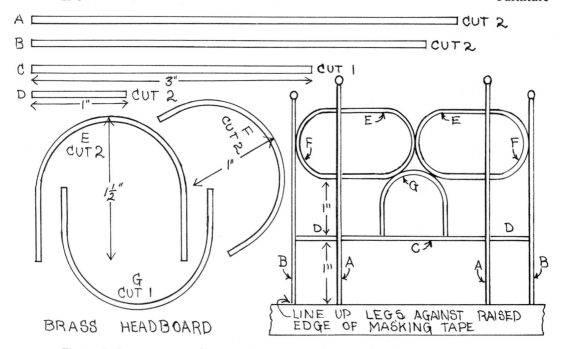

Fig. 19-8   Pattern parts and construction sequence for brass headboard.

along inside of base at glue line. This is for support.

6. Cut out ¹⁄₁₆″ piece of wood or cardboard to fit within bed area. Glue onto (G) strips of wood.

7. Cut a rectangle of foam rubber for mattress and cover. Keep height level with side rail.

How to Make a Brass Headboard

Since the pieces for the headboard (Fig. 19-8) are glued together, there must be a perfect fit and sometimes extra cuttings are necessary to achieve this fit. They could also be soldered together if one has such equipment.

Materials: Five wire hangers (allow for more in case of error in cutting); four small gold beads.

Directions:

1. Use the strongest contact glue available or an epoxy glue. Line up the brass pieces, as shown in drawing, on top of waxed paper that's been taped down onto a board or heavy cardboard. Mark with red the areas of contact and sand these areas with steel file.

2. Proceed to glue wire pieces together. Don't move anything. Leave overnight to dry.

3. Glue beads to top. This is a delicate piece, but with tender loving care it will hold up once it's placed into position.

✤ 20 ✤

Dressers, Chests and Cupboards

Everyone's personal acquisitions need a place to hide, away from eyesight or exposure to soil. Hence the chest of drawers came into being. Prior to the time that bedroom suites were introduced, chests of drawers were acceptable and used in any part of the house. The bureau came into use when a fixed mirror was added to the framework. There are three-drawer chests, four-drawer chests and five, six or seven tiers of graduated drawers that stretch out to be called tall chests of drawers. And then we have the chest-on-chest, chest-on-frame (sometimes called highboy), straight front, bow front and serpentine front and, unless I miss my guess, you'll be starting with the straight-front chest for crafting.

Chests were forerunners of the chest of drawers and personal belongings were originally stored away in these boxlike cabinets. The first crude, though sturdy, containers for household linens and wearing apparel served their purpose. In time, appearance and crafting improved as chests were either decorated with moldings, handsomely carved or beautifully hand painted.

The chest acquired a drawer at the bottom and also assumed a new name: blanket chest. The dower chest was very special since this was often decorated with stylized designs and a personally inscribed woman's name—hence the marriage chest.

Chests, being one of the first household items, revealed significant differences in style as set forth by people from various parts of the Old World. Each brought a little of himself, reflecting the trend of his former homeland and the style that predominated in his country. Although these furnishings are from out of the past, chests are still sought after and can assume a respectable place in your little house, too.

While chests were designed to hold personal items, cupboards were primarily utilitarian pieces, used for storing household and kitchen necessities. They became very special in name, use, location and construction. Cupboards can be very small or quite large, open or closed, free standing, wall hanging or built-in, and they enhance many a wall or snuggle into a corner.

The open cupboard, also known as the hutch cupboard, is a tall piece. The upper part is open and the lower portion is enclosed with either one door or a double

191

Fig. 20-1 The ball-foot chest of two woods (walnut and birch) features painted decoration, imitating elaborate marquetry. It's really beautiful.

door. The closed cupboard differs, with the upper portion being enclosed with glass or wooden doors (see color Fig. 4).

The wardrobe was a necessary closet for storing full-skirted dresses and other fashionable clothing. A standard in bedroom furniture, the wardrobe had either a single or double door, sometimes with full paneled mirrors attached to them. A small version is also the wardrobe-on-chest which is obviously a combination of the two pieces. The armoire, which is the European derivative, is sometimes used in contemporary homes where closet space is inadequate.

How to Make a Decorated Three-Drawer Chest

Follow pattern in Figure 20-5 for this chest, made of walnut and birch.

1. Bevel front and sides of base piece (B).

2. Cut a piece to fit in back out of $^1/_{16}$" wood (measure front area).

3. Glue sides (D) and back piece onto base (B).

4. Paint design on each drawer front. Scroll work is dark brown and leaves are olive green.

5. Glue two spacer pieces (C) into place, making sure they are level. Make pencil marks on sides (D), according to pattern.

Fig. 20-2 A chest-on-chest is constructed in the simplest manner. False drawers keep it easy. Made of balsa wood, it's painted brick red in color.

Fig. 20-3 Made of walnut, this blanket chest with a pull-out drawer and lift-up top looks distinguished in either a period room or a traditional home setting. Stuff it with your own little linens.

6. Fit and glue each set of drawers (E and F) together. Cut bottoms to fit for each drawer and glue bottoms into place.

7. Bevel sides of top (A) and glue in place.

8. Add ball feet to bottom—four seed beads and four large round beads. Paint feet dark brown, and add tiny gold beads for knobs or whatever you like. Spray chest with clear acrylic.

How to Make a Chest-on-Chest

The pattern pieces are all cut from balsa; note different thicknesses used (Fig. 20-6).

1. Bevel sides and front of middle base piece (C).

2. Glue front (A) and sides (E) to base.

3. Glue front (B) and sides (F) to bottom of base.

Fig. 20-4 Cherry wood makes up nicely into a serpentine open-top corner cupboard. It's an enjoyable piece to make, but the greatest satisfaction comes from seeing it finished. The wall covering is some leftover drapery-slip cover material.

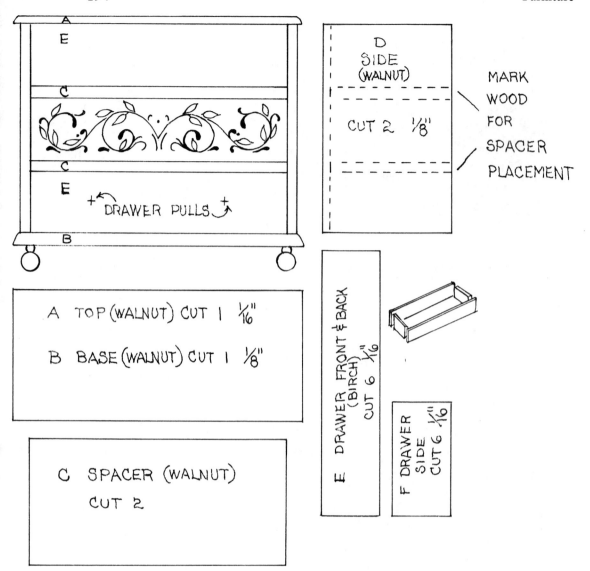

Fig. 20-5 The decorated chest is made of walnut and birch.

4. Cut and fit upper and lower back pieces. Glue into place.

5. Glue top piece on after beveling front and sides.

6. Glue six false drawers (G and H) into respective positions.

7. Paint the chest a brick red color.

8. Add drawer pulls.

How to Make a Blanket Chest ca. 1750–1775

This walnut chest (Fig. 20-7) is cut from $1/8''$ and $1/16''$ wood.

1. Bevel front and sides of base piece (B).

2. Glue sides (D) and back (L) together and to base (B). Back is flush with base.

3. Glue front piece (C) and "strip"

Fig. 20-6 Pattern parts and construction techniques for the chest-on-chest.

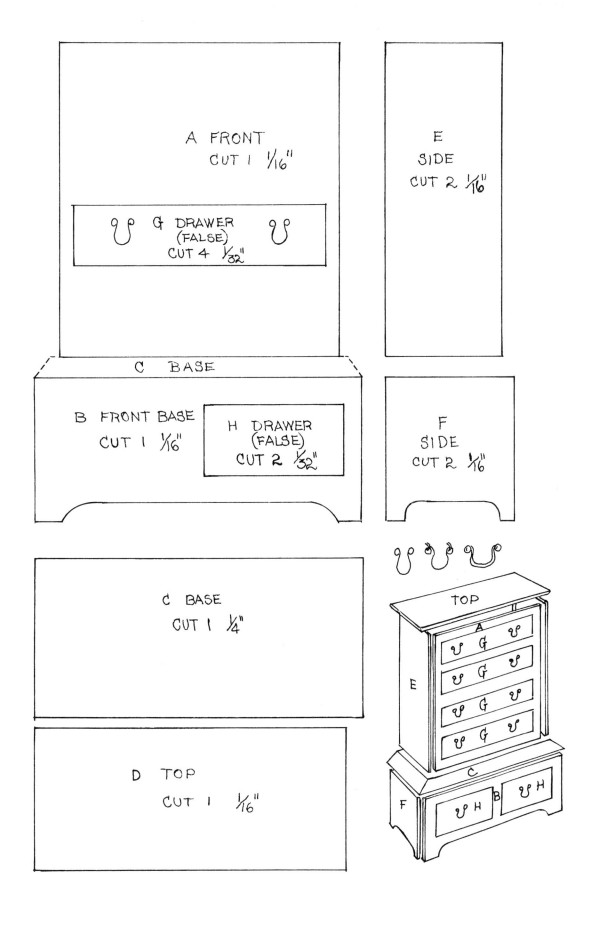

A FRONT
CUT 1 1/16"

G DRAWER
(FALSE)
CUT 4 1/32"

E SIDE
CUT 2 1/16"

C BASE

B FRONT BASE
CUT 1 1/16"

H DRAWER
(FALSE)
CUT 2 1/32"

F SIDE
CUT 2 1/16"

C BASE
CUT 1 1/4"

D TOP
CUT 1 1/16"

TOP

A
G
G
G
G

E

C

F B H

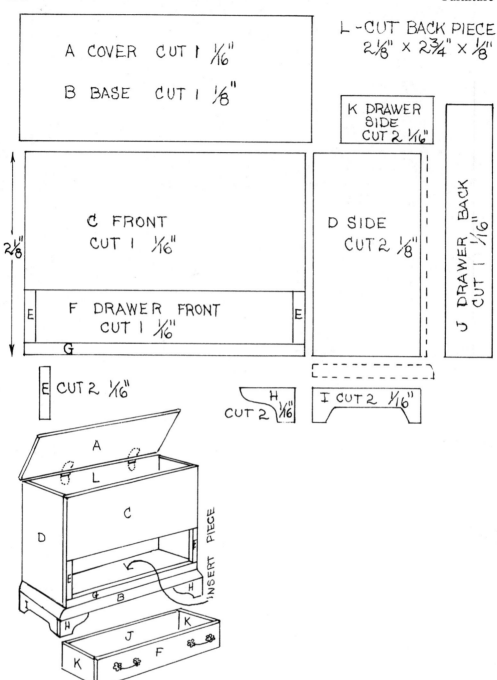

A COVER CUT 1 1/16"

B BASE CUT 1 1/8"

L - CUT BACK PIECE
2 1/8" × 2 3/4" × 1/8"

K DRAWER SIDE CUT 2 1/16"

C FRONT CUT 1 1/16"

D SIDE CUT 2 1/8"

J DRAWER BACK CUT 1 1/16"

2 1/8"

E

F DRAWER FRONT CUT 1 1/16"

E

G

E CUT 2 1/16"

H CUT 2 1/16"

I CUT 2 1/16"

Fig. 20-7   Walnut blanket chest, ca. 1750–1775.

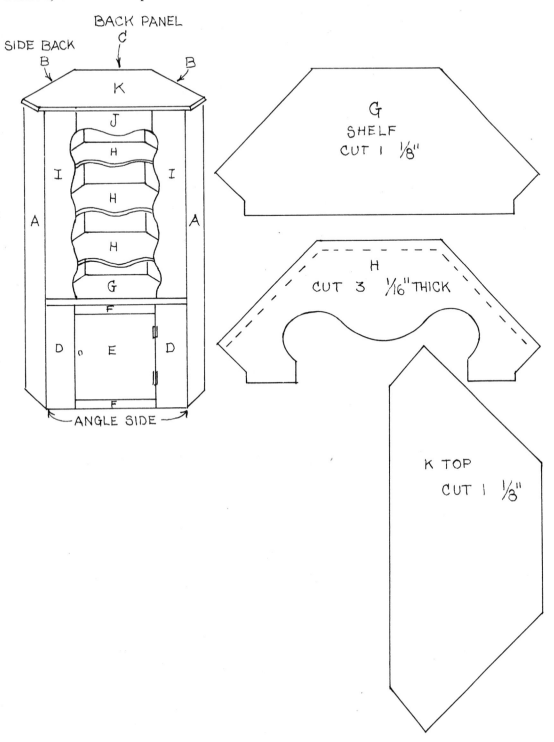

Fig. 20-8   Pattern for serpentine corner cupboard, made of cherry with an open top.

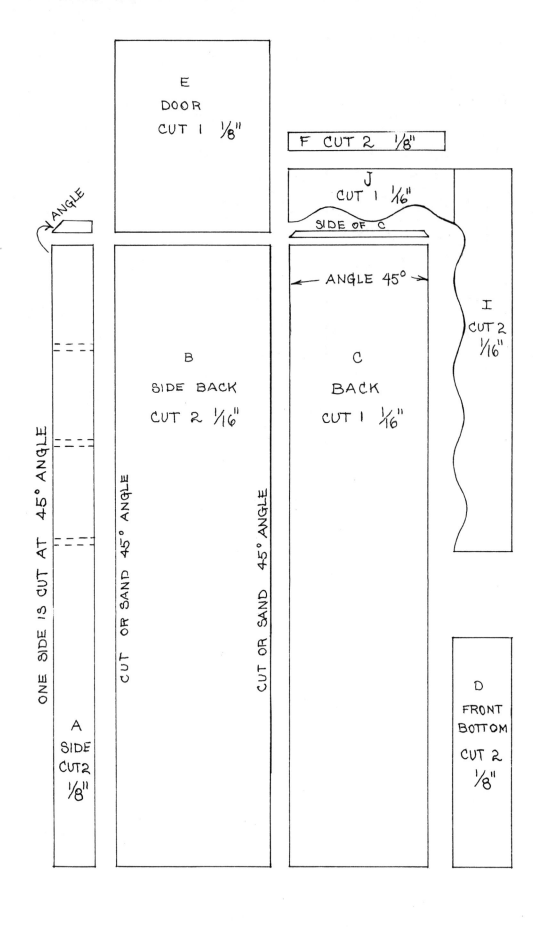

E

DOOR

CUT 1 1/8"

F CUT 2 1/8"

J

CUT 1 1/16"

SIDE OF C

ANGLE

ANGLE 45°

I

CUT 2

1/16"

B

SIDE BACK

CUT 2 1/16"

C

BACK

CUT 1 1/16"

ONE SIDE IS CUT AT 45° ANGLE

CUT OR SAND 45° ANGLE

CUT OR SAND 45° ANGLE

A

SIDE

CUT 2

1/8"

D

FRONT

BOTTOM

CUT 2

1/8"

sides (E) and "strip" bottom (G) into place.

4. Cut an insert piece from balsa wood ⅛″ thick to fit within and on bottom (see arrow).

5. Construct drawer from pieces (F), (J) and (K). *Cut* a bottom piece to finish off drawer. Try for fit and glue together.

6. Cut and add a ¹/₁₆″ bottom for inside of storage area of chest; this can be balsa. Glue in place.

7. Glue front (H) and side (I) legs to base (B).

8. Hinge the cover (A) to back, gluing hinges to inside of chest.

9. Add two pull handles to drawer.

How to Make a Serpentine Corner Cupboard

Follow Figure 20-8 to make this eighteenth-century cherry open-top corner cupboard.

Materials: two small hinges; 6″ Northeastern DCC-16 molding (if desired); cherry wood.

Directions:

1. Place flat down on waxed paper and glue front side pieces (D) to top and bottom cross pieces (F). Try door (E) for fit before gluing together. Sand door edges if necessary.

2. Glue side pieces (A), angled side, to pieces (D).

3. Rout out areas for dish rests on all three shelves (H). Place steel-edge ruler on shelves as indicated by dotted lines and, using a "rat-tail" steel file, gouge out the lines.

4. Try shelves (G and H) for fit. Sand and adjust and glue into place. Dotted lines in drawing (A) indicate shelf placement.

5. Glue side backs (B) and back (C) into position.

6. Try scalloped pieces (I and J) for fit. Glue together, dry well and glue against side pieces (A).

7. Glue hinges on door (E) and to right side piece (D).

8. Cut DCC-16 molding, 2⅜″ long, for two pieces to be glued on top of pieces (D). Stain molding cherry (or dark oak is close in color). This is purely added decoration, but is not necessary.

9. Round underneath area of top piece (K) and glue onto top.

10. If you wish, cut out a thin piece of wood to fit into bottom of cupboard and glue into place.

11. Add a little knob to door (cut off round pin head) and a small keyhole below knob. Glue a small "door stop" inside cabinet at the top.

Fig. 20-8 (cont'd). Pattern for serpentine corner cupboard, made of cherry with an open top.

Tables

More than any other piece of furniture, the table has come into use in a variety of ways, each casting a different shadow in design and special purpose.

The removable trestle-type table used for dining in the Middle Ages established the need for a dining table and that was the beginning of table variance. Tables became classified as expanding, center-opening and drop-leaf; leg construction was adapted to the needs of the table.

A rundown of tables, not necessarily in the order they were conceived, will give the reader an idea of their great variety. Aside from dining tables, we have the console table, writing table, side table, dressing table, wine and drinking tables, work, tea and game tables, tavern table, library table, refectory table, lazy susan table, tilt-top table, candlestand table, center table, davenport table, pier table, card table, poker table, end table, hutch table, chair table, bedside table, occasional, cocktail and coffee tables, nested tables and the "stand"—any small table used for displaying an object.

Most of these tables, by their names alone, suggest their usage. Early side tables were an auxiliary piece for dining. Fastened to the wall, they accommodated

the necessary liquor and utensils for entertaining. When the side table was replaced by the buffet, side tables become smaller and, although still used as servers, they also became useful as writing and dressing tables and consoles. The decorative console table, placed against a wall, is either free-standing or fastened to the wall. The dressing table made additional use of the mirror and lighting (see color Fig. 12).

But most tables were intended to accommodate the comforts of basic home life. Branching out into specialized adaptations of their counterparts, they added greater dimension to one's way of life and even a touch of luxury.

One day my husband inquired about his topless shaving lotion bottle. It was a beautiful wooden barrel-shaped top and I saw possibilities for a magnificent Oriental hand-decorated table. So I swiped it! Wouldn't you? (see Fig. 10-4).

Yes, all those extra occasional tables can be made from many oddities. Coasters take on a new perspective when turned into a small tabletop. How you dress them up and which legs you choose to use will give them their own identity.

Egg holders that the eggers use to display their beauties are often perfect for a

200

Fig. 21-1 A collection of small tables and pedestals line up. From the left they are a simple block of stained balsa; a coaster and bead table; a curtain clip table; a glass bottletop table, upside down; an Indian brass ashtray on egg stand; a decorated lotion bottletop. The bust rests on a pedestal, the remains of a cut pickle fork handle, already turned, attached to two shaped wooden plaques. The large console table begins with cut frame molding and an added piece of wood is finished to match and glued on top; the bottom is cut from a jewelry clip. Other wall-hung pieces suggest possibilities for tabletops—enameling on round copper disk; a hand-painted Chinese miniature tray; a square of ceramic tile; a jewelry box becomes a display tabletop, revealing seashells; flat turquoise gemstones are pushed into modeling compound adhered to a copper disk; round inlaid wood design is purchased. Free-form stone slabs come in an assortment of colors and sizes: visit the next gem and mineral show—the "stands" become excellent table bases.

base. Topped with a glass or something else, they become elegant. They also make handsome plant stands.

Another novel and eye-catching table is to create a see-through tabletop, featuring a variety of tiny objects—seashells, polished semiprecious stones, mosaic of tiny seeds, dried flowers, or another miniature hobby. It can start out with any unusual boxtop, shallow in depth. Turn upside down and arrange the inside to your liking. If the outside needs a covering of veneer, glue accordingly. Add a glass top and legs.

Helpful Hints

- Tabletops can be slabs of rock, marble, petrified wood—cut very thin to $1/8''$ thickness. Free-form shapes produce good modern styles.
- Use small tiles for a mixing table (wine and drinking table).

Fig. 21-2 The game table provided many hours of competition and relaxation. This table is made with a reversible top and an inner area provides space for storage of checkers or chess pieces.

Fig. 21-3 Second side of game table shows smooth-surfaced top.

✔Other tops can be an enameled design, inlaid wood design, trays, flat pebbles or gemstones, stained glass, medallions or decoupaged designs.

✔Cocoa tin covers and tin bottoms from

Fig. 21-4 The lazy susan tabletop was originally a cigar box and the simple, turned legs are constructed from dowel, stained to match the cedar wood.

packaging can be painted and decorated for "pie-topped" tables.

✔If tin is unappealing, then build up layers of papier mâché. Paint or decorate the finished piece.

✔Mini plaques, purchased in craft stores, come in assorted shapes. Large ones can be tables and smaller ones can become pedestal tops.

✔Use gold filigree or gold embossed designs to decorate your Empire style tables.

✔Cutting through frame moldings can produce good legs for console tables, vase-shaped slab sides, three-legged tables and supports for brackets. Experiment.

✔Black hairpins may resemble wrought iron legs.

✔Dowel sticks provide good strong support. Make them more interesting with a few turnings or with tapering.

✔Spool-turned legs can be acquired by stringing beads on a corsage pin. Paint.

✔A large treble fish hook can become a center base for a table—put some beads over the three points so your little people won't get "punctured."

✔Handles of hors d'oeuvre forks are sometimes turned and can become table legs, or one alone becomes the base for a pedestal.

How to Make Lazy Susan and Game Tables

The game table in Figure 21-10 is made of walnut; the lazy susan of cedar from a cigar box.

GAME TABLE

Materials: Walnut in thicknesses of $1/16''$, $1/8''$ and $1/4''$ (the $1/4''$ thickness can be balsa or pine, but should be stained to match other wood).

Directions:

1. Glue pieces (C) and (B) together as indicated. When dry, glue onto bottom (A), centering it.

2. Glue pieces (D) and (E) together.

3. Line inside of (C) and (B) area with leather, felt or attractive paper.

4. Glue top (D and E) onto center section. There should be a ridge all around for checkerboard to rest on.

5. Lay out checkerboard drawing on piece (F) and fill in with india ink (test first for bleed) or black acrylic paint.

6. Shape each of the legs slightly as shown in drawing. Be sure legs are even. Glue legs onto bottom. For checkers, there are the proverbial seed beads.

LAZY SUSAN TABLE

1. Cut legs (D) from $3/16''$ dowel and turn legs at bottom. Stain to match cedar wood.

2. Center piece (C) onto piece (A) and glue down.

3. Rout out small round area on bottom center of piece (B) for head of nail to be inserted and glued securely (see F).

4. In center of pieces (A and C) drill a hole large enough to allow nail to fit through and rotate.

5. Fit four pieces (E) and four legs (D) into position on bottom of table (see G). Mark positions and glue into place.

How to Make a Chair Table, Dressing Table and Pedestal

Figure 21-11 supplies patterns for three divergent table styles.

Fig. 21-5 The Victorian era was often known for its busy, ostentatious decor, and a dressing table of lace, glitter and ribbons testifies to a very fussy accent of this period. The gaudy mirror was part of a cosmetic set and tiny handmade bottles and atomizers adorn the tabletop.

CHAIR TABLE (PINE) 1/16''

This piece of furniture demonstrates for the novice how to build up the thickness of wood by gluing a few pieces together. The pattern is cut from $1/16''$ pine.

1. Glue three pieces of $1/16''$ wood (all $3/4'' \times 3''$) together to attain $3/16''$ thickness. Repeat for second piece. Press together well and wipe away excess glue. These must be thoroughly dried, so place

of seat. Glue seat (C) into position on both sides. Glue cross pieces (D) into place. Dry well.

5. On side pieces (A), find equidistant area from top and back for placement of holes—see dotted lines on drawing. Drill hole at corner junction. Place support piece (E) alongside side piece (A), center it and mark where hole is. You can do this by placing (E) inside chair and drilling through both pieces. Also drill hole through both pieces at front. Repeat process on other side of chair.

6. Cut two small toothpick pegs, 3/8″ long, to be inserted through holes.

7. Now comes the tricky part: using the pegs to hold (E) and (A) in position, center the tabletop (F) against supports (E). Indicate with pencil their position. Dislodge pegs and glue tabletop and supports together. Dry well. (You may arrive at your own method for putting the piece together.)

VICTORIAN DRESSING TABLE

Materials: 3/16″ mahogany wood; 15″ of panel lace for table; 16″ of panel lace for top; colored material for table; ribbon trim; dowel legs (optional).

Directions:

1. Glue two small supports to back support, as indicated by dotted lines.

Fig. 21-6 Back up, it's a chair. Back down, it's a table. This one is made of pine with a poly-urethane satin finish. On the seat, a puppy has found a nice safe place to stay, waiting for something to eat; there's a loaf of bread and baskets of apples and eggs—hardly the fare he's looking for.

Fig. 21-7 One of the most diminutive tables is made with a base of cafe curtain clips. Clipped, twisted and glued together and topped with glass, it's a decorative piece. It also looks nice holding a planter.

these under heavy books and leave over-night. Be sure the slippery glue doesn't slide the pieces out of place when doing this.

2. Next day, cut pattern for feet (B). Shape and sand the corner areas as shown in drawing.

3. Glue side pieces (A) to feet (B), cen-tering them. Dry well.

4. Dotted line on (A) indicates height

Fig. 21-8 Two wooden coasters are combined with three gold decorative beads to become a tiered cocktail table. The top coaster is metal rimmed, giving it a pie-topped look, and also has a gold decoupaged paper decoration for an extra attraction.

2. Glue this structure to underside of tabletop.

3. Depth of skirt is 2½″. If panel lace is too wide, fold over forward before shirring, so extra edge of lace shows on top. Panel lace and colored material are shirred together to fit around three sides of tabletop.

4. Glue skirt to edge of table.

5. Cut second panel of lace in half, shirring two top areas to fit around a 1¼″ diameter half circle of balsa. Glue lace trim to edges (see Fig. 21-5).

6. If table will be glued to wall, legs are unnecessary. Otherwise, add four dowel legs to fit.

7. Add thin ribbon trim where desired.

Note: For directions regarding matching stool, see Figure 18-14.

PEDESTAL

1. Shape a simple turning on the dowel support, as shown. Stain.

2. Gouge out center area underneath tabletop (A) and center of square base (B). Glue support into each.

3. Glue four small round beads to corners of base.

How to Make a Cafe Clip Table

When we moved into our present home, the windows somehow did not lend themselves to cafe curtains, which had helped decorate the previous homestead. So now I was laden with umpteen sets of cafe curtain clips, all neatly packaged and hiding in a drawer. One day I took them out, looked at them and decided it was time they came out of retirement. After a few minutes of consideration, the "wheels began to turn" and, if you don't agree that they make the most elegant legs for a low cocktail table or plant stand, then I'll put them back into retirement. Figure 21-7 shows the finished table; techniques shown in Figure 21-12.

1. Using a chisel edge cutter, snip through each side, separating clip from hinge area.

Fig. 21-9 A barrel chair needs a barrel table, which is conceivably the easiest piece of furniture to make. Simply glue a ⅛″ round of wood (3½″ to 4″ wide) on top of a barrel. If you like, add a lazy susan top. Another suggestion is to cut a door in the barrel and attach with hinges.

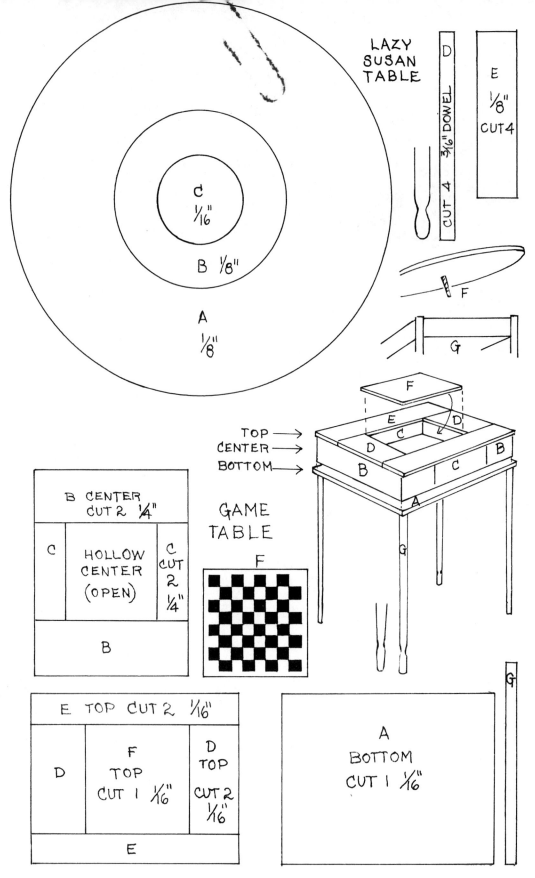

Fig. 21-10 Patterns for walnut game table, and a lazy susan table made out of the cedar from a cigar box!

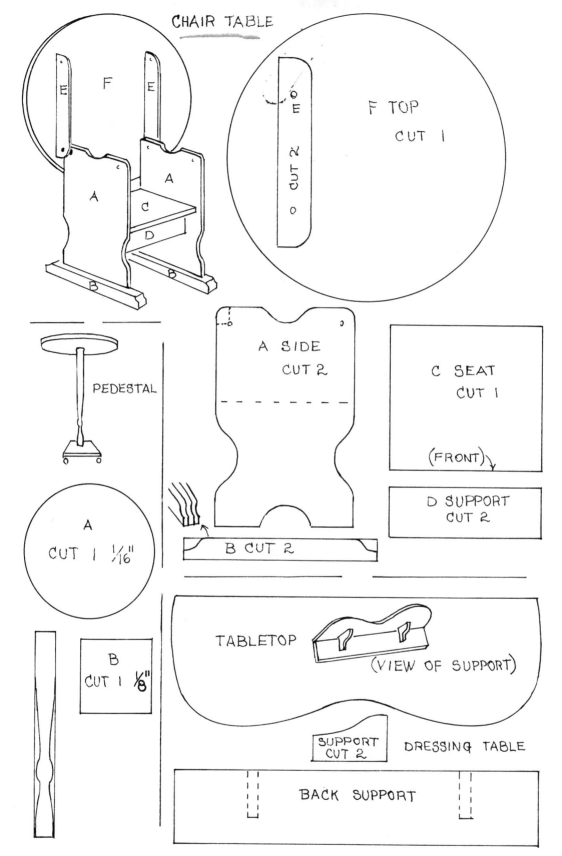

CHAIR TABLE

E F E

A A

C

D

B B

F TOP
CUT 1

E
CUT 2

PEDESTAL

A SIDE
CUT 2

C SEAT
CUT 1

(FRONT)

D SUPPORT
CUT 2

A
CUT 1 1/16"

B CUT 2

B
CUT 1 1/8"

TABLETOP

(VIEW OF SUPPORT)

SUPPORT
CUT 2

DRESSING TABLE

BACK SUPPORT

Fig. 21-11 This drawing supplies the patterns and assembly sequence for the chair table, Victorian dressing table and a pedestal table.

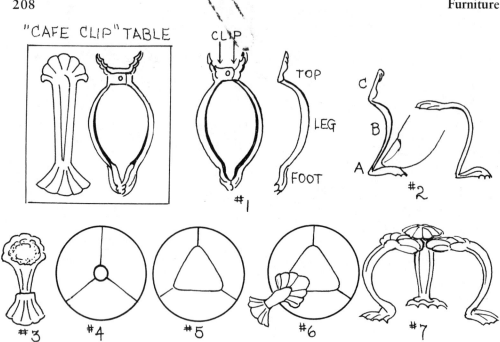

Fig. 21-12   Construction sequence for the "cafe clip" table—a unique design.

2. Clip will be reshaped by pressing and pushing. Place finger on "foot" (A); pull back legs with other finger (B); push top to horizontal position (C).

3. Apply white glue to inside of top area. Stuff small amount of cotton into glue, making it solid and filling in area.

4. On top of 1"-diameter spool, mark three lines, equidistant from each other. Set down on table.

5. Place cutout triangle of gold cardboard on top of spool. Cover triangle with craft glue.

6. Place first leg (top) on glue of one

Fig. 21-13   This design is planned for the top of an 8-ounce bottle of English Leather lotion (see Fig. 21-1). There is also a 4-ounce size. Colors to be used are: birds—two shades of turquoise blue; large bottom flowers—rose; small tree flowers—red; tree limbs and leaves—bright green; lower pointed leaves—olive green; top and bottom border design—black; and there are accents of gold throughout. This design could also be used for a wall mural or embroidery.

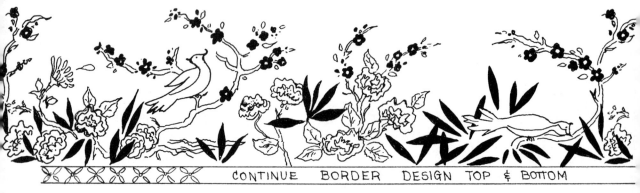

CONTINUE   BORDER   DESIGN   TOP & BOTTOM

corner of triangle. Hold. Repeat with second and third corner. Allow to set.

7. When thoroughly dry, test for standing ability. If legs need a little help in standing flat, carefully twist for correc-tion. Now it's ready for a top and I do recommend a glass one, since it would be shameful to cover over that beautiful design.

❖ 22 ❖

Shelves and Bookcases

The intended use of a shelf will influence its size, shape and architecture. The smallest shelf, which is bracketed, usually holds a single item—a beautiful clock or an ornamental object.

Other shelves placed within an architectural framework become bookcases. Before the seventeenth century, bookcases were unknown and books were stored upon shelves in closets. The advent of the detached bookcase produced new architectural challenges and the artistry of Chippendale, Adams, Hepplewhite and others produced some of the best (see color Figs. 6 and 13).

The breakfront gained popularity in France and England and the many unique ways in which it was designed produced singularly beautiful pieces of furniture.

Bookcases were especially popular in the Victorian period. Whether the structure consisted of simple open shelves, the breakfront or an elaborate style with glass doors, bookcases proliferated as book publishing increased. The bookshelf is smaller in size and can range from its own simple stand to variations of attached revolving stands, book tablestands and book racks attached to writing tables.

Built-in shelves date back many centuries, but they are a popular and functional style of our contemporary society and, in many cases, an absolute necessity to accommodate all the trivia that families collect. As this style strengthened in popularity, there were built-ins flanking fireplaces, around studio beds and some even obliterating entire walls. Built-ins can fit comfortably into a room of period flavor. Appropriate moldings and proper choice of wood will add authenticity. Whether open storage or covered storage, built-ins can be an integral part of a well-planned, up-to-date miniature room.

The whatnot or etagere (French) is a series of shelves usually supported by four corner columns or posts (Fig. 22-3). Although the Victorian whatnot departed from this rectangular shape and branched off into more circular and corner designs, the function remained much the same, that of displaying curios and bric-a-brac. Empire vied with Victorian for popularity in this furniture piece. There was a lull for many years, but the mid-twentieth century has seen a return of the popular etagere as the perfect piece of furniture for showing off today's collectibles.

Fig. 22-1 When I showed my mahogany English Regency bookcase console to visitors, a few reacted with disbelief, saying that perhaps I "really didn't make it." Well, I *did,* and you can too! The mirrored top, frame molding doors and filigree trim are the attractive distinguishing features.

Helpful Hints

✔ Acrylic of ¹/₃₂″ thickness is a good substitute for glass shelves and glass front doors.

✔ The daguerreotype outer case can be fitted with tiny shelves for curios (Fig. 22-4).

✔ Large copper staples can be made into brackets for wall shelves.

✔ A metal pouring spout can become a modern wall bracket. Cover perforated areas with card or Contact paper.

✔ Two of the same pouring spouts can be bracket supports for half of cut bottom from square frozen package container. This lipped shelf would be nice in a bathroom to hold towels or whatever.

✔ Seashells, long used in architectural design, can be used in furniture decoration. Use a scallop shell as base for a bracket. Paint everything white or gold.

✔ Metal spread eagles are also good for brackets.

✔ A collection of small, assorted square plastic containers can be grouped together for modern cubbyhole shelving. The same thing can be done with small boxes, matchboxes and round containers such as pill bottles.

✔ Small metal storage cabinets have clear plastic drawers with dividers. A bookcase or storage shelves can be improvised by standing drawer up vertically or extending it horizontally—use the metal insert or cut new ones of wood veneer for shelves.

Fig. 22-2 An open-front bookcase makes it easy to place books and other items upon the shelves. Although this specific type was made during the mid-nineteenth century, simplicity of style enables one to improvise with this piece, making shorter, taller and wider versions, including the built-in bookcase. Handmade books and Spanish miniature charms are placed within. The window is devised from a plastic supermarket container and the table chair is described in Chapter 21.

Fig. 22-3 With only four lengths of wire dress hanger, five shelves of acrylic and four small gold beads, you can complete a lovely modern etagere, ready to show off a collection of curios. In this instance, blown glass animals find their perches.

How to Make an English Regency Bookcase Console

Different thicknesses of wood have been used for various sections of pattern, supplied in Figure 22-5.

Materials: Picture frame moldings (Northeastern PFA-6 and PFA-8); acrylic for glass; four small hinges; ¼″ dowel stick; mirror; metal filigree and gold embossed paper; ¹/₁₆″, ¹/₈″ and ¹/₄″ mahogany.

Directions:

1. Stain dowel posts dark mahogany. Bevel upper sides and front of base piece (A). Bevel front underside of top piece (C).

2. Glue sides (B) to base (A). Glue top (C) on top of side pieces (B); top will project forward. Cut, fit and glue front piece (D) into place.

3. Cut frame moldings to size indicated for doors. Check for fit in cabinet. Glue four sides together. Dry very well. Cut away areas of both frames (see illustration) to accommodate barrels of hinges for swivel. Remember, the size of *your* hinge may vary. Glue hinges onto doors. Glue acrylic (glass) into back. Dry very well. (Use molding PFA-8.)

4. Line up hinged doors with walls of cabinet and glue second side of hinge to inside wall. Work from open back of cabinet. Dry very well.

5. Try shelves (E) for fit. Adjust, if nec-

Fig. 22-4 Extra ornamentation on the outer case of a daguerreotype frame, plus some added little accessories, help dress up a wall.

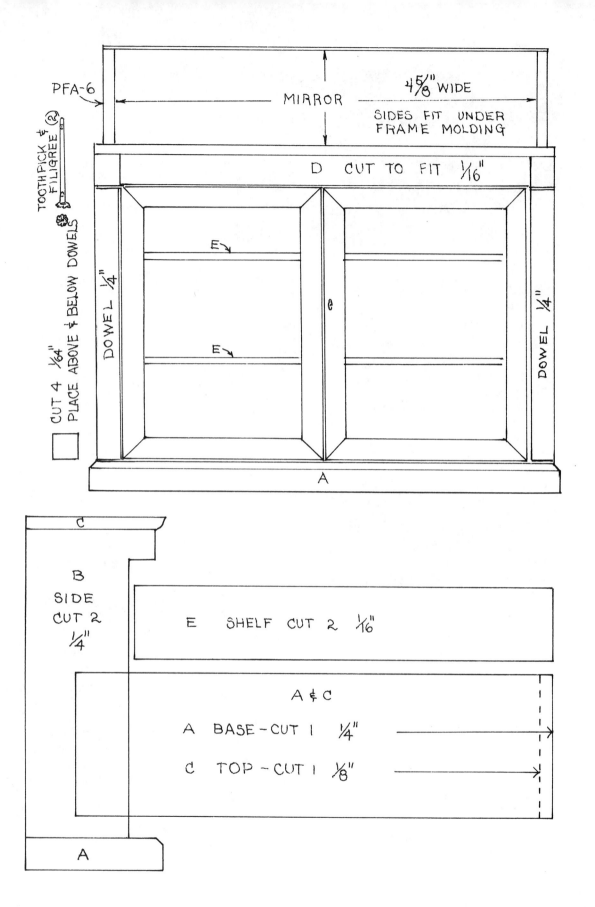

PFA-6

TOOTHPICK & FILIGREE (2)

MIRROR

4⅝" WIDE

SIDES FIT UNDER
FRAME MOLDING

D   CUT TO FIT   ¹⁄₁₆"

CUT 4 ¹⁄₆₄"
PLACE ABOVE & BELOW DOWELS

DOWEL ¼"

E

e

E

DOWEL ¼"

A

C

B
SIDE
CUT 2
¼"

E   SHELF CUT 2   ¹⁄₁₆"

A & C

A   BASE - CUT 1   ¼"

C   TOP - CUT 1   ⅛"

A

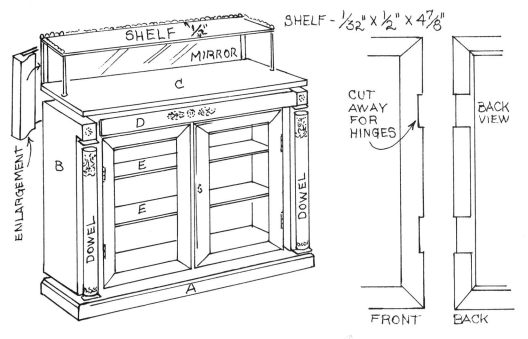

SHELF - $\frac{1}{32}$" X $\frac{1}{2}$" X $4\frac{7}{8}$"

Fig. 22-5   Pattern for English Regency bookcase console, an outstanding addition to your mini home.

essary. Mark positions on sides (B) with pencil. Glue into position.

6. Cut and fit one piece or two pieces of wood for back of bookcase. If you are not using mahogany for back, stain pine dark mahogany. Glue.

7. Glue a decorative border of gold embossed paper around top of each dowel and a tiny rim of gold around bottom of each. Note that $\frac{1}{32}$" squares of wood are placed at top and bottom of each dowel. These are glued down first and dowels, which must fit precisely, are than inserted and glued into position.

8. Mirror sides are glued to picture frame molding (PFA-6); glue to back top. Add shelf, which is supported by two front toothpick posts. See drawing for filigree trim on toothpicks.

9. Add rest of filigree trim to front and include a tiny keyhole on the door.

10. Under each shelf glue small pieces of wood for extra shelf support and add a small block of wood at front center on bottom shelf to prevent doors from swinging inward too much.

11. Glue tiny metal filigree chain around sides and back of top shelf above mirror.

How to Make an Open-Front Bookcase ca. 1840–1880

All pieces in Figure 22-6 are cut from $\frac{1}{8}$" cherry wood, except for pieces (C) and (F), which are $\frac{1}{16}$" cherry wood.

1. Glue front and back base pieces (A) to side bases (B).

2. Bevel three sides of top of base (C) and glue on top of (A) and (B). Front and sides will extend forward.

3. Glue sides (D) to back (E).

4. Glue back and sides onto base.

5. Glue undertop (G) on top, followed by top (H) which has been previously sanded and curved on three sides.

6. Check shelves (F) for fit; these must be snug. Glue into position, separating them evenly.

7. Glue two legs (I) to front and four legs (J) to sides.

Fig. 22-6 Pattern parts and construction sequence for an open-front bookcase, ca. 1840–1880.

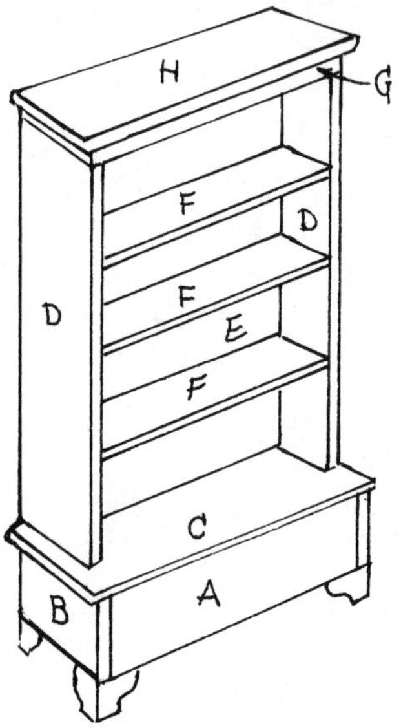
H
G
F
D
D
F
E
F
C
A
B

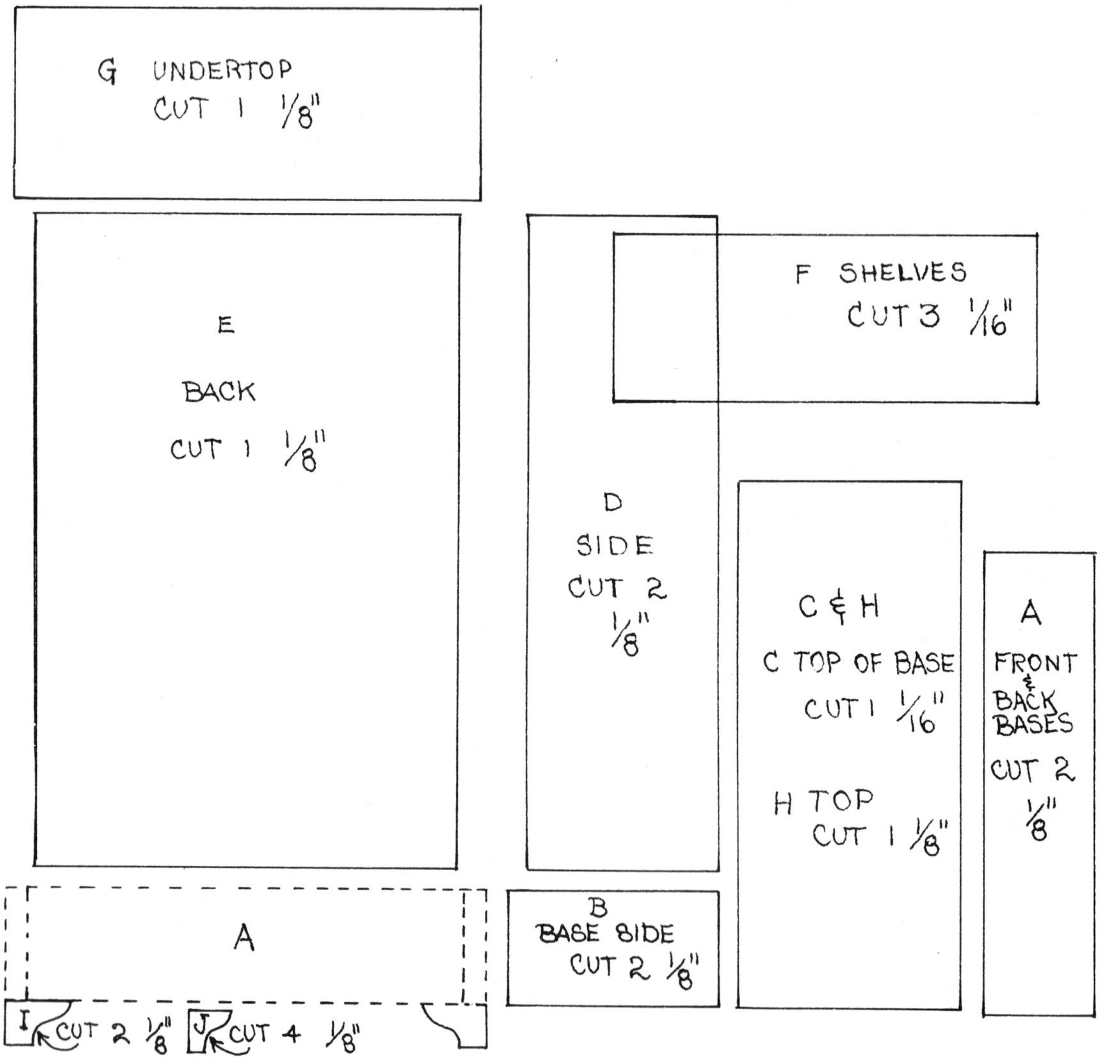
G UNDERTOP
CUT 1 1/8"
E
BACK
CUT 1 1/8"
D
SIDE
CUT 2
1/8"
F SHELVES
CUT 3 1/16"
C & H
C TOP OF BASE
CUT 1 1/16"
H TOP
CUT 1 1/8"
A
FRONT & BACK BASES
CUT 2
1/8"
A
I CUT 2 1/8"
J CUT 4 1/8"
B
BASE SIDE
CUT 2 1/8"

How to Make an Etagere

Figure 22-7 supplies assembly techniques for this etagere.

Materials: Wire dress hangers (cut four 6″ lengths); five pieces of acrylic, ¹/₁₆″ thick; four gold beads.

Directions:

1. Pierce each corner on four acrylic shelves by heating the curved part of a hanger and quickly pushing into the corner as shown. Practice on a few corners.

2. The rods fit *into* the corners of *four* acrylic pieces. The fifth piece fits onto the top, as shown in drawing. Glue the rods into position on one side. Dry well. Glue other side. Dry well.

3. Glue top piece on and glue beads at each corner.

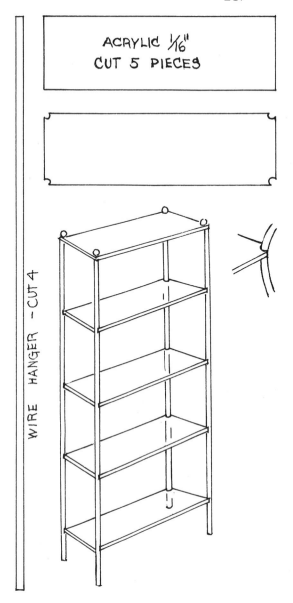

Fig. 22-7 Pattern and assembly guide for a handsome etagere.

Folding Screens and
Room Dividers

I've never been able to arrive at a conclusive decision as to whether screens are used more to hide something or to be a decorative accent in a room. Whichever, they do add an extra touch of "something" to the decor and there are a variety of ways in which they can be decorated and used. So consider their possibilities and take your pick—or do all of them: divider, background, accent piece, photo stand, hobby stand, memorabilia stand, a substitute for drapery (see color Fig. 15).

There are two ways of making a screen: the easy way which consists of folding cardboard back and forth for the number of panels that you desire; or the method of cutting or creating individual panels and securing them together with tiny hinges.

Casual or elegant, a screen is frequently the focal point in a room. A screen can be rectangular in shape or arched at the top, conceived of polished wood or fancy fabrics, or a blend of the two. It can scream with cascading color or quietly retreat into the background with subtle blending. Your screen can become a canvas. Treat it as a piece of art and decorate it attractively and tastefully.

To construct a simple folding screen which needs a firm stand, it's important to start with a good grade of cardboard; I suggest using illustration board purchased from an art department. This cardboard is useful for many other pieces of work, too.

Decide how many panels you need for a particular screen and carefully cut to size, using a steel-edge ruler and sharp knife to obtain straight, clean edges.

1. For cutting fold, place steel-edge ruler on fold line; using razor blade or knife cut only *slightly* through cardboard.

2. For second fold, turn cardboard over and again cut cardboard only slightly through.

3. For third fold, return cardboard to first side and again cut through slightly, etc.

Helpful Hints

✔Paint each panel of the screen a different shade or tint of one color for monochromatic tones.

✔Paint all panels gold. Then varnish, and stick on petite dried, pressed flowers

Fig. 23-1 A pair of two-panel screens (felt, topped with lace trim) set off a window with casement styling. A sterling filigree box sits in front of window.

while sticky. Spray with acrylic when dry. Or press flowers between two thin pieces of acrylic.

✔ Cover screen with same pattern of material or paper used on walls.

✔ Cover a screen with leather, then add gold decorative trim to corners or other areas.

✔ Show four seasons on four panels.

✔ An old straw hat can be cut into panels for a beautiful woven screen.

✔ Make a montage of faces. Boldly paste lots of heads all over the panels.

✔ Decorative tape trim comes in different widths and is the perfect answer for many screens.

✔ For a very ambitious project use the heads of straight pins as "nailheads" for decorating the edges of material or leather-covered panels.

How to Make a Reversible Folding Screen

Patterns and assembly sequence are provided in Figure 23-5 for the two-sided screen shown in Figures 23-2 and 23-3.

Materials: $\frac{1}{32}''$ balsa wood; four hinges; 2″ width of ribbon trim; three pieces solid color material, $6\frac{1}{4}''$ long (lining was used); wood stain.

Fig. 23-2 The hinged folding screen is reversible. The plaid background is ribbon trim, bordered by birch-stained balsa wood.

Fig. 23-3 The reverse side of the folding screen in Figure 23-2 reveals three hand-painted floral designs on soft green material which was leftover skirt lining.

Fig. 23-4 These three folding screens are just a small sampling of what can be done with this versatile accessory. The top screen is a greeting card: if you do choose a card, select a picture that can be folded without the scene being mutilated at the fold line. Notice how each panel looks like a scene in itself. The bottom left screen has a red background color, and an embroidery ribbon trim of pink roses has been cut and glued in the center of each panel. The little wicker planter (formerly the top from a wine bottle), holds real greenery from the rock garden. It's kept fresh within a plastic pill container of water, which is hidden inside the basket. The bottom right upholstery-covered screen shows how your family can come alive. In the photos on the left, my son, stepping high with his high school band, comes close, closer and closest. The frames consist of a box filler, curtain rings, a square plastic boxtop, a button, a metal decoration and jewelry jump links.

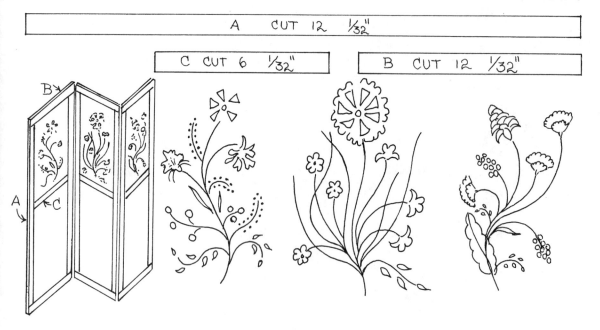

Fig. 23-5 Pattern and design motif for a two-sided folding screen.

Directions:

1. Stain balsa wood; the screen in Figures 23-2 and 23-3 was stained birch.

2. Glue strips of wood (A and B and C) into position over ribbon trim as shown in drawing.

3. On other side, glue solid-color material along edges, onto back of ribbon trim.

4. Glue strips of wood into position, just as you did on the opposite side.

5. About 1″ down from top and 1″ up from bottom, cut out areas of wood to allow hinges to fit.

6. On solid-color material, transfer flower designs from pattern and color with acrylic paint.

7. Glue hinges into place.

24

One-of-a-Kind Furnishings

Grouped together in this chapter are other items of furniture, mostly unrelated to each other, but significant for the unique use that each brought to its own particular era. A few that come to mind, not necessarily in order of importance, are such useful pieces as the washstand, umbrella stand, desk, cellarette, wine cooler, easel, music stand, shaving stand, lectern, piano and other musical instruments.

Before the innovation of household plumbing, the washstand was a standard piece in bedrooms (Fig. 24-1). Whether the design was open or closed, simple or elaborate, it served as a storage unit for a wash basin and washing accessories.

Umbrella stands became more important and conspicuous during the mid-nineteenth century. Adapted for holding umbrellas, canes, hats and possibly coats, they assumed their rightful position in the front hall. The advent of closets seemed to put them "out of business" but they still make nice conversational pieces and can be used in a traditional miniature home, too.

Desks are variable. Starting with the primitive writing box—a chest with a sloping lid—they branched out into many styles adaptable for various needs. Reversing the lid hinge produced a whole

new concept and the slant-front and fall-front styles came into being. Slant fronts were the upper parts of turned frames or bureau bottoms. The eighteenth-century bureau desk provided extra storage space, a welcome addition. When an enclosed cupboard or bookcase top was added, this taller structure became a secretary, and the lower inner area was divided into sections of small drawers, shelves, dividers and cubbyholes. Ladies' desks were table-like, small and delicate. Other structures are defined as kneehole desks, kidney desks and tambour roll-top desks. Of course there are office desks, too.

Other extra furnishings are all interesting features, designed to help make a little house more adaptable and functional. If you have a music room, then musical furniture is a must. If you have a sewing room, then furniture for these needs becomes important.

Decision making in miniature is less traumatic these days. Since this hobby has expanded, there are more furnishings, more plans and more ideas abounding than ever before. We are living in a Golden Era for miniaturists and there is much that is available for you to use—lucky, lucky you!

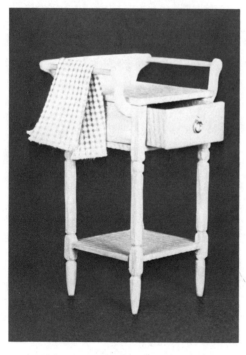

Fig. 24-1 The open washstand, ca. 1840–1880, was made from a variety of woods. This one is made from ash, but others of the period were also constructed from birch, maple and black walnut. Usually they were painted. Designed to hold washing accessories, they were standard equipment in everyone's bedroom.

How to Make an Umbrella Stand and Open Washstand

Patterns and assembly guides for these furnishings are provided in Figure 24-6.

VICTORIAN UMBRELLA STAND

All pieces are cut out of ¹/₁₆″ walnut, except (I) which is ³/₁₆″ walnut, and (J) which is ¹/₃₂″ walnut.

1. Bevel the front and sides of piece (H).

2. Glue two sides (G) to front base (F); glue on top (H), which will protrude forward.

3. Glue pieces (A, B, C, D and E) together as indicated in drawing.

4. Glue six corner pieces (J) into positions.

5. Cut thin, small strips of wood to fit on top of (H) as shown in drawing; fit and glue into position.

6. Glue side pieces (I) into place. Drill a little hole first on each side of circular area for rod.

7. Walnut stain a few round toothpicks. Make a turning in center of one, which is rod. Cut seven pieces, ¼″ long, for hat pegs. Glue these into position.

8. In back, add a fitted piece of wood to fill in bottom base area.

Please note that many Victorian pieces made much use of fret work and, although I did not use it for this, pieces (J) and side pieces (I) would be even more enhanced with some cutout design.

Fig. 24-2 The Victorian hat and umbrella stand will prove to be very useful for the entrance hall, especially if you have umbrellas and canes that need a place to repose.

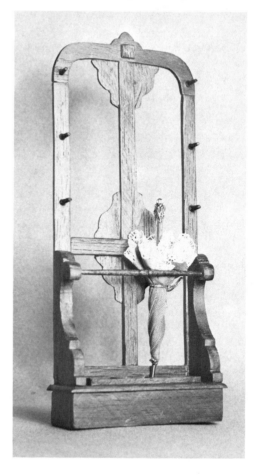

Fig. 24-3 This is a delicate piece and, since it's called the Martha Washington desk, it's obviously meant for a lady. The drawers don't pull out, but at least there are lots of cubbyholes to fill. Although there are no plans for this, I thought it would be nice to include, pictorially. After you've made a few pieces of furniture on your own this one shouldn't be too difficult. Why not give it a try?

OPEN WASHSTAND

Legs are partially turned (see Fig. 24-6).
Materials: $1/16''$ ash wood, $1/8''$ ash wood: all pieces are cut from $1/16''$ wood except legs, which are $1/8''$.
Directions:
1. Glue two side pieces (D) and back piece (D) to top surface (B) and piece (C).
2. Glue turned legs (K) into position and also glue shelf (C) below in place.
3. Try drawer pieces (E, F, G) for fit; glue together.
4. Round left and right front sides of drawer front (H) and glue to (E, F, G) combination.
5. Glue (A) to back.
6. Glue scroll-like ends (I) into place.

Fig. 24-5 The dressing glass is the "extra" on top of the dresser. The little pull-out drawer can be filled with tiny personal items, but do add a shaving cup and brush on top or some jewelry or some handkerchiefs or some bottles or. . . .

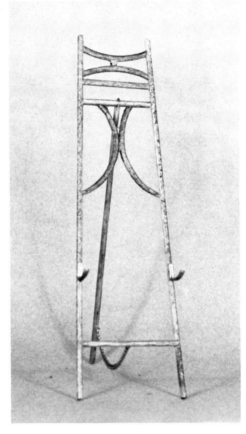

Fig. 24-4 Although different in design, this easel was inspired by my own and, since my home is anything but Victorian, it sends out a message that bentwood doesn't have to be confined to the Victorian era—you *can* "do your own thing."

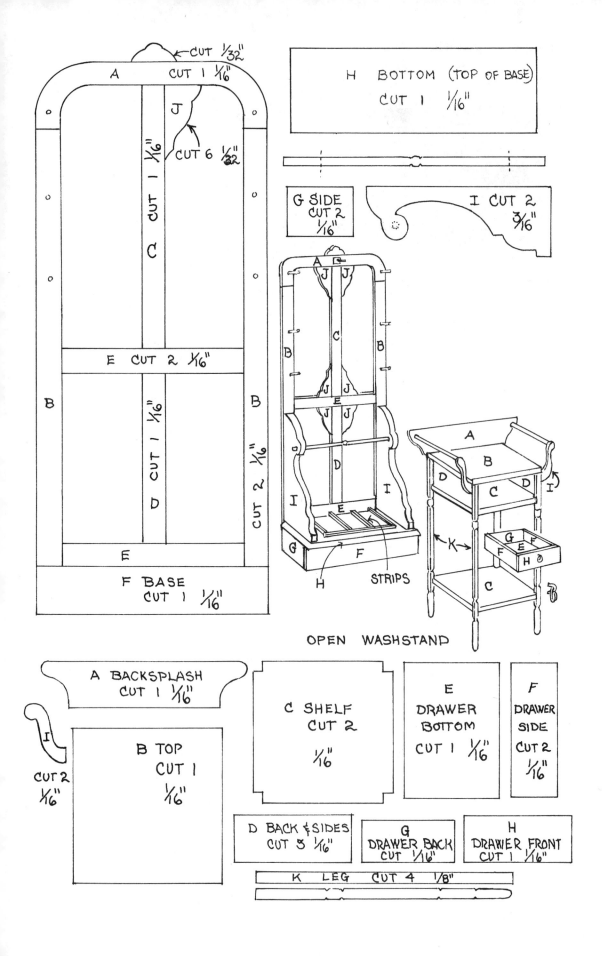

CUT 1/32"
CUT 1 1/16"
A
J
CUT 6 1/32"
CUT 1 1/16"
C
E CUT 2 1/16"
CUT 1 1/16"
B
B
CUT 2 1/16"
D
E
F BASE
CUT 1 1/16"

H BOTTOM (TOP OF BASE)
CUT 1 1/16"

G SIDE
CUT 2
1/16"

I CUT 2
3/16"

A
J J
C
B B
J J
E
J J
D
I I
E
G F
H STRIPS

A
B
D C D I
K
G E F
F H
C

OPEN WASHSTAND

A BACKSPLASH
CUT 1 1/16"

I
CUT 2
1/16"

B TOP
CUT 1
1/16"

C SHELF
CUT 2
1/16"

E
DRAWER
BOTTOM
CUT 1 1/16"

F
DRAWER
SIDE
CUT 2
1/16"

D BACK & SIDES
CUT 3 1/16"

G
DRAWER BACK
CUT 1/16"

H
DRAWER FRONT
CUT 1 1/16"

K LEG CUT 4 1/8"

7. Cut antiseptic sticks for two towel bars to fit and glue between (I) and (A), as shown.

8. Drill two small holes in drawer and add two jump links for a pull (see drawing).

How to Make a Bentwood Easel

The construction techniques for this easel are shown in Figure 24-7.

Materials: Antiseptic sticks; round toothpicks; fine chain, 2″ long; two gold necklace hooks; three short eye pins; oak stain.

Directions:

1. Submerge eight toothpicks in boiling water (I allow for extra in case of breakage). Soak thoroughly one hour.

2. When ready, gently curve toothpicks around small round bottle, 1½″ diameter or less. With masking tape, secure curved toothpicks to bottle and allow to thoroughly dry—perhaps overnight.

3. Round both ends of front uprights (A) and bottom end of back upright (B). Drill a tiny hole into top of back upright (B). Glue into hole a "much shortened" piece of eye pin. The ring part will eventually encircle crossbar (D) for swivel. Drill small hole into back upright, ⅝″ up from bottom, and in the center of bottom crossbar (C). Abbreviated eye pins can be glued into these areas, to be connected with a chain later on.

4. Stain all cut pieces, both antiseptic sticks and curved toothpicks, with oak stain.

5. You may bevel some of the cross pieces that will be glued to the uprights for more secure fit. Glue (C) to uprights (A). Glue two (D) crossbars to uprights (A). One (D) may need a little trimming.

6. Cut curved toothpicks to fit into areas as shown in drawing, then glue in place. Note the small ball-shaped piece that separates two top curved pieces.

7. Shape two necklace hooks into Ls, discard ends with holes, and glue L shapes onto uprights as shown.

8. Attach eye pin from top of back

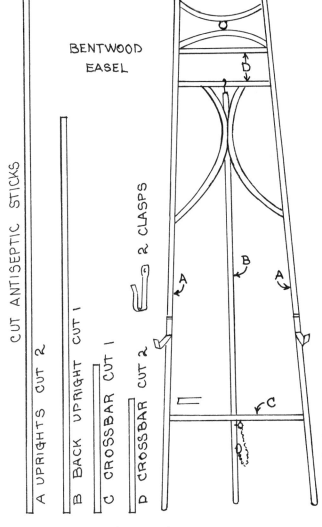

Fig. 24-7 Pattern and construction sequence for bentwood easel.

upright (B) around crossbar (D) as shown in drawing. This allows easel to fold.

You might think of some other ways to create your bentwood design. Tightly curved areas can be cut out with a jigsaw, then shaped and sanded.

How to Make a Dresser Glass

An addition to the well-dressed vanity, this piece is made of walnut (Fig. 24-8).

Fig. 24-6 Patterns and assembly guides for Victorian umbrella stand and open washstand.

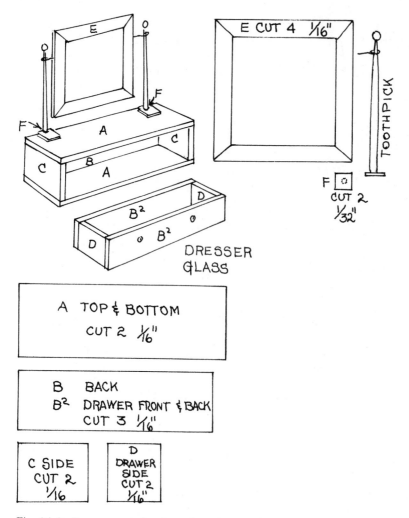

Fig. 24-8 Pattern parts for the walnut dresser glass.

Materials: Two toothpicks; mirror; two small gold beads; two white seed beads; 1/16″ and 1/32″ walnut.

Directions:

1. Glue top and bottom (A) to sides (C).

2. Glue back piece (B) in place.

3. Fit and glue drawer front and back (B2) to drawer sides (D). Cut and fit a piece for bottom and glue.

4. Fit four sides of pieces (E) and glue together. Cut a mirror to fit within and glue mirror and frame onto cardboard.

5. Cut one toothpick for each side to size indicated and glue bottom into piece (F), which has been routed out.

6. Add a cut eye pin over top of toothpick. Glue on gold bead. Simultaneously, glue (F) to rear of top (A). Insert and glue eye fastener between card and wood. Glue two white seed bead "knobs" onto drawer front.

Sources of Supply

Sources of supply means different things to different people. Since this book is devoted to crafting, the few supplies that are listed deal with projects or raw materials needed to help the craftsperson complete her work. Sources for other tools, lumber, trims and kits are further available through the advertisements in publications and newsletters. Include large, self-addressed stamped envelope (SASE), if inquiring.

BOOKS ON DOLLHOUSES, MINIATURES AND DOLLS.

Paul A. Ruddell, 4701 Queensbury Road, Riverdale, MD 20840. (Catalogue free)

BUTTONS, BEADS, FINDINGS AND NOTIONS.

Boutique Trims, P.O. Drawer P, 21200 Pontiac Trail, South Lyon, MI 48178. (Catalogue #106, $3)
Fabric-Craft Outlet, Donna Murray, 37A, Lisbon, NY 13658. (No catalogue)

ELECTRICAL APPLIANCES.

Illinois Hobbycraft, 12 South Fifth Street, Geneva, IL 60134. (Catalogue 25¢ and SASE)

GUIDE BOOK OF SOURCES.

Guide to American Miniaturists, Jane Haskell, 31 Evergreen Road, Northford, CT 06472. (Softbound book is $4.25 plus 75¢ postage; hardbound book is $8 plus $1.50 postage)

KITS FOR DOLLHOUSES.

Doreen Sinnett Designs, 418 Santa Anna Avenue, NPT Beach, CA 92660. (Send SASE)
Joen Ellen Kanze, 26 Palmer Avenue, North White Plains, NY 10603. (SASE)
My Uncle, 133 Main Street, Fryeburg, ME 04037. (SASE)
The Doll House Factory, Robert V. Donkanics, President, 157 Main Street, P.O. Box 456, Lebanon, NJ 08833. (Catalogue, $1)

KITS FOR NEEDLEWORK.

June Dole Hodges, 1280 North Stone Street, West Suffield, CT 06093. (Cross-stitch Kits—brochure, 20¢ and SASE)

KITS FOR SHADOWBOXES.

Braxton Payne, 60 Fifth Street, N.E., Atlanta, GA 30308.

METAL TRAYS FOR PAINTING.

Crafts Manufacturing Company, 72 Massachusetts Avenue, Lunenburg, MA 01462. (Booklet and Folder—25¢)

SEASHELLS.

> *Florida Supply House,* P.O. Box 847, Bradenton, FL 33505. (Catalogue available)

TOOLS.

> *Brookstone Company,* 120 Vose Farm Road, Peterborough, NH 03458. (Catalogue $1, includes six issues)
> *Dremel Manufacturing Division,* 4915 21st Street, Racine, WI 53406. (Use local dealer)

WOOD (COMMERCIAL).

> *Albert Constantine and Sons,* 2050 Eastchester Road, Bronx, NY 10461. (Catalogue 50¢)

Craftsman's Wood Service, 2727 South Mary Street, Chicago, IL 60608. (Catalogue 50¢)

WOOD (DOLLHOUSE AND STRUCTURAL).

> *C. A. "Chuck" Newland,* 600 South Raymond Street, Fullerton, CA 92631. (SASE)
> *Northeastern Scale Models, Inc.,* Box 425, Methuen, MA 01844. (SASE for Catalogue or Catalogue and Samples, $1)
> *Shaker Miniatures,* 2913 Huntington Road, Cleveland, OH 44120. (also tools; catalogue, $1.50)

Newsletters and Publications

The Doll House and Miniature News, 3 Orchard Lane, Kirkwood, MO 63122. Publishes monthly except summer, 10 issues; 8½" x 11"; $8.50 for third class; $9.50 for first-class mailings.

International Dolls' House News, 56 Lincoln Wood, Haywards Heath, Sussex, RH16 ILH. Publishes quarterly; 8" x 10"; overseas $8 (bills) or $8.75 (check).

Miniature Gazette (publication of National Association of Miniature Enthusiasts), P.O. Box 2621, Brookhurst Center, Anaheim, CA 92804. Publishes quarterly; 8½" x 11"; send SASE for membership information which includes *Gazette.*

The Miniature Magazine, Carstens Publications, Inc., P.O. Box 700, Newton, NJ 07860. Annual, $1.

Miniature Makers Journal, 409 South First Street, Evansville, WI 53536. Publishes quarterly; 5½" x 8½"; $12 yearly.

Miniature Reflections, 409 South First Street, Evansville, WI 53536. Publishes quarterly; 6¾" x 10"; $12 yearly.

Mott's Miniature Workshop News, P.O. Box 5514, Sunny Hills Station, Fullerton, CA 92635. Publishes annually; send SASE for information.

Nutshell News, Clifton House, Clifton, VA 22024. Published bimonthly; $12 annually.

The Scale Cabinetmaker: A Journal for the Miniaturist, Dorsett Miniatures, P.O. Box 87, Pembroke, VA 24136. Good for scale modelers. Publishes quarterly; 8½" x 11"; $12 yearly; single copy $3.75.

Small Talk, P.O. Box 334, Laguna Beach, CA 92651. Publishes monthly; 8½" x 11"; 12 issues for $12 yearly, international rate is $15.

Bibliography

GENERAL BOOKS

Aronson, Joseph. *The Encyclopedia of Furniture.* Crown Publishers, 1965.

Bassermann, Jordan/Bertile. *The Book of Old Clocks and Watches.* Crown Publishers, 1964.

Blum, Stella. *Victorian Fashions and Costumes from Harper's Bazaar: 1867–1898.* Dover Publications, 1974.

Christensen, Edwin O. *The Index of American Design.* MacMillan, 1950.

Drepperd, Carl W. *Handbook of Tomorrow's Antiques.* Thomas Y. Crowell, 1953.

Idem. Pioneer America—Its First Three Centuries. Doubleday and Co., 1949.

Idem. Primer of American Antiques. Doubleday and Co., 1944.

Idem. First Reader for Antique Collectors. Garden City Books, 1954.

Foley, Dan. *Toys Through the Ages.* Chilton Books, 1962.

Foster, J. J. *Chats on Old Miniatures.* T. Fisher Unwin, Ltd.

Gottshall, Franklin H. *Simple Colonial Furniture.* Bonanza Books.

Gould, Mary Earle. *The Early American House.* Medill McBride.

Harbeson, Georgiana Brown. *American Needlework.* Bonanza Books, 1938.

Hughes, Bernard and Therle. *Small Antique Furniture.* MacMillan, 1958.

Klamkin, Marian. *Hands to Work:* *Shaker Folk Art and Industries.* Dodd, Mead and Co., 1972.

McClintock, Inez and Marshall. *Toys in America.* Public Affairs Press, 1961.

Newman, Jay H., Lee S., and Thelma R. *The Frame Book.* Crown Publishers, 1974.

Nutting, Wallace. *Furniture Treasury.* MacMillan, 1954.

Ormsbee, Thomas H.: *Field Guide to Early American Furniture,* Little, Brown and Co., 1951.

Idem. Field Guide to American Victorian Furniture. Bonanza Books.

Strange, Thomas Arthur. *English Furniture Decoration, Woodwork and Allied Arts.* Bonanza Books, (n.d.).

Williams, Henry Lionel. *How to Make Your Own Furniture.* Avenel Books.

The Antiques Book. Edited by Alice Winchester and the Staff of *Antiques* Magazine. Bonanza Books, 1950.

The Antiques Treasury of Furniture and Other Decorative Arts. Edited by Alice Winchester and the Staff of *Antiques* Magazine. E. P. Dutton & Co.,

DOLLHOUSE BOOKS

Jacobs, Flora Gill. *A History of Dolls' Houses.* Charles Scribner's Sons, 1965.

Idem. Dolls' Houses in America. Charles Scribner's Sons, 1974.

Idem. A World of Doll Houses. Rand McNally & Co., 1965.

Johnson, Audrey. *Furnishing Dolls' Houses*. Charles T. Branford Co., 1972.

Latham, Jean. *Dolls' Houses*. Charles Scribner's Sons, 1969.

MacLaren, Catherine B. *This Side of Yesterday in Miniature*. Nutshell News, 1975.

O'Brien, Marion Maeve. *The Collector's Guide to Dollhouses and Dollhouse Miniatures*. Hawthorne Books Inc., 1974.

Thorne, Mrs. James Ward. *American Rooms in Miniature* (1941) and *European Rooms in Miniature* (1962), The Art Institute of Chicago.

Worrell, Estelle Ansley. *The Dollhouse Book*. D. Van Nostrand Co, Inc., 1966.

Dollhouse Miniatures. Carstens Publications, Inc., 1975.

Index

Page numbers in *italics* indicate information
found in illustrations.

(Jack Ruthberg, photograph)

Helen Karp Ruthberg

Early drawings foretold the future career of Helen, who was born, reared and educated in Syracuse, New York, and ultimately acquired her art training at Syracuse University, where she majored in illustration. She drifted into advertising and worked in such diverse areas as department store advertising art, pharmaceutical advertising and free-lance designing of greeting cards and shopping bags.

Domestic life brought her into community service. A past president of the Woman's Auxiliary to the Medical Society of Orange County, she has on many occasions used her "gift of talent" to benefit numerous organizations with decorations, craft work, paintings, murals and creative hobby auctions.

Helen started miniaturing in the early 1960s and later set this aside to develop other skills, including seashell arrangements and dried pressed flowers under glass. Using her talents and taking up the pen, she became the contributing author of several articles for *Creative Crafts* magazine and *The Miniature Magazine*. A member of The National Association of Miniature Enthusiasts, she returned to miniaturing and the accomplishment of her dream . . . this book.

In addition to creating heirloom crafts, she is a fine artist, enjoying the medium of watercolor. Her miniature paintings have been exhibited in national shows and have received awards from The Miniature Painters, Sculptors, and Gravers Society of Washington, D.C.

Married to a physician, she resides in Middletown, New York, and has one son, a medical student.